Ministry to Families

WITH TEENAGERS

By Dub Ambrose and Walt Mueller

Loveland, Colorado

From Dub:

*I dedicate this book for families to the family
to which I am dedicated . . .
to Cathy, Bree, Jeremy, Chap and Delindy.
You are "all the diamonds in the world
that mean anything to me."*

From Walt:

*I dedicate this book to my wonderful wife
and co-worker in our family ministry, Lisa,
and to our three great kids,
Caitlin, Joshua and Bethany.*

Ministry to Families With Teenagers

Copyright © 1988 by Dub Ambrose and Walt Mueller

First Printing

Credits

Edited by Eugene C. Roehlkepartain
Cover designed by Jean Bruns

Scripture quotations are from the Holy Bible, New International Version.
Copyright © 1973, 1978, 1984 International Bible Society. Used by permission of Zondervan Bible Publishers.

Library of Congress Cataloging-in-Publication Data

Ambrose, Dub, 1951-
    Ministry to families with teenagers / by Dub Ambrose and Walt Mueller.
        p.   cm.
    Bibliography: p.
    ISBN 0-931529-54-9 (soft)
    1. Church work with families. 2. Church work with teenagers.
I. Mueller, Walt, 1956- . II. Title.
BV4438.A46   1988
259'.23—dc19   88-21158
                                                                           CIP
Printed in the United States of America

Acknowledgments

From Both Authors

We first want to thank Eugene C. Roehlkepartain, the editor of this project, for his enormous effort in combining our thoughts and ideas into one readable book.

We also thank the following people who contributed programs to this volume:

- Esther Bailey, for "The Burning-Coals Approach to Confrontation" and "Hearing Assistance Lab."
- Roy Crowe, for "Let's Make a Deal."
- Dean Dammann, for "Getting Along With Parents."
- Walter Mees Jr., for "Parent Appreciation Night."
- Arlo Reichter, for "Getting Them Through It."

From Dub

Thanks to Dad, Mom and George Anne, for filling my mind with fond memories and unlimited possibilities.

From Walt

Writing this book couldn't have been done without the help and support of the skilled persons who've surrounded me through the process.

I am first and foremost grateful to Dan Jessen, a wise professor at Gordon-Conwell Theological Seminary. In the context of a brief conversation, he convinced me to make a deliberate and conscious effort to reach families within the context of youth ministry. His wisdom has taken root and grown in my life. The families of Supplee Presbyterian Church in Maple Glen, Pennsylvania, have been most cooperative as I have translated my ideas and convictions into "real ministry."

Thanks to those who lent their helping hands in many different ways: the staff at Supplee Presbyterian Church (Marie, Arlene, Sylvia and Dad), who gave time and computer assistance. Thanks to the youth ministry staff at Supplee, who carried the ball while I was busy (Dave, Linda, Lisa, Sue, Dave, Jill, George, Jeff, Doris, Arlene and Doris).

And finally, thank you to Lisa, Caitlin, Josh and Bethany, four people who make up the greatest family and who always seemed to understand when Daddy came home tired after a day in front of the computer.

Contents

Introduction **6**

Part 1: Why Minister to Families With Teenagers?

Chapter 1:   Families: Youth Ministry's Missing Link **10**
Chapter 2:   The Changing Family **25**
Chapter 3:   The Church and the Family **44**
Chapter 4:   Families in Need **61**

Part 2: Elements of a Successful Ministry

Chapter 5:   Designing Effective Family Programs **84**
Chapter 6:   Supporting and Educating Parents **102**
Chapter 7:   Building Credibility With Parents **122**
Chapter 8:   Reaching Out to Unchurched Parents **136**
Chapter 9:   Helping Families Communicate **149**
Chapter 10: Helping Families Through Conflict **160**
Chapter 11: Involving Parents as Youth Ministry
                       Volunteers **171**
Chapter 12: Letting Go: When Should You Refer? **197**

Part 3: Building a Ministry to Families With Teenagers

Chapter 13: Deciding to Build: Sharing the Ministry
                       Vision **208**
Chapter 14: Surveying the Land: Assessing Families'
                       Needs **223**
Chapter 15: From Blueprint to Building: Designing
                       Your Ministry **254**
Chapter 16: The Housewarming Party: Beginning
                       Your Ministry **278**

Part 4: Programming Ideas

Chapter 17: Programs for Parents and Teenagers Together
             Bible Study: Getting Along With Parents **296**

Meeting: Parent Appreciation Night 304
Retreat: The Family: Past, Present and Future 308
Retreat: Let's Make a Deal 321

Chapter 18: Programs for Parents

Meeting: Rx for a Healthy Family .333
Meeting: The Thrill of Parenting 340
Retreat: Getting Them Through It .351

Chapter 19: Programs for Teenagers

Meeting: Hearing Assistance Lab .368
Meeting: Excuses, Excuses 374
Lock-In: The Burning-Coals Approach to Confrontation 384

Resources for Family Ministry 395
Notes 403

Introduction
Welcome to the Family

What makes teenagers act the way they do? As youth workers, we have asked that question many times as we see young people mature, change and do crazy things. We've pinpointed many different forces in teenagers' world—peer pressure, the media, the educational system. But as important as these forces may be, they don't compare to a force we've sometimes ignored: the family.

In recent years, youth workers have begun putting the pieces together. If we want to influence kids for the good and want parents to have the most influence, then maybe we should start trying to influence parents too.

Ministry to Families With Teenagers grows out of this connection. Both Dub and Walt are veteran youth workers who realized that the only effective way to make a difference in young people's lives is to make a difference in their families' lives. Their experiences had a tremendous impact on their youth groups, their churches and their own ministries. In this book, they share their experiences, insights and advice with you.

The book is divided into four sections:

- **Why Minister to Families With Teenagers?** These four chapters lay a foundation for your ministry. They show how ministering to families helps youth ministry; how changes in today's families require us to rethink our ministries; how the church can—and should—help families; and family needs in today's complex world.

• **Elements of a Successful Ministry.** These eight chapters suggest specific issues and needs to address in your ministry to families with teenagers—and practical ways to meet those needs. The topics range from how to design an effective program to reaching unchurched parents to involving parents as youth ministry volunteers. Each chapter includes lots of ideas you can use and adapt for your own ministry.

• **Building a Ministry to Families With Teenagers.** This section has step-by-step plans for organizing your "customized" ministry to families with teenagers. It includes how to get congregational support, how to assess needs in your congregation and community, how to design a solid, well-rounded ministry, and how to introduce your new ministry to families. Each chapter includes a complete meeting to help a task force of parents and teenagers plan the ministry.

• **Programming Ideas.** This section consists of 10 meetings and retreats for families on family subjects. Included are programs for parents and teenagers together, programs for parents, and programs for teenagers. Each meeting and retreat is ready to use, and each offers a concrete model for designing your own effective and creative programs.

*H*ow to Use the Book

We've written this book as a hands-on manual for youth workers to use in their own congregations. The book can be used in several different ways:

• **Read it yourself.** You will find useful information and ideas as you work to improve your ministry to teenagers. It will help you understand them, their parents and their needs. In the process, it will give you the information you need to convince your congregation of the need to minister to families.

• **Use it with the planning task force.** Part 3 of the book offers a step-by-step plan for beginning this kind of ministry in your congregation. Planning task force members can read this book. It will help them understand the rationale for the ministry, and it will give them ideas for your own ministry. Use material in the book as a basis for your discussions.

• **Share it with parents and teenagers.** Some parents and teenagers may have a keen interest in understanding families and family needs. Have them read the book. Find out if they think the analysis and ideas in the book fit their own perceptions.

• **Pass it on to other church staff.** Ministering to families with teenagers crosses lines among traditional ministry structures in congregations. Ask other church staff to read the book and assess its appropriateness for your congregation. Their support and ideas are invaluable to planning your ministry.

A Challenge

We hope this book challenges your congregation to rethink its ministries and develop a ministry to families with teenagers. We hope it will provide new ideas and helpful encouragement to your congregation if it already ministers to these families. And, above all, we hope this book will be a catalyst through which your congregation makes a difference in families' lives.

Part 1

Why Minister to Families With Teenagers?

Chapter 1
*F*amilies: Youth Ministry's Missing Link

*F*ourteen-year-old Mike had been an active member of his junior high group for two years. But as Walt got to know Mike, he realized the young teenager came to church only because his parents wanted him to.

During confirmation classes, Mike made it clear that he'd rather be playing football than studying scriptures. In fact, Walt found out that neither Mike nor his parents were concerned that he understand what it means to be a Christian. His parents wanted him to become a member of the church only so he could be a well-rounded person. Mike's dad sees church as nothing more than another activity—like work, watching football and taking care of his sports car. And Mike's mom enjoys church only for the social contacts she makes there.

Walt has tried again and again to help Mike develop a realistic and personal understanding of the Christian faith. But despite all efforts, Mike's attitude has never changed. Like his parents, Mike now comes only to worship services, avoiding all other church activities. He's following his parents' example—an example that's difficult to overcome.

• • •

Marie's parents have a rule: "You must go to church

until after eighth grade. After that it's up to you." Sunday after Sunday Marie's mom would climb out of bed, throw on her bathrobe, drop Marie off at church and go back home for another couple of hours of sleep.

Marie seemed to enjoy church and her time there with her friends. But then she finished eighth grade. She could choose for herself. Not surprisingly, she decided Sunday school and church were for kids. How did she reach this decision? She learned from her parents that sleeping in on Sundays is more important than going to church. Now Marie and her parents come to church only on Christmas and Easter.

• • •

Sandra was in 10th grade when Anita invited her to the "Spaghetti Explosion," an overnight outreach event put on by the high school youth group. That evening Sandra made new friends, heard the gospel and soon became a Christian. She has been an active member of the youth group ever since.

Despite her Christian growth, Sandra has a problem. Her father disapproves of her church involvement. When she tells him what she's learning at church, he openly challenges and ridicules her beliefs. As a result Sandra has trouble understanding or accepting the demands of the gospel. And her father's skepticism has made her cautious about getting more involved.

• • •

Kerry is the envy of her high school friends. Her parents have given her a new car, nice clothes and money to burn. A fresh romance, straight A's, a new outfit and a full wallet keep her exciting and upbeat. Her dad is a real go-getter who works late into the evenings at his growing business. Her mom also works full time and is involved in prominent community activities.

Kerry appears to be carefree and content. But she has tried to kill herself twice within six months. When pressed, she says her life is empty and meaningless. All she wants is "to be loved," she says as she stares at the floor.

Yet in spite of her suicide attempts and her pleas for love, her parents continue to work long hours to "shower her with blessings." "After all," they say, "work is so important . . . and she knows we love her." Kerry has learned from her parents that material prosperity is what gives meaning and purpose to life.

Just Like Their Parents

Like most teenagers, Mike, Marie, Sandra and Kerry have been influenced much more by their parents than by church. They have been shaped primarily by attitudes and behaviors they see at home. Moral and faith development are influenced first and foremost by the family. Inevitably, those clumsy 12-year-olds in the junior high group blossom into mature adults who are strikingly like their parents.

This parental influence is sometimes difficult for youth workers to accept. *We* want to influence teenagers! When Walt graduated from college, he was ready to take on the world. He went to his first youth ministry position convinced that he could single-handedly (with divine help, of course) build the biggest and best youth program Pennsylvania had ever seen.

His efforts were pretty successful. The group was big and the program worked smoothly. Everyone was pleased. Yet despite apparent success, Walt knew inside that most of the kids weren't growing spiritually as they should. They lacked the depth of commitment to keep them in church when youth group no longer attracted them or when they left for college. What was wrong? Their spiritual growth wasn't being nurtured and supported by their families.

As youth workers, our influence on teenagers is limited—and it's certainly less than parents' influence. Numerous studies show that parents are the primary influence on teenagers. In a survey of *Teenage* magazine readers, 66 percent of the teenagers surveyed said their family has the most influence on their lives, while only 27 percent said friends do.[1] Youth workers weren't even on the list!

It follows then, that when the principles of Christian living are taught and modeled only at church and not in the home, it's tough for teenagers to understand, accept and apply these principles in their own lives. "For good or for ill," Paul Borthwick writes in *Organizing Your Youth Ministry*, "[teenagers'] values, beliefs, attitudes, and commitments [are] remarkably similar to those of their parents." As a result, he continues, "If I am going to have a substantial, long-term effect on the youth, I have got to try to affect the parents as well."[2]

Years of experience in youth ministry have convinced us that a key ingredient for successful and effective ministry to teenagers is ministry to and with their parents. When we seek to evangelize, disciple, support, train, educate and equip parents to fulfill their roles as Christian parents, the odds are greater that our group members will develop a meaningful commitment to Christ that's characterized by long-term spiritual growth.

This perspective changes our responses to the stories at the beginning of the chapter. In order to minister most effectively to those teenagers, we need to minister to their families. The best way to challenge Mike's casual attitude toward church is to challenge his parents' attitude. If Marie's parents become excited about church, chances are good that she'll become active again too.

Sandra doesn't need a crash course in apologetics to help her argue with her dad. Rather, the church needs to reach out to her father, sharing with him the gospel's relevance to his own life.

And one-to-one counseling with Kerry will never give her renewed hope in life. Instead, the whole family needs to hear God's word of redemption for a self-destructing family that has accepted our culture's mixed-up values.

Defining Our Ministry

These examples illustrate the many ways youth ministry can and should involve ministry to families. It's important, therefore, to establish a definition of the scope and goals of such a ministry. Otherwise we risk fragmenting rather than uniting our ministry efforts. The following definition suggests key ingredients a ministry to families with teenagers should include: *Ministry to families with teenagers is a process of supporting and strengthening families by bringing parents and teenagers together in the church and equipping them to live their faith in their relationships with one another and in all areas of life.*

Let's examine the various elements of this definition.

• **Ministry to families with teenagers is a process.** No one can give us a magic formula for successful ministry to families. There aren't any fast-and-easy methods that will work all the time in every setting or situation. Programs that work at First Church may be disasters down the street at Grace Church. Each congregation must constantly rediscover specific family needs among its members and in the community. Then it must plan a strategy, set goals, implement specific programs and evaluate each effort in light of those needs. Moreover, churches must be flexible enough to change their approach when change is needed.

• **It supports families.** Our role as youth workers in ministry to families is not to take over the family but to support it. "No matter what the family situation is like," youth worker Jim Burns writes in *The Youth Builder*, "you can never take the place of the parent. Don't even try."[3] Too often we think we know so much about teenagers that we feel it would be more efficient—not to mention effective—simply to go into a family and tell it how to operate. Not only will this approach fail, but it simply isn't consistent with our roles as youth workers.

• **It strengthens families.** Because families are the primary influence on teenagers, our ministries should help make families strong and healthy. Thus we must identify what makes a family strong and healthy then augment those traits through our ministries.

This strengthening may take many forms. Often it will involve counseling and nurturing, particularly for families in crisis. Other times it will involve training. Both parents and teenagers must learn the skills that help develop healthy families. Family members may need to learn many interpersonal skills—how to communicate, resolve conflict, express their faith, and fulfill their roles as parents, spouses or teenagers—to name just a few.

• **It brings parents and teenagers together in the church.** Picture the typical family going to church on a Sunday morning. All four car doors open as family members climb out and head for the church door. As soon as they step inside, they scatter, going different directions to different Sunday school classes. An hour later they each go to the sanctuary. They may greet each other as they go in, but they each sit with their peers. After the service they converge on the car and head home together.

Most church programming is divided by ages, separating families and keeping them from any meaningful interaction at church. Programming is almost always age specific. And events billed as family events (such as "family worship") are all too often geared for adults so that teenagers just endure them.

Churches that minister to families break this pattern. They bring parents and teenagers together whenever possible to strengthen their relationships. They carefully monitor their programming to ensure that it brings families together rather than pulls them apart.

• **It's faith-oriented.** Ministry to families with teenagers isn't psychological counseling or therapeutic social work. It's *ministry*. It recognizes spiritual needs and addresses them in a spiritual context. Not only does it ask, "What's good for families?" but also, "What would God have the family be?"

One aspect of this element of family ministry is that it reaches out to unchurched families. It's sometimes easy to assume that if teenagers are Christians then their parents must be too. Often, though, this isn't the case. In a survey of more than 1,400 teenagers from evangelical churches, only 56 percent said their father is a committed Christian, and 75 percent said their mother is.[4] As the church reaches teenagers beyond the church family, it's important that they share the gospel with the rest of their families.

• **It equips parents and teenagers to live their faith in their relationships with one another.** Despite (or because of) their importance, family relationships are sometimes the most difficult to "be Christian" in. At home we "let it all hang out," and too often we hurt the people we love the most. For some people, the hurt may result from relatively minor outbursts of anger. For others, though, it results from physical violence and abuse.

The challenge for Christian families is to let their faith transform not only their actions but their character, making family members Christlike in their actions and their deepest being. Thus, ministry to families should ask families to grapple with questions such as:

How does faith affect our family life? What does it mean to be a *Christian* parent? How do *Christian* teenagers relate to their parents and siblings?

• **It equips parents and teenagers to live their faith in all areas of life.** As important as it is to improve family relationships, this shouldn't be the ultimate goal of family ministry. Successful family ministry gives families the strength to support their members as they seek to minister and live their faith in all areas of their lives. A family that ministers together to others is a powerful witness. And that ministry can build significant and important bonds between family members.

Changing Our Attitude

As important as this ministry is, it's not always easy to think about youth and family ministry instead of just youth ministry. Adding to the problem, as youth workers, we often adopt attitudes that decrease rather than increase, our effectiveness. These make it difficult—if not impossible—to carry out an effective ministry to families. Here are some inappropriate attitudes that come to mind:

• **The Lone Ranger.** "Lone Ranger" youth workers saddle their horses and—with a mighty "heigh-ho, Silver"—gallop into the adolescent world to fight evil and promote righteousness . . . *alone*! They're not alone because they've been deserted. Rather, they *want* to be alone.

When Walt started in youth work he thought this way. He thought he was the kids' greatest resource. He could identify needs, address problems, be a trusted friend and provide impeccable guidance. If the parents would provide food, clothing, money and shelter, he could single-handedly care for their children's spiritual needs.

In other words, Walt believed he could fulfill a parental role better than any parent. After all, he was a young professional in tune with teenagers' needs—not like those old-fogy parents who, frankly, weren't equipped to do their jobs.

This arrogant approach to youth ministry is dangerous, and it can severely limit—even destroy—the youth worker's credibility with parents. What parents would trust and respect someone who assumes he or she can do a better job meeting their teenager's needs? If we take this approach, it isn't long before we find ourselves becoming Lone Rangers (whether or not we want to be), with parents resenting rather than supporting our influence and work.

• **The horse with blinders.** Unable to see what lies to the left or right, the "horse with blinders" trots forward with his or her eyes fixed only on the destination: the spiritual growth and nurture of teenagers.

While the Lone Ranger consciously avoids contact with parents, the horse with blinders unconsciously avoids that same contact by overlooking the fact that teenagers' needs are intricately intertwined with a complicated bundle of needs at home. Many times what appears to be a problem for the teenager is only a symptom of a problem at home. By failing to remove our blinders, we often miss opportunities to address the real issues in kids' lives.

Part of the blame for this obstacle should be placed on churches that hire youth workers to work only with young people. But, as youth workers, we must share the blame if we believe and act as though working with parents is not our job.

Walt remembers a group member named Rodney, who almost overnight became unusually disruptive and hostile during youth group meetings. A "slap on the wrist" or even a caring reprimand never solved the problem. Walt couldn't figure it out. But after spending time together, Rodney began to open up to Walt. He told about his dad's deteriorating health and how, as a result, his dad had been unusually angry and short-tempered. Once he saw the whole picture, Walt not only understood Rodney's behavior but was able to address the real problem by ministering to Rodney's whole family.

• **The misdirected minute manager.** Why should youth workers add another responsibility? "I already work 60 hours a week to pull off a youth program, meet with kids and attend meetings," we say to ourselves. "And now I'm supposed to add 10 more hours to my schedule for family ministry. Ha! I barely have time to take a shower, much less visit with my spouse."

Youth workers are certainly busy enough already. We really don't need anything else to do. But the problem with the "misdirected minute manager" is not necessarily one of poor time management or even having too few hours in a week. Rather, it's a problem of misdirection.

When Walt began working full time in youth ministry, he realized "full time" was a misnomer. His job wasn't full-time; it was double-time. He sometimes worked more than 80 hours per week. But this double-time ministry became unthinkable when he married and had children, so he cut back to 40 or 50 hours per week.

At first he felt guilty. "After all, the kids in the youth group really need me." Yet he has found that his ministry is far more effective and successful now than when he worked twice as many hours. When he began focusing his time and effort on both parents and teenagers, he began to see greater results. By helping the most influential people in teenagers' lives fulfill their roles, Walt, in turn, became more effective in his own role as youth worker.

• **The ice treader.** The "ice treader" says: "Working with parents scares me. They constantly question my plans, second-guess my decisions and criticize my programs. Besides, they don't like me. I'd prefer to spend my time with kids rather than feel like I'm always treading on thin ice."

Every youth worker remembers stories that scare the ice treader. One Sunday morning when he was walking to worship service, Walt was confronted by Dan, a father of a junior higher. With concern in his voice, Dan asked, "What happened on the hayride last night?"

Somewhat puzzled, Walt replied, "Well, we had a great time."

"Mark told me he had a terrible time," Dan retorted, "and that all the leaders were picking on him."

Walt was shocked. He told Dan that Mark appeared to have a great time. In fact, he made a point of "stuffing" all the leaders with hay. Dan looked at Walt in disbelief. His son would *never* do such a thing!

How should Walt respond to Dan and other parents like him? It's sometimes tempting to withdraw and avoid these encounters with parents. It's true that parents can be intimidating. But our ministries will be much more effective if we try to build relationships with parents, attempt to understand them, and work to gain their trust and support.

Of course we have to realize that no matter who we are, where we work, how much kids love us or what we accomplish, some parents still won't like us. On the other hand, though, our extra effort will often build bridges to more effective ministries.

• **The uninformed amateur.** Mrs. Williamson appeared outside Walt's office one day and asked if she could talk with him . . . privately. He was excited that a parent had actually come to him to share a problem. She began: "Things aren't good at home. I wanted to let you know in case Jennifer says something or doesn't seem to be herself."

Walt was caught off guard. He had no idea the Williamsons were experiencing marital problems. He swallowed hard. He had no idea what to do or say. Suddenly, in the midst of a difficult situation, he had an opportunity to help—but he didn't know what to say or do. Sure he was a "professional" in working with kids. But when it came to working with parents, he realized he was an amateur.

As youth workers, we must overcome our lack of confidence and expertise. We need to take time to educate ourselves in order to understand parents and to be confident in working with them. If we say, "I can't," we won't see our ministries expand to help families in need.

*R*eaping the Benefits

Elements of each of these attitudes are probably present in most youth workers. But as we work to overcome them, we open doors for significant benefits to our ministries and churches. Here are some of many benefits we reap when we minister to families with teenagers:

• **We develop new opportunities for significant ministry.** Our experience supports all the research: parents desperately want help. When they know someone is ready, willing, trustworthy, understanding and able to help, they'll respond. Initiating communication with parents gives them, in turn, the opportunity to approach us. This open communication enables us as youth workers to have a significant impact on the lives of teenagers and their families.

• **We develop a team ministry.** When we include parents in our youth ministry, it shifts from being "my ministry" to being "our ministry." Parents and youth workers become co-workers and partners in ministry to teenagers. We work together to see teenagers come to faith and mature in their faith. Together we develop a respect for each other and a realistic understanding of how we can complement each other in ministry. By knowing we're working together, we gain a strong sense of shared vision and camaraderie. No longer do we feel in competition or conflict with parents; now we work together.

• **We increase our understanding of teenagers.** Parents are youth workers' greatest resource. Nobody knows Brian better than Brian's parents do. When he struggles with dropping grades, his parents can share with a youth worker their perceptions and opinions about the problem. As a result, the youth worker can be of greater service to Brian as they sit down and talk about grades.

Not only do parents help us understand specific situations with specific kids, but their perspective on teenagers in general gives us insights we might not otherwise have—particularly if we've never been parents of teenagers ourselves. What we learn from parents can balance and deepen our own understanding of and ministry to teenagers.

• **We observe long-term spiritual growth.** There's nothing more frustrating for youth workers than to invest time and energy in a high school student only to see him or her leave for college and, at the same time, leave his or her faith in the church youth room. What seems to be real spiritual growth turns out to be short-term and shallow. By working with families to create a faith-filled and nurturing home environment, we greatly increase our chances of seeing long-term, in-depth spiritual growth in teenagers.

• **We maintain our sanity.** What would we do if 50 kids signed up for a junior high retreat but only two adults agreed to go as leaders? And what if those two adults were the youth worker and his or her spouse?

Including parents in our youth ministry helps us avoid this kind of nightmare. We can communicate program needs—for drivers, chaperons, discussion leaders, cooks or teachers—and chances are good that we'll always have more than enough volunteers. Too often our good intentions tempt us to "do it all," leaving us burned out and frustrated. Parents are willing and able to carry some of the responsibility for the youth ministry program. After all, their kids are the ones who benefit. Once we as youth workers learn to make parents active co-workers in ministry, our programs will be stronger and our sanity will be maintained.

• **We build community in the congregation.** Bringing families together with other families fosters new friendships. As a result, the church begins to grow closer together as a family of faith. It becomes a friendlier place where people know and care for one another. Visitors are attracted to this spirit of fellowship in the congregation.

• **We experience church growth.** Not only do individuals grow in their faith when we minister to families, but the church begins to grow numerically. When families in the community learn that a church can help with their needs, they'll often come to the church without being invited. They want to discover what's offered. Thus they're challenged by the gospel, and they respond to the challenge and become active members.

Walt has seen dozens of families begin attending—and eventually join—the church because of its outreach to families. And these families aren't from other churches. Rather, they're families that haven't been active in church for a long time—if ever. The ministry has drawn them in, and the church is growing as a result.

• **We develop a positive reputation in the community.** Since Walt's church began working with families, its reputation in the community has improved dramatically. People who previously avoided church heard about the family programs. Because they were struggling as parents, they came to the programs. They got involved once they saw what was happening in the church, and many are now active members.

Getting Started

Fifteen-year-old Sally and 17-year-old John are every youth worker's dream. Their knowledge of the Christian faith is exceptional. Their spiritual maturity expresses itself in their leadership abilities and their Christian lifestyle.

It's easy to see where their commitment was nurtured. They come from a home where the Christian faith is central to all of life. Their parents model a Christian lifestyle and, in the process, instill in Sally and John a desire to do the same.

This story—and hundreds of others like it—shows how much parents really do influence their teenagers. It also reveals the tremendous needs, opportunities and challenges of ministering to families with teenagers. By understanding the changes and stresses in today's families and seeing how the church can address their concerns, we open the door for a significant new area of ministry. The needs are obvious. And the potential benefits to teenagers, families and the church are immeasurable. So let's begin.

Chapter 2
The Changing Family

*I*t was time to start recruiting teenagers to plan the youth group's annual retreat. Dub had asked for volunteers, then suggested that youth council members contact each person to arrange a planning session.

What Dub thought would be a simple task turned out to be quite complicated. On the evening all the contacts were to be made, Dub's phone kept ringing as council members tried to figure out what to do.

"I can't find Terry's phone number," the council president fretted. "She lives with her mom and step-dad, and their last name is different from hers. What should I do?"

The phone rang again. "I reached Cory," the council secretary said. "He'd love to help, but he's only with his dad every other weekend. So he's not sure when he can meet."

"Frank has to babysit his little sister after school each day," the vice president explained. "His folks don't get home until 8 p.m. and he has to fix dinner for the family before that. So it's almost impossible for him to meet during the week."

That evening spent trying to organize a single planning meeting emphasized the need for us as youth workers to understand the changes that have taken place in families in the past 30 years. Otherwise, we risk overlooking the real needs and concerns of today's families.

*L*ooking Back

Actually, the family has been in transition since the Industrial Revolution, which began about 200 years ago. Before that time, the typical family was the farm family. These families were large extended families in which everyone—both men and women—spent his or her days working in the fields simply to provide basic necessities.

With the Industrial Revolution and its accompanying urbanization, a middle class developed that could afford the luxury of having what we now call the "traditional" family. Women could now stay home and raise children. Thus, as sociologist Tony Campolo writes: "The 'traditional' family is largely a bourgeois invention that did not manifest itself until the 19th century . . . It was not until technology spawned the Industrial Revolution and improved productivity that it was possible for women to be free to actually concentrate on child rearing."[1]

Perhaps the most dramatic changes that directly shaped today's families, though, have taken place because of the women's movement and the sexual revolution. Born in the early 1960s, the women's movement has reshaped women's roles in society, giving them the option to develop their own careers and identities separate from the kitchen and nursery. These changes have reshaped the way men and women relate to each other and their roles in the family.

Like the women's movement, the sexual revolution—coupled with effective contraception—brought similarly sweeping changes in the family. These changes go deeper than the rapid increase in sexual promiscuity in all age groups. The sexual revolution has changed people's understanding of sexuality, relationships and choices. In his book *The Christian Response to the Sexual Revolution*, sociologist and marriage counselor David R. Mace describes the revolution this way: "The Sexual Revolution . . . represents a radical change in our *thinking* about sex. The change has proceeded from a negative attitude to a positive attitude; from the suppression of serious discussion to the encouragement of study and investigation; from a strict and rigid control of sexual expression to a tolerant and permissive attitude toward it."[2]

These two changes have had a dramatic impact on families, as households have readjusted their perceptions, responsibilities and expectations. And whatever our personal views on the morality or appropriateness of these changes, their impact is unquestionable. These two movements have specifically affected families in several ways that deserve mention.

• **Working women.** Perhaps the most obvious result of the women's movement is the influx of women into the work force. Sociologist Janet Huber Lowry goes so far as to say, "The participation of women in the labor force has had the most dramatic impact on the family of any social force in our society today."[3] In 1960, 34.8 percent of all women worked outside the home. By 1986, the percentage had increased to 54.7 percent. Moreover, in 1986, 68.4 percent of women with children aged 6 to 17 worked outside the home.[4]

Having a working mom is generally a positive experience for teenagers. By a 67 to 26 percent margin, 13- to 17-year-olds say they prefer having a working mom.[5] However, these families do face unique stresses that we'll discuss later in the chapter.

• **Divorce.** The sexual revolution has directly contributed to the dramatic increase in the number of divorces. Some Americans apparently no longer feel obligated to stay in a marriage that is no longer fulfilling. Some divorce because the marriage has deteriorated and become destructive or abusive. In 25 years, the divorce rate in the United States increased by 127 percent—from 2.2 divorces for every 1,000 people in 1960 to five divorces for every 1,000 people in 1985.[6] As a result, the United States now has the highest divorce rate in the world.

At the same time, researchers believe the divorce level has peaked and may actually be declining. They attribute the reversal to several factors. First, since people are waiting until they are older to marry, they tend to be more mature and thus more ready for the adjustments of marriage. Also, as they have seen the effects of divorce on other families, younger couples appear willing to spend more time working out differences instead of simply breaking up their marriage.

Even with the predicted decline in the divorce rate, we'll still find ourselves ministering to teenagers from broken homes. Psychologist David Elkind believes that a teenager going through a parental divorce "becomes so preoccupied with the issue that he or she focuses solely on the divorce and neglects the age-appropriate concerns related to the construction of a healthy identity." Moreover, the divorce "changes the teenager's status not only within the family but also outside it," thus complicating the task of identity formation. Elkind concludes, "The teenager in effect must start over when the struggle is the hardest."[7]

Other research has found that these young people often have difficulties with relationships because of their parents' breakup. They tend to be lonelier and have a greater fear of betrayal, hurt and abandonment. They experience anxiety about relationships with the opposite sex and marriage. In general they and their families need particular care and compassion from their church.

The high divorce rate has also resulted in a dramatic rise in the number of single-parent and blended families. We'll discuss these and other family arrangements later in this chapter.

• **Postponed marriage and childbearing.** As young men and women place more importance on careers and personal fulfillment, couples have also postponed marriage. In 1960, the median age for a first marriage was about 20 for women and about 23 for men. Twenty-six years later, the median age for women was 23.1 years and 25.7 for men.[8]

Many young couples also choose to postpone childbearing and have fewer children. In 1960, only 10 percent of married women in their mid-20s and early 30s didn't have any children. Today, one in four of these married women don't have children. When they do have children, they have fewer of them. Today's average mother has 1.8 children, compared with 3.5 children in 1960.[9]

Many researchers believe this trend bodes well for the future of families. "Women are entering motherhood much later because they have other things on their own agendas," sociologist Glen Elder says. "Most of the evidence suggests that older parents are more effective parents."[10]

This trend will have a direct impact on youth ministry. Put simply, there will be fewer kids in the future. The number of teenagers has already fallen dramatically, and demographers predict that it will fall to 13 million 14- to 17-year-olds by 1990—from the 1985 level of 14.9 million.[11] Moreover, since the dynamics of small families differ from those in larger ones, we'll minister to more families and teenagers dealing with the unique concerns of having or being an only child, or being a small family.

*N*ew Family Forms

Families live in the wake of these and other societal changes that have swept across the country in the past generation. Today's young people live in families that reflect these trends. A Roper Poll of teenagers found that only 64 percent live with both natural parents. Another 23 percent live with one parent, while 10 percent live in blended families. A final 3 percent are adopted or live in other kinds of relationships.[12] As sociologist Larry Bumpass says, "It is simply not possible to talk about 'the American family,' and, indeed, many children might have difficulty answering the simple question: 'Who is in your family?' "[13]

Not long ago Dub and a volunteer youth worker were designing a "Personal Information Sheet" to help keep track of kids and their backgrounds, interests and activities. In the process, Dub realized that he would receive incomplete information if he simply asked for the names of the teenagers' parents. To be accurate, he needed to expand part of the form to ask for the following information:

Personal Information Sheet

Father's name (first) _____ (last) _____
Mother's name (first) _____ (last) _____
I currently live with (check all that apply):
☐ my father   ☐ my mother
☐ stepfather   ☐ my stepmother
☐ my guardian (or other)
Stepparent's name (first) _____ (last) _____

The need for this extra information reflects the diversity of today's families. While some families still fit traditional patterns, many are quite different; some don't even look like families. As a major national study by Ethan Allen Inc., on the family concluded, "Undoubtedly, the family does not look as it did just a few decades ago." It continued: "A typical family scene today might include a single working mother, harried and stressed, rushing home to relieve the babysitter, or children living with their father and a new stepfamily. Or perhaps, even more common, is the dual career family, with mother and father both arriving home from work at the end of the day, tired and unprepared for their children's pressing demands."[14]

In order to minister effectively to families, we must first understand the many shapes and sizes of families today. In doing so, though, our purpose is not to judge different structures, but to understand and minister to them. As Joe Leonard Jr. writes: "Preoccupation with the form of families is unhelpful. A more helpful concern, one with a clear biblical foundation, is the quality of relationships within familial households. Planners of family ministry need to ask themselves: What are the facts about family relationships today and what are the needs and opportunities for ministry?"[15]

Let's look at family structures we encounter in youth work, along with the particular stresses and needs common within these families.

• **Traditional families.** The traditional "nuclear" family—a breadwinning husband, homemaking wife and at least two children—is the picture that usually comes to mind when we think of "the family." However, with the growing number of other family arrangements, this traditional family structure is gradually claiming a smaller percentage of the total population. In 1960, 61 percent of married women stayed home; in 1986, only 32 percent did.[16] Some researchers say that less than 5 percent of American households fit this image of the family.[17]

Even though their numbers are declining, traditional families still make up a sizable proportion of the population and church membership. And they have particular needs and concerns.

—These families are often strapped financially because they don't have two incomes sometimes needed to support a family.

—Because society often doesn't value their work, homemakers may feel pressured to work outside the home. The church needs to support and affirm parents in whatever roles they choose.

—Teenagers with homemaking mothers may have difficulty respecting what their mothers do because of the value our society places on jobs in the work place. Churches can help families communicate about the choices they make.

—Homemakers often become so involved in nurturing and supporting others that they neglect self-identity and self-care. Moreover, they may have difficulty letting go of a child who graduates and moves away from home.

• **Two-career families.** The most common family today is the two-income family. About 56 percent of families had two or more wage earners in 1984—a total of 26.2 million families, compared to 17.9 million single-income families.[18]

Whatever our opinion of whether women should work, as youth workers we must admit—and adapt to—the reality of two-career families.

Several years ago Dub decided it would be a great idea to have a weekly after-school program for junior highers. They'd have refreshments and fun mixers followed by Bible study and a service project. It would be over by 6 p.m. so the kids could be home for supper.

What should have been a great idea failed. Yes, the program was good. Yes, it was creatively publicized. And yes, the kids wanted to come. But they couldn't. In planning the events, Dub hadn't taken into account the fact that kids with working parents don't have anyone to shuttle them to church activities during the day. Unless the church could arrange transportation, the kids simply couldn't get to the programs.

With more women working, churches must also adjust their programming to fit families' even tighter schedules. Many families spend evenings and weekends trying to stay caught up with housework. And because they're not home in the daytime, parents often covet the evenings as quality family time—time they're reluctant to give up for a committee meeting or a church program.

An important side effect of the increased number of working women is that an increasing number of adults prefer equality in marriage to traditional patterns. As a result, many families are redefining the roles of different family members. In 1974, most Americans defined a traditional marriage as the most satisfying marriage, by a 49 to 45 percent margin. By 1985, they had changed their position, with a 57 to 37 percent majority of women and a 50 to 43 percent majority of men believing that the best marriage involves a husband and wife equally sharing work, housekeeping and child care responsibilities.[19] Moreover, a survey of 1,062 American men found that 84 percent believe a father's child raising role is as important as the mother's. And 73 percent of those surveyed rate their family as the most important area of their life.[20]

Living in a two-income home greatly affects children and teenagers. Girls from these homes see themselves having careers as adults. Both boys and girls have more liberal views of sex roles in the home and society.[21] But as young people reject old stereotypes, they may be left without specific role models and guidelines.

These changing patterns and attitudes require that we as youth workers, and the church, guard against making assumptions about families that may no longer be true for most of them. These concerns call for particular sensitivity and leadership from the church.

For instance, does our church programming assume that moms are available in the daytime to help with planning, cooking or other activities? When we call to ask a teenager's parent a question, do we always ask for "so-and-so's mom"? These slips may be harmless, but they also have the potential of unnecessarily alienating many families.

• **Single-parent families.** About 22 percent of families with children under 18 (almost 7 million families) are single-parent households. This figure represents a 100 percent increase in the proportion of single-parent families since 1970, when single-parent families constituted 11 percent of all households.[22] That means as much as 60 percent of the children born in 1986 will spend at least part of their childhood in a single-parent home.[23] These families are four-and-a-half times more likely to be headed by a woman than a man. About 11.7 percent of all households (including non-family households) are headed by a single woman, compared with 2.6 percent of households headed by a single man.[24]

These families are confronted by an array of problems and stresses. Perhaps the most obvious problems are financial. While the median income for all families is more than $26,000 per year, the income for single-parent households headed by a woman is less than half that amount ($12,800 per year). In fact, black, female-headed households have the highest poverty rate of any group in the United States (51.7 percent).[25]

Other stresses single-parent families face include:

• A lack of role models for children. A mother raising a son can't provide the male role model needed to help him develop a healthy view of his own identity and sexuality.

• Time pressures. Because there's only one adult in the house, this parent finds herself or himself trying to meet parenting, financial and home care responsibilities single-handedly.

• Unresolved tensions from separation or divorce. Since most single-parent situations result from divorce or separation, many of these families face additional stress that lingers after the initial breakup. David Elkind writes that single parents sometimes place unreasonable demands on children and teenagers, thwarting the development of their self-identity.[26]

• Inability to share parenting and personal concerns. Unlike couples, single parents don't have someone around the house to discuss parenting problems with or to share in an adult personal relationship. This lack of adult contact can leave single parents feeling isolated and frustrated.

Single-parent families need particular understanding from the church. As youth workers, we must ensure that the cost of youth activities doesn't exclude group members from single-parent families with limited incomes. And we must be sure our "family activities" reflect a sensitivity to these families and their needs.

Churches can also develop specific ministries to meet these families' needs. These could include a support group for single parents of teenagers to share the unique concerns of their parenting role. Or they could include mentor programs that give young people appropriate role models missing at home.

• **Blended families.** The prevalence of divorce has given rise to another type of family: the "blended," "reconstituted" or "step" family, in which one or both of the spouses brings children from a previous marriage into the new marriage. A full 72 percent of remarried men and 57 percent of remarried women have children from a previous marriage.[27] As a result, one in five children is a stepchild. Researchers estimate the number of stepfamilies and single-parent families together will outnumber traditional families by the early 1990s.[28]

Perhaps the most immediate need for blended families is the need to sort out the new relationships in the family. Psychologist Judith Wallerstein estimates it takes two to four years to resolve the inevitable problems and role confusions when families are blended.[29]

Teenagers in blended families are confronted with a host of people who are suddenly part of their family. Understanding roles and how to relate to each other can be extremely stressful, sometimes even leading to the parents' eventual divorce. Teenagers don't know how to relate to their new "mom" or "dad"—much less their new stepbrothers and stepsisters. Their role in the family invariably changes, shaking established elements of their personal identity.

Complicating the matter for some teenagers is their relationship with their non-custodial parent. Spending weekends at "Dad's place" interrupts a teenager's social and church life. "Understanding time in reconstituted families is essential to youth programs and general weekend participation expectations for all family members," Janet Huber Lowry writes. "Multiple relationships demand time to preserve them, and these compete with typical church time. Those who can't be part of everything shouldn't be left behind."[30]

The church can have an important ministry in helping blended families learn to communicate together and sort out family roles.

• **Unmarried couples.** With the sexual revolution also came an increase in the number of unmarried couples who openly live together. Though these cohabiting couples constitute only 4.1 percent of all households, their number has increased by an incredible 342 percent since 1970, when they constituted 1.2 percent of all households. The U.S. Census Bureau estimates there are 2.22 million unmarried-couple households in the United States.[31] About a third of them have children under age 15.[32]

Of course, many of these couples consider cohabitation a "trial run" for marriage—particularly better-educated and upwardly mobile couples. This partly accounts for the disproportionate percentage of young adults who live together. About 21 percent of cohabiting couples are under age 25, and 82 percent of such couples are younger than 45.[33]

Whether or not we accept these couples' lifestyle, we'll inevitably come in contact with them and their children through our ministry. Their lifestyle presents a particular challenge to the church. How can we minister to their needs without condoning their behavior? What particular struggles do they and their children face because of the lifestyle they've chosen? How can the church help them understand the importance of covenant relationships based on their existing informal sense of commitment?

*F*amilies in the Future

Some observers look at the many shapes of the family and conclude the institution is falling apart. They advocate rolling back the clock to the time all families followed traditional patterns, and members within each family followed traditional roles.

Even if this approach were appropriate, its concern is probably misplaced. Though the family has changed, it's still a critical part of our society. "Underneath these changes in the working patterns of women, in the divorce rate, in the number of unmarried couples, and in the number of single-parent households," Joe Leonard Jr. writes, "there are deep and stable currents of family life which shape the experiences of most of us."[34]

Surveys of Americans repeatedly show that they are satisfied with their families and that they affirm family values. Four out of five people surveyed say their family is very close, adding they greatly value time they spend together as a family. The survey report concluded: "Despite statistics, despite what they hear on the news or read in the popular press, most Americans feel good about their own family life. And while recognizing that the family unit has undergone outer structural changes, a majority of the public does not believe these changes have undermined the value of the American family."[35]

Nostalgia for past family patterns is also destined to fail. The changes in family structures that have taken place aren't likely to be reversed. In *The Third Wave*, Alvin Toffler predicts that in the future, "No single form will dominate the family mix for any long period." He continues: "Instead we will see a high variety of family structures. Rather than masses of people living in uniform family arrangements, we shall see people moving through this system, tracing personalized or 'customized' trajectories during the course of their lives . . . This does not mean the total elimination or 'death' of the nuclear family. It merely means that from now on the nuclear family will be only one of the many socially accepted and approved forms."[36]

*F*amilies in the Bible

How will we as youth workers respond and minister to these different family structures? Will we shut them out because they don't fit our traditional notions of the family? Or will we focus on building and strengthening relationships and commitments in many different family structures and situations?

When we look to the Bible for specific direction on this matter, our first impression is that the Bible doesn't say a whole lot about the family. And when it does speak on families, the passages sometimes seem to conflict with each other. First we read the Creation story in Genesis and learn that God created the family as the foundation for society (Genesis 2:18-24). But then we turn to Luke where Jesus says: "If anyone comes to me and does not hate his father and mother, his wife and children, his brothers and sisters—yes, even his own life—he cannot be my disciple" (Luke 14:26). That statement doesn't appear to be an unconditional endorsement of the institution!

However, a closer reading reveals that scripture is filled with information about what the family is and isn't. To get a better understanding of the relationship between families and the church, let's examine how scripture portrays families.

• **Focus on family relationships.** The first thing we notice about families in the Bible is that they're rarely what we call traditional or nuclear families. Rather, families often included a father, mother (or mothers, if polygamous), grandparents, other relatives, servants, concubines and even long-term visitors (Genesis 46:5-7).

This reality presents problems for people who look to the Bible to defend a particular family structure. Indeed, the Bible says little about specific family structures. When it does talk about them, it usually reflects the common structures of the day for both believers and non-believers.

While it doesn't talk much about family *structures*, the Bible does say a great deal about family *relationships*—regardless of the family structure. How should a husband relate to his wife? How should a wife relate to her husband? How should parents treat children and children treat parents? What are family members' responsibilities to one another? These questions were much more important to the biblical writers than questions about specific family structure.

Think of all the Old Testament stories about family relationships. First there's the story of Cain and Abel—a dramatic illustration of the tragedy of sibling rivalry. The book of Ruth gives glimpses into the private life of one family and Ruth's selfless love for her mother-in-law. Then in the life of David we see the destructiveness of unrestrained passion for Bathsheba followed by the agony of David as the parent of rebellious Absalom (2 Samuel 18:33). Each story teaches us about our relationships within our families and God's redeeming work through those relationships.

• **Importance of family.** From the beginning of the Bible, the family is vital. In the Creation story, God created Eve because "it is not good for the man to be alone" (Genesis 2:18). Later the family became the building block of Hebrew society. The "house of the father" was the foundation for the larger social order of clans, tribes and eventually the nation of Israel. Indeed, as the Old Testament genealogies testify, the Hebrew people's very identity was tied to their family ancestry as children of Abraham, Isaac and Jacob (Exodus 3:15; Isaiah 51:2; Matthew 3:9; John 8:39-41).

Even when the Hebrew people settled into communities, they vigorously maintained the institution and centrality of their family structure. In addition to providing an identity for the Israelites, families were the vehicle for passing their history and faith from one generation to the next. The home was seen as the setting for a child's most important learning, and parents were admonished to bring up their children in the faith (Deuteronomy 6:7-9).

In the same way the family sustained early Hebrew culture, the early church also relied on families as it struggled to establish itself. Scholars believe that the first Christian churches were house churches where

Christians gathered in the home for communion, hymn singing, scripture reading and prayer.

Paul's missionary work illustrates the family's importance to the early church. Throughout his travels, Paul stayed in Christian homes (Romans 16:3-5). Among his early converts were Priscilla and Aquila, whom Paul relied on for hospitality and support (Acts 18:3). When Paul and Silas were miraculously set free from prison, the guard was converted and the two missionaries went to his home and baptized the entire family (Acts 16:25-34).

• **Family as a symbol.** We also can see the centrality of the family in the Bible by looking at the many ways biblical writers used analogies from family life to talk about God, the church and fellow Christians.

Consider the many ways family relationships are evoked to symbolize relationships with God. Hosea compares God to a faithful husband who searches for his errant wife Israel. Isaiah describes God as a nursing mother who comforts her child (Isaiah 66:12-13).

Imagery from family relationships also permeates the New Testament. Jesus calls God "Abba"—Father—and he instructs his followers to do the same. Perhaps his best-known parable, the prodigal son, portrays God as a patient, loving father. The early church continued to use family imagery to describe itself and its relationship to God. Believers considered themselves "children of God" (1 John 3:1), and Paul calls the church Christ's bride (Ephesians 5:32).

• **Tension between family and faith.** When we turn to the life of Christ, though, we see what appear to be conflicting messages about the family. On one hand, Jesus supported the traditional importance of the family in the Jewish world. He approvingly quotes the Jewish law on divorce and the command to honor your parents, thus supporting the traditional

family structure and responsibilities (Matthew 19).
And when he was on the cross, Jesus acted on his
own responsibility as firstborn to his mother by en-
trusting her to the care of his beloved disciple (John
19:26-27).

On the other hand, though, Jesus himself didn't always have a good relationship with his own family.
In fact, his family didn't even support his ministry;
John writes that "even his own brothers did not believe in him" (John 7:5). Then there's the dramatic
confrontation between Jesus and his family (Mark
3:31-35):

Then Jesus' mother and brothers arrived.
Standing outside, they sent someone in to call
him. A crowd was sitting around him, and they
told him, "Your mother and brothers are outside
looking for you."

"Who are my mother and my brothers?" he
asked.

Then he looked at those seated in a circle
around him and said, "Here are my mother and
my brothers! Whoever does God's will is my
brother and sister and mother."

This tension in Jesus' views of the family leads us
to a critical—and often difficult—understanding of the
family's place in the Christian faith. As we have seen,
families can be a central part of God's work and reve-
lation. But when family loyalties conflict with loyalty
to God, our obligation is to God.

If family becomes more important to us than the
demands of our faith, then the family has become an
idol we worship rather than a vehicle for God's
work. As Judith Kovacs writes: "Jesus expects us to
give good gifts to our children, to support our parents, to remain loyal to our husbands and wives, but
above all to follow him and to seek God's reign on
earth."[37]

It may seem odd to emphasize this side of the biblical teaching on families in a book on family ministry. But it's critical that we keep this balance in mind in our ministry. Our purpose in ministering to families is not to save the family or nation or just to add members to the church—though these goals could be side effects. Rather, our purpose in ministering to families is to help them corporately and individually live out God's will in their lives through their relationships to one another, to their world and to their God.

Chapter 3
The Church and the Family

*W*alt was leading a workshop on ministry to families with teenagers. To start the discussion he said, "Let's begin by sharing what we're doing in our individual churches in ministry to families with teenagers."

The normally talkative group of youth workers was dead silent.

"Anyone? . . . Go ahead . . . Speak up . . . Don't be shy."

Still no response.

Finally one person spoke. "Nothing," she said. "Our church isn't doing anything at all."

Gradually all the group members admitted they weren't making any conscious efforts to minister to these families. They saw the need and wanted to do something, but they weren't doing anything.

Though only a few youth workers were in that workshop, their response was fairly typical. While most churches claim to be "family churches," few shape their ministries with families in mind. Indeed, churches have sometimes actually pulled families apart through their programming.

Where the Church Has Failed

Much of the programming and structure in a typical congregation is guided by a "we've-always-done-it-this-way" tradition. While tradition can be useful, it sometimes needs re-examination and re-evaluation to ensure that our ministries stay relevant and fresh.

Let's look at what churches implicitly say to families through their programming and structures. Each mistake is a lesson in how not to minister to families. Each one points to more appropriate ways to meet family needs.

• **There's no place like church.** Allan needed to spend time at home. His mother had died of cancer six months earlier, and the family needed to be together to rebuild relationships and work through their grief.

But Allan was spending all his time at church. He was involved in youth group on Sunday nights, choir on Tuesdays and Bible study on Wednesdays. He also helped lead the junior high meeting on Fridays. He spent his free evenings with friends from church. His father didn't know what to do. "We need to be together," he told Walt, "but he's always at church." Instead of pulling together during their grief, he felt the family was falling apart.

All too often, youth workers equate a busy ministry with a successful ministry. We fill calendars with meetings, retreats, lock-ins, trips and special events. Then in exhaustion we look at the schedule and admire everything we're doing to help kids grow spiritually.

Of course many of these programs do help kids grow. And many contribute significantly to the life of the church. But something's wrong when parents complain that their kids are never home because they're always at church.

Like most teenagers, Walt's youth group members wanted to do everything everywhere. At school they were involved in clubs, athletics, drama and band—not to mention classes and homework. They participated in community clubs and activities. They had part-time jobs. They had active social lives. They were also involved in youth group activities and planning. As a result, when the church scheduled numerous activities throughout the week, it found itself competing with dozens of other activities. The church activities usually lost.

Once they realized the problem, the youth group leaders changed courses. They cut down the number of activities and concentrated on providing a few high-quality programs for young people. Now the junior highers meet only on Friday nights for fellowship meetings and special events. The senior highers meet twice a week—Sunday nights for fellowship and Wednesdays for Bible study. Since older teenagers have more freedom, the church occasionally schedules special events on weekends.

The change has proved that more isn't necessarily better. The group has continued to grow—both spiritually and numerically. The youth staff has had more time to develop quality programs for those few activities.

Of course youth programs shouldn't take full blame for kids spending all their time at church. Families themselves must learn to make choices and limit their involvement. But we can help by not over-programming then making kids feel guilty when they can't attend everything. Instead we should support family times, encouraging kids to be with their families.

Many activities, organizations and commitments steal time from families. If the church really wants to be a "family church," it must facilitate family unity and growth rather than demand the family's time and energy.

• **The family that prays apart . . .** Recently Walt attended a church family picnic. Dozens of families came. Yet as soon as families arrived, they split. Children ran to play with other children. Teenagers headed toward their group of friends. Parents sat in a circle of chairs under the trees to hear the latest news.

While such groupings are natural for most people, Walt assumed the picnic planners would bring families together for structured activities. Instead they had specific activities for each age group. Young children played games for young children in one corner of the park. Teenagers had their own activities in another. The adults headed to the other end of the field for adult games.

If this family picnic was designed to bring families together, it failed miserably. Everyone may have had fun, but family members didn't get to know one another any better.

All too often, our good intentions in church programming keep family members from being together. Children don't worship with their families on Sunday mornings. Teenagers have their own activities. Parents spend all their time with other adults. Kids and parents don't even have a chance to get together for retreats, picnics, potlucks, workdays or other informal activities.

Of course there's certainly a place in our programming for age-specific activities. It would be impossible, impractical and, possibly, counterproductive for families to be together for all church activities. But there's a place for both kinds of activities in the church. It's time we plan activities that unite families and promote family fellowship and spiritual growth in addition to age-specific activities.

Many churches have been able to plan regular family events every month or so. Other congregations schedule all their weekly activities for one night so that families have the other evenings for themselves. Other churches make special efforts to keep families together for fellowship meals and worship. The possibilities are endless. With a little creativity, church activities can bring families together for quality time rather than pull them apart.

• **Youth group is where the heart is.** Several years ago Walt asked Debbie, a youth group member, to be part of the annual youth-led Christmas Eve service. She agreed and began to learn her part. Two days before the service, Debbie called Walt. Her mother didn't want her to be in the service. She wanted her to be home for their annual family Christmas Eve dinner.

Walt initially was angry. Of all the nerve, asking Debbie to break her commitment! She said she'd be there, so she should be.

But as he thought about the situation and his reaction, he realized he had made a serious mistake. He had assumed it was more important for Debbie to be with the youth group than with her family. But she needed to be with her family more. Christmas Eve was an important family time, especially since home life was difficult because of marital tensions. The family needed to be together much more than Debbie needed to be in the youth program.

In the midst of trying to build community and commitment in the youth group, we sometimes forget that group members' primary relational commitment is to their family. While friendships and commitments in youth groups are vital, they aren't as important as family relationships. It's dangerous to allow—or even ask—kids to become so involved and preoccupied with the youth group that they forget about family life.

• **Youth worker knows best.** How many times have we said to ourselves: "John's parents are so inept! They don't know how to discipline. They don't encourage him. They have lousy theologies. If I were his parent . . ."

We may not articulate these sentiments, but we feel them. As a result, churches and youth workers sometimes step in and try to replace parents. Many parents gladly give up their responsibilities. All they do is get the kids involved in church activities and get them there on time. They expect the church to do the rest. And, too often, it tries.

Though intentions are good, this approach hurts more than it helps. The church, the youth group and the youth worker never can be adequate substitutes for parents. Most children grow in their faith more from watching and living with models of that faith at home than they ever will from youth group meetings, retreats and sermons put together. Any youth group program that usurps the parents' role and responsibility is doomed to failure.

Rather than trying to replace parents, the church and youth worker must discover ways to support parents in their roles. In this way the youth worker becomes a partner—or consultant—with parents in the spiritual growth and development of teenagers.

• **The squeaky family gets the ministry.** In some churches, family ministry equals crisis ministry. If youth workers and the church ever reach out to families, it's in times of crisis. The ministry may be intense—and intensely needed—but it's short-lived. After the crisis has been resolved or the family has been torn beyond repair, the church moves on to other concerns.

This approach has two major problems. First, in their concern about being "respectable," many families actually may not seek help until it's too late. As a result, youth workers can do little to heal deep wounds that may have festered within the family for years. Second, it fails to help families face inevitable day-to-day struggles.

As important and unavoidable as crisis ministry to families may be, it alone is not an adequate response to family needs. By broadening our ministry to families beyond crisis ministry, we have opportunities to nurture and support families before crises hit—which will actually make more difference in more families. As Joe Leonard Jr. writes in *Planning Family Ministry: A Guide for a Teaching Church*: "Of course, it is important for the church to respond to families in crises. It is equally important for the church to respond to the needs of all families with planned educational programs so that the families are more able to meet the issues of daily life and resolve them before they *become* crises."[1]

• **Don't practice what we preach.** Week after week people come to church. They hear tremendous biblical expositions. They participate in challenging Bible studies and stimulating Sunday school classes. They know the Bible backward and forward. They may even know whether Adam and Eve had bellybuttons.

But ask them how their faith affects their day-to-day family life and you're likely to get a blank, puzzled stare. They've been programmed with impressive biblical and theological data, but they've never been equipped or challenged by the church to translate that data into real life. When the church does challenge people to apply their faith to their lives, it's usually limited to inner, personal concerns, not to the network of relationships that include friends and families.

Does being a Christian make any difference in our family life? We all agree it should, but does it? What does it mean to be a *Christian* parent? What does it mean to be a *Christian* child, sister or brother? How should Christians respond to family issues such as conflict, divorce, cohabitation, stress or media use? When the church fails to help families deal with these questions, it falls short of its calling.

One of the most beneficial ministries a church can offer is to address family problems and issues from a faith perspective. Churches that don't have periodic sermons on family concerns, Sunday school classes on parenting and family life, family activities or other family-oriented programs miss tremendous opportunities for ministry.

• **Freedom, sweet freedom.** What do parents think when they drop off their teenager at a youth group meeting? Many breathe a sigh of relief and say to themselves: "Ahhhhh . . . I've been looking forward to this all week. Two whole hours of freedom!" Or: "Now I can get something done. Thank the Lord for youth group."

Some parents see youth group as little more than a free babysitting service. The church is partly to blame for this misperception. Many times youth workers communicate—however unconsciously—to parents that we're just trying to give kids something to do on Friday nights so parents can have a little peace and quiet.

We communicate this in many subtle ways. We haphazardly throw together programs at the last minute. We sponsor activities with no real substance just so kids will have something to do. "So there won't be any trouble," we ask parents to chaperon meetings where they sit at the back and act like babysitters.

This babysitting syndrome sends parents harmful messages. It tells them the church doesn't care enough about their participation to do careful and creative planning. It tells them they need not go to church since it doesn't have anything substantive to offer them. It teaches parents that we really don't deserve their respect and support. Thus it becomes impossible to build good relationships with them. Finally, it neglects families' personal and faith needs, and it doesn't give them any guidance or direction.

For ministry to families with teenagers to be effective, we must communicate to teenagers and their parents that we do what we do for a reason. Once parents understand our ministry's purpose and goals, they'll be challenged to get involved—beyond driving to and from church each Friday night.

• **It's better than nothing.** The church board was discussing priorities for the next year. Mr. Smith had decided the church should start a youth program. Why? "First off," he said, "we're the only church in town without one. All our kids go on retreats with kids down the street. Lots of our kids grow up and leave the church for no apparent reason. If we had a youth program, they'd probably be here."

Then Mr. Smith played his trump: "And another thing. Look at all the problems teenagers have today. If we don't do something soon, all the teenage boys in church will be on drugs, and all the girls will be pregnant."

Almost everyone would agree with Mr. Smith's belief that youth ministry should be an important part of a church's ministry. Many people would agree with his concerns. However, establishing a youth program on Mr. Smith's arguments alone would be disastrous. Jealousy, guilt and fear are simply the wrong reasons for starting a youth ministry.

A program based on these concerns—as legitimate as they may be—won't focus on meeting teenagers' spiritual needs. No program that's started "just because it's a good idea" will have a solid enough foundation to sustain a long-term, well-rounded youth ministry. Also, it's unlikely that it will ever take the family's needs seriously.

Before we can reach out effectively to families, we must know why our ministry exists. Shaky foundations must be replaced with a solid understanding of ministry. As we seek to meet teenagers' needs effectively, we will inevitably see the need to reach their families too.

*R*ole Confusion

At the heart of each of these problems is confusion about the differences in the roles of families and churches in relation to each other. Where do family responsibilities end and church responsibilities begin, and vice versa? This question isn't easy to answer, since specific situations often require unique and creative responses. However, we can make some distinctions between the responsibilities of families and churches.

*T*he Family's Responsibilities

Often when we think of the family's responsibilities, we begin with lists of dos and don'ts. We comb scriptures to find specific guidelines for various issues. Should parents spank children? Who's in charge of whom in the family? Who has what responsibilities? Though such an approach is useful at times, it's important that we first understand the general biblical responsibilities that should guide family life. Let's look at a few of these issues as they relate to the church.

• **To live under Christ.** Everything families do should be guided by the belief that Christ is head of the household (Ephesians 5:23). More than 200 years ago Jonathan Edwards wrote: "Every Christian family ought to be as it were a little church consecrated to Christ, and wholly influenced and governed by his rule."[2]

Having Christ as the head of the household has profound implications on how family members should relate to one another and to the world. "In a Christian family Christ is the head of the household and all members of the household are mutually responsible to one another and to Christ," Leonard writes. "Mutual submission to Christ provides the framework within which the duties and responsibilities of each household member are spelled out."[3]

• **To provide companionship.** Christian marriages are built on the belief that "the two will become one flesh" (Matthew 19:5b). This intimacy is central to what it means to be a Christian family. Not only does it meet the deep human need for acceptance and joy in relationships, but it provides a supportive environment for Christian growth, outreach and service.

It follows, then, that a primary way churches can support families is to nurture, celebrate and affirm relationships within families. As youth workers, we can celebrate birthdays, anniversaries and other significant events within families. We can provide opportunities for families to learn skills to enhance interpersonal communication and conflict resolution.

• **To nurture faith in children.** Deuteronomy 6:6-7 reminds us that the primary arena for spiritual growth is the family—not the youth group, the breakfast club or Sunday school. Parents are called to educate their children in all they do.

Ephesians 6:4 says, "Fathers, do not exasperate your children; instead, bring them up in the training and instruction of the Lord." Parents' highest duty is to bring up their children in the Christian faith. The emphasis here is not on what we call a "Christian upbringing" that just makes sure Johnny and Suzie are in church and Sunday school every week. Rather, building faith should be central to every element of family life.

Moreover, teaching isn't just verbal instruction. Parents are called to model their faith through everything they say and do. "The faith is passed on," Leonard writes, "not through prepared speeches, but through the ordinary activities of life, which have all been marked in some way by reverence for God and remembrance of God's teachings."[4]

Too often churches take this responsibility from the family rather than support and educate the family so it can fulfill its own role. As youth workers, we can provide parents the skills to articulate their own faith to their children then challenge them also to live that faith at home.

• **To participate in the larger family of faith.**

Perhaps the most important pattern families can develop is regular and committed membership to a local congregation. Through the church community, families gather the nurture they need to fulfill their roles as Christian families. The web of supportive and caring relationships within a family of faith can sustain small families that might not have the resources or energy to meet the demands and crises of contemporary life.

Sociologist Peter Uhlenberg believes a supportive faith community provides the answer to those who say nuclear families aren't strong enough for today's world. He writes in "Adolescents in American Society: Recent Trends and Proposed Responses":

An unhealthy overemphasis upon individualism has led to a general neglect of the importance of a Christian community. Not only are the lives of individuals in nuclear families to be linked together in intimate and committed relationships, but also the lives of all persons in a local church are to be linked in similar ways . . . Such families are not restricted to their own limited resources during times of need, but can call upon a much greater supply of material, emotional, and spiritual resources.[5]

As youth workers, we need to encourage families to become active participants in church life. Through the local church, families can find the support they need, and they can work with other Christians to fulfill their primary calling as Christians: to love and serve God.

The Church's Responsibilities

As we read the list of family responsibilities, we may wonder, "What's left?" We've given families responsibility to live under Christ, provide companionship, nurture faith and participate in the local church. Why can't the church sit back and watch families fulfill their responsibilities?

Of course such a simplistic question is both unrealistic and irresponsible. Just as families have important responsibilities to fulfill as followers of Christ, so the church has important responsibilities as Christ's body to minister to families. While we could examine dozens of specific responsibilities (many of which are covered in other places in this book), let's focus now on foundational responsibilities that should guide our relationship to families.

• **To be the family of God.** It may seem obvious to say the church's primary responsibility is to be the church. However, we as youth workers sometimes get so caught up in doing things—planning retreats, scheduling meetings, providing counseling—that we forget that our first calling is to be God's family.

In *Faith and Families*, theologian Sang H. Lee says, "Families need to be transformed by the good news of God's gracious act of redemption in Jesus Christ, and the church must faithfully fulfill its role of proclaiming that good news in word and in deed." He continues: "Members of the church . . . have a high responsibility to extend support and care to individual families and their members especially when certain families are having difficulties in fulfilling their affectional function and also when certain individuals are without the support of a family."[6]

This emphasis may seem simple, but it challenges us to rethink what we do in our youth and family ministries. How can our ministries effectively model what it means to "be a family" together as Christians? Does our structure help build relationships and communication? Do our ministries reflect the good news of Christ, offering individuals and families a place of forgiveness and redemption? As youth workers, we should constantly think through such questions that reflect responsibilities we have as the family of God.

• **To teach families to be Christian.** Perhaps the church's most important educational task is to help families understand what the Bible teaches about families. Too often churches ask families to be Christian without ever teaching them what a Christian family is. We have discussed the responsibilities of families. The church's role is to support and educate families as they seek to fulfill those responsibilities.

This role involves both pastoral and prophetic ministry. Pastoral ministry involves standing beside and supporting families as they struggle with real-life issues each day. Prophetic ministry calls families to move beyond where culture tells them to be so they can model a biblical lifestyle. For example, Uhlenberg writes, "A solid Christian critique of our society's ideals of individual self-fulfillment and autonomy from constraining commitments is essential if we are to understand God's basic design for family relationships." He suggests several areas in which cultural values for families need to be challenged by the church: "The contrast of the Christian ideal of life-long commitments in relationships with the popular ideal of maintaining relationships so long as they are considered to be personally rewarding must be made . . . The contrast of sacrificial love in relationships with the popular ideal of self-first must be made."[7]

• **To support families.** Hospitals across the country have formed support groups for people coping with cancer. Each week, cancer patients gather to encourage and support one another. Though the cancer isn't going away, participants say the support they receive from the group members helps them cope better than they would alone. They have chosen to go through their trauma together.

Though parenting a teenager can be joyful and exciting, it also can be painful. With the support of other parents of teenagers, the pain can be lessened and the joy shared more deeply. By providing families—parents and teenagers—support structures of peers within the church, we as youth workers provide a valuable and important ministry to families as they seek to live their Christian faith together.

• **To provide information for families.** In their book *Five Cries of Parents*, Merton P. Strommen and A. Irene Strommen report that one of the major needs of parents is to understand themselves and their teenagers. This desire for understanding is particularly strong among single parents.[8] Merton Strommen says, "If youth leaders recognize this desire, they can provide opportunities for a parent to achieve a fuller understanding of what's happening in their home, and their role in it."[9]

Churches in general and youth workers specifically are in a unique position to help meet this need for understanding. The church is one of the few places where both generations gather together each week. From this perspective we can help parents understand teenagers and parenting roles, and we can help teenagers understand parents. By framing our information from a biblical perspective, we not only provide families with information, but we also help them grow in their faith.

• **To reach beyond the church.** When we think of ministry to families with teenagers, we usually think about the needs of the families within the congregation. While this is important, we also need to reach out to the community to provide services to families that are not part of the church.

Not only does this give the church an outlet for Christlike service to the world, but it provides an important opportunity for outreach and evangelism. Because the church has a message of spiritual hope for all people, Uhlenberg writes, ". . . those outside of the church should always be invited and encouraged to be-

come members of a Christian community. Incorpora-
tion of hurting individuals and families within the
church is the most effective and significant outreach
ministry that is possible."[10]

• **To forgive families.** As we have seen, the Bible
has high standards for marriage and family life. The
church has a responsibility to prophetically challenge
families to live up to those standards. We must call
families to repentance and work with them toward
reconciliation and restoration.

Unfortunately families aren't and can't be perfect.
They don't always fulfill their responsibilities and calling. For whatever reasons and despite best efforts,
families will make mistakes. They will fail—sometimes
tragically.

When families fail—even when they're at fault—the
church is called to respond as Christ would respond:
with compassion. We can look to Jesus' conversation
with the woman at the well (John 4:4-26) and his
refusal to condemn the woman caught in adultery
(John 8:3-11) as our models. While Jesus didn't con-
done sinful behavior, he forgave the women and
challenged them to "go and sin no more."

In our ministry to families with teenagers, this same
attitude should prevail. In most cases, parents already
feel guilty about their failures—whether real or perceived. By offering the forgiveness, redemption,
reconciliation and restoration that Christ offers, we
can be instruments of healing in broken and hurting
families.

*T*he Challenge to Families and Churches

Dora had never been to church before. Her parents
never thought church was important, and her dad
needed the car Sunday mornings to get to work. As a
junior in high school, Dora started coming to church

with her friends. Before long, she was active in the youth group and rapidly growing in her faith.

One month Walt's youth group planned a family fun night at a local gym with the sole purpose of providing a non-threatening event where unchurched families would feel comfortable. Walt invited Dora's parents, and they agreed to come. That evening Walt made a special effort to spend time with Dora's parents. They were delightful people, and they seemed to have a great time. They met several church families.

During the next two years, Dora's family slowly became involved in church. First they participated in youth events as chaperons and helpers. Then they started coming regularly to family nights. Much later they began attending Sunday worship. Now the whole family is involved in church and Sunday school.

Looking back, it would've been easy to write off Dora's parents. After all, they were busy and expressed no interest. Instead, the church intentionally reached out to this family, providing programming designed to meet their needs.

God worked through the church to bring this family to personal Christian commitment and active participation in Christ's body. By fulfilling its responsibility to families, the church now enables families like Dora's to fulfill their responsibilities of serving Christ and nurturing faith in their children.

Chapter 4
Families in Need

*T*he Johnstons were a pillar family in the congregation. Larry was a trustee and Margie coordinated the Christian education program. Their son Bob, a high school junior, was the youth group president.

You could always count on the Johnstons. During the three years Dub served the church, they always supported the youth program. They took every opportunity to share their faith and promote strong family life.

About a year after Dub moved to another church, he learned the Johnston family had fallen apart. Margie found out Larry had supported a mistress for more than 10 years. She also discovered he had gambled away the entire family savings.

No one at church suspected the Johnstons were having problems at home. From the church's perspective, the Johnstons seemed like the perfect Christian family.

*M*asks of Serenity

When families come to church, they're on their best behavior. Seldom do we see the struggles and pain that sometimes are hidden beneath masks of serenity.

Why do families wear those masks? Perhaps they

don't want to unload their personal problems on other church members. It's more likely, though, that they feel they have to live up to the image of the "perfect Christian family" to be accepted at church. Too often the church suggests simplistic solutions to family problems. When families try the solutions and they don't work, they feel guilty or inadequate.

Not long ago Dub watched a televised religious program where the speaker told people in the audience their family difficulties would disappear if they would simply make Jesus the head of the household. If they were struggling in their family, the speaker concluded, either Jesus wasn't really Lord of their home or they were under attack by the devil. Easy. Simple. But wrong. Jesus doesn't promise to take away our struggles and tough times. But he does promise to be with us through them.

It takes a lot of work for families to function in healthy ways—even when Christ is the center of home life. But the church is sometimes guilty of glossing over real-life struggles in families, thus offering them no help when they need it. "If sons or daughters get into difficulty—do something disreputable or scandalous— we try to cover it up with a coat of respectability," writes professor J.C. Wynn in Christian Ministry magazine. "In fact, some of us are so preoccupied with our precious respectability that our reputation is more important to us than caring for one another and working out some stability within the home."[1]

Dolores Curran, in her book *Stress and the Healthy Family*, says it's unhealthy for churches or society to expect families to be perfect. "This idealized view of family produces great guilt in parents who live with everyday family stresses," she writes. "Rather than acknowledging such pressures as valid, we submerge them and feel as if we have failed as spouses and parents when they erupt."[2]

Curran suggests that families are like delicately balanced mobiles hanging from the ceiling. When everything goes well, the pieces remain in balance. But stresses from within or outside the family can throw the family mobile out of balance. Sometimes the stresses are outside gusts of wind such as inflation, a move or peer pressure on teenagers. Other times the pressures are within the family—a new baby, a divorce—all of which can shake the mobile and thus require adjustments.[3]

If we as youth workers want to minister effectively to families with teenagers, we must realize that all families inevitably deal with problems and stresses. Our task is to minister to families in the midst of those struggles, sharing the grace, liberation and challenge the gospel offers families.

What stresses do families, parents and teenagers face? What causes these stresses? What problems develop in families—often as a result of these stresses? What do families need? What makes a family healthy and strong? This chapter examines these questions. It's divided into the following sections:

- Stresses on Families
- Stresses on Teenagers
- Serious Family Problems
- Healthy Families
- Healthy Families With Teenagers

Stresses on Families

All families deal with a variety of stresses. But many of these stresses are magnified during the teenage years. These years are simply a period of life when a young person's body, relationships, intellect and emotions are rapidly growing and maturing.

All the changes can be frightening not only to teenagers but also to their parents. How many times have we as youth workers been approached by concerned parents who say something like: "I don't know what's gotten into Clarice. She used to be so tidy and cooperative. But lately her room looks like the city dump. I can't get her to do anything. What's wrong with her?" How often have we wanted to say: "Congratulations! You're the parent of a normal, growing teenager"?

Researchers now believe parents may be overly worried. As psychologist Anne C. Petersen writes in Psychology Today, ". . . although the early teen years can be quite a challenge for normal youngsters and their families, they're usually not half as bad as they are reputed to be."[4] Parents and teenagers need to hear the good news that more than 50 percent of all teenagers have no serious problems during their early teenage years, when kids go through the most dramatic changes.[5]

Even though these changes are normal, they're still stressful. A survey of Canadians found that parents see the teenage years as the most difficult years of parenting.[6] Relationships change. Kids mature. Parents and teenagers face issues of control and independence. As a result, family conflict usually increases and communication decreases. In a Group Publishing survey of parents of teenagers, 47 percent of the parents surveyed said raising a teenager is harder than they expected it to be, and 75 percent said it's harder today than it used to be. At the same time, 90 percent said it's worth the effort.[7]

• **Money, money, money.** Almost every family survey points to financial pressure or budgeting as the top stress on families. For instance, in a survey of 30,000 Better Homes and Gardens readers, 48 percent said finances cause the most difficulty in their family.[8]

As one parent responded to a survey question: "The top ten stresses in our family all have to do with money. Money may not be the root of all evil, but it sure is the root of all stress."[9]

Interestingly, the problem isn't necessarily that families don't have enough money. Families in all income levels name money as the top family stress. Though families often attribute stress to inadequate funds, stress appears really to come from how to manage and spend money.

At the same time, low-income families face more family problems than wealthier families. Single mothers point to issues such as insufficient funds, keeping up with inflation, not receiving anticipated child support and temporary unemployment as areas of greatest financial stress. Other families mention retirement funds, inflation, scaling down expenses, savings, credit cards and college spending as greater stresses.[10] Teenagers from low-income homes are generally less content with their home life than other teenagers. While 93 percent of other teenagers said they are generally happy at home, only 81 percent of those from lower-class homes do.[11]

Churches and we as youth workers have a great deal to offer families in dealing with financial stress. For many family members, an important need is to learn how to communicate among themselves about financial priorities and values. Other families struggle with finding and accepting a comfortable and modest lifestyle in an upwardly mobile society. The church has an important role in challenging families to use appropriate stewardship with all their resources—and supporting them when they make difficult faith commitments.

Our youth programs must also keep in mind the difficult financial situations of many families, particularly single-parent families. Are special events and workshops too expensive for disadvantaged teenagers and parents to participate in? Are scholarships or other resources available that allow low-income people to participate in trips and leadership training events? What advocacy roles can our youth programs and the church play in addressing the needs of poor families for services, educational opportunities and crisis intervention?

• **Stopping the clock.** With two working parents (or just one parent), working kids, long commutes and numerous time-consuming activities, American families are busier than ever. A major study by the National Research Center of the Arts found that the amount of time Americans give to jobs, school and housekeeping has increased dramatically in 14 years. In 1973, Americans said they spent an average of 40.6 hours per week on these chores. In 1987, the average amount of time spent on these activities increased to 46.8 hours, resulting in a 37 percent decline in leisure and relaxation time.[12]

Dub recently talked with a parent who typifies the stress of having too much to do. She was worried that she was losing touch with her teenage son because all the different family schedules meant she saw him only in passing. Her family's tradition of having dinner together had long since vanished, and now her family was lucky to have just one meal together each week.

Curran writes that time pressures are particularly significant stresses since they generate and intensify other stresses. She explains:

When a couple suffers from lack of time together, communication suffers. When communication suffers, couples are less able to deal with issues like children's behavior and financial worries. When personal time gets squeezed out by work, family, and excessive community activities, predictable feelings like fatigue, tension, and a sense of futility give rise to sharp retorts, temperamental outbursts and an atmosphere of walking-on-

eggs at home. [13]

Rather than minister to these stresses, many churches and youth programs augment them. Just look at church and youth group newsletters from around the country. If teenagers and families participated in everything offered, they'd be at church most week nights, all day Saturday and until bedtime Sunday. While churches say they offer diverse options to appeal to different people, they often publicize the options with a not-so-subtle message such as "If you really want to support the church and be part of the program, you need to participate in everything."

As we seek to minister to families with teenagers, we must keep their schedules in mind. We must listen to their needs and plan quality programming that will make them feel that participating is worth their time. Moreover, we need to affirm their decisions to say "no" to options or responsibilities at church in order to spend time together or fulfill other obligations.

• **Independence and control.** What limits should parents set for their teenagers? What do parents do when their teenagers go beyond those limits? When should parents let their teenagers fail? How should they respond to those failures?

Perhaps the most difficult parenting issues during the teenage years lie in the tension between autonomy and control. "During a child's adolescence, parenting issues hinge on an ability to allow the adolescent independence while still setting limits," writes Bettie B. Youngs in *Helping Your Teenager Deal With Stress.* "A parent has the difficult task of providing experiences that keep the parent-child relationship healthy at a time when the adolescent is screaming for autonomy but still needs guidance." [14]

Stress comes for parents from two directions. First is the stress of feeling they're "losing" their son or daughter as he or she develops an identity and independence distinct from the family. Second is their concern for their child's physical and emotional safety and well-being as he or she makes choices and tests options in the world away from home.

As youth workers we can help parents through these types of stresses. We can provide opportunities for young people to affirm their parents, thus easing the feelings of loss as the teenager develops his or her self-identity. We can also work with youth group members to teach them ways to assure parents of their love. We can help families develop open lines of communication so parents can know where their kids are and that they're safe.

• **Relating to teenagers.** As children grow from infancy to childhood to adolescence and to adulthood, parents must learn how to relate to them at each stage. Sometimes the "generation gap" becomes the "generation chasm" as teenagers identify with the music, fashion, food and activities of their youth culture.

These changes and others leave both parents and teenagers wondering how to interact with and relate to each other. How many times have we witnessed that awkward moment before a youth group trip when parents say goodbye to their son or daughter? No one knows exactly what to do or say. A mother may lean forward to kiss her son goodbye, only to have the boy stick out his hand for an "appropriate" handshake. Or a father may exchange nonchalant waves with his daughter and leave the room, only to have her slip out to catch Dad for one more hug.

Because of the changes they're going through, teenagers are often unpredictable and difficult for parents to understand. As Richard D. Parsons writes in *Adolescents in Turmoil, Parents Under Stress: A Pastoral Ministry Primer*, "At times it seems they are the epitome of positive energy and innocent optimism; then at other times, they show themselves to be abruptly cynical and immobilized in worlds to which adults don't seem to have access."[15]

As youth workers who specialize in adolescence, we can help parents understand this unique and confusing stage in their child's development. We can assure them that the changes they see in their child are not cause for alarm, but normal stages of growing up. And we can act as mediators and interpreters to help parents better understand the culture that helps to shape their child.

• **Feelings of inadequacy.** Several years ago Dub participated in a local panel discussion after a national TV program on crises facing today's teenagers— substance abuse, pregnancy, running away and dropping out. In the midst of the discussion, a mother in the audience said: "I'm hearing that one of the core issues is a teenager's self-esteem. I try to encourage my daughter, but knowing how insecure she is and how vicious her world can be, I wonder whether what I say makes any difference at all."

Dub responded by telling the mother not to underestimate her influence on her teenager. While parental influence does decline as teenagers get older, it's always a major factor in teenagers' decisions. Moreover, a recent study found that parental influence on teenagers is gradually increasing after bottoming out in the 1970s.[16]

Other researchers have confirmed that parents do have a great deal of influence on teenagers. A Search Institute survey of 8,000 young adolescents found that when faced with various problems, they turn to parents for help much more often than they turn to peers. Forty-eight percent of the junior highers said they turn to parents for help with problems, compared with 18 percent who turn to friends.[17]

Yet parents don't always know how to respond to their teenagers and their teenagers' world. They worry about their child getting involved in problem behaviors. They feel inadequate to meet the many demands of being a parent today.

Youth programs can offer parents ways to deal with their feelings of inadequacy. In everything they do, churches can work to support and enable parents to be more effective in their parenting roles. Through workshops, newsletters and discussions, churches can help parents understand their teenager. Churches can provide opportunities for learning parenting skills. They can sponsor support groups where parents can share their own ideas, frustrations and concerns with one another.

• **Confusion in a changing world.** In the past 30 years, Western culture has gone through dramatic changes. At the heart of these changes has been a shift in values regarding several issues, including sexuality. Parents who grew up knowing one cultural value system suddenly find their teenager living in another.

For instance, pollster and social commentator Daniel Yankelovich argues that older parents grew up with a "social role" orientation in which personal desires were often overshadowed by family, employer and societal needs. However, this philosophy has been replaced by a "culture of narcissism" that searches for self-fulfillment among the many options of today's world. David Elkind writes in his book *All Grown Up & No Place to Go*, ". . . we as adults and parents are caught in the crossfire of these two social philosophies."[18]

The differences in parents' and teenagers' values show up in a Search Institute survey that compares what parents think is important with what young people think. While both generations place the most importance on having a happy family life, their other values differ. Young people place more importance than their parents on six of the 10 values, including fun, money and freedom. Moreover, young people aren't as strongly opposed to such behaviors as lying to parents, teenage beer drinking and teenage abortion.[19]

Caught in the middle, parents feel pulled between protecting their child and accepting the new social code. And teenagers sometimes interpret their parents' ambivalence as license. As Elkind writes: "Because we are reluctant to take a firm stand, we deny teenagers the benefit of our parental concern and we impel them into premature adulthood. We say, honestly, 'I don't know,' but teenagers hear, 'They don't care.' "[20]

The church has a tremendous opportunity—indeed, responsibility—at this point to help families in their confusion. We can help guide teenagers and their families through the many value shifts in the culture. What cultural values can be affirmed by Christians? What cultural values conflict with Christian values? What are appropriate choices for Christians in today's world? By allowing families to ask these kinds of questions, we not only foster communication within the family, we help families grow in their faith and commitments.

Stresses on Teenagers

Just as their parents encounter the stresses of parenting and maintaining a family, teenagers grapple with the stresses of their changing bodies, relationships and thinking abilities. The same things about adolescence that confuse parents also confuse teenagers.

In the midst of these and other stresses, though, teenagers are generally content with their family and parents. A full 90 percent of young people say they're happy at home. Moreover, the particular structure of the young person's family makes little difference in this overall positive attitude. (The only factors that lessen this contentment are divorce and poverty.)[21]

At the same time, some teenagers identify areas

where home life causes stress. When asked what would make home life better, teenagers listed getting along better with siblings (39 percent), talking openly with parents (39 percent), being treated more as an adult (37 percent), having more time with parents (35 percent), having more money in the family (34 percent) and having more responsibility (32 percent).[22]

Let's look at some of these and other stresses on teenagers in the home.

• **Do everything.** School. Sports. Jobs. Extracurricular activities. Church. Dating. Today's teenagers are busier than ever. While many teenagers choose their activities, they also get involved because they're expected to. "There is an enormous amount of peer and parental pressure to be involved in everything," says child psychiatrist Bennett Leventhal. "We expect kids to have their life goals set at 14. They feel there is too much to get done in too little time."[23]

Wanting the best for their children in a complex world, parents often push their children to achieve beyond their abilities. As a result, more than two-thirds of affluent teenagers surveyed say they're convinced they can't live up to their parents' expectations.[24] It's not surprising that school performance topped the list of teenagers' concerns in a Group Publishing survey.[25]

A youth group member once told Dub that whenever he takes his report card home his parents reprimand him for any grade below "B." And when he tries to get credit for good grades that he worked hard for, the response is always the same, "Well, that's expected, of course." Instead of getting needed affirmation, the teenager only hears about his failure.

The pressure to achieve can be particularly strong in single-parent families. Since single parents often need help with the family, they place heavy demands on their teenagers and often ask them to be "adult" companions. "It isn't that such children are required to do more work than generations before them," Elkind writes. "The problem is that the child is taking on parental responsibilities. Children of years ago worked hard, but usually had mothers and fathers to take on the real worry and care of the family."[26]

As youth workers, we need to be aware of teenagers' busy schedules and avoid simply adding to the time pressures they already feel. We need to help them make wise choices among their many options. At the same time, the church needs to be a community where kids don't feel the need to impress their peers in order to be accepted. Finally, as we work with parents we should remind them not to send mixed messages to their children that say in effect, "We love you for what you do and what you achieve."

• **Relationship with parents.** Many people assume parent-teenager relationships are always bad. One author goes so far as to write to teenagers: "One of the greatest sources of stress, if not *the* greatest source of stress in your life as a teenager, is your relationship with your parents."[27]

However, most research doesn't support this negative opinion. Search Institute found that a minority of young adolescents report major conflicts with parents. While conflict increases slightly through junior high, ". . . the phenomenon of out-and-out rebellion against parents or rejection of parental values is relatively rare."[28]

There are, however, inevitable stresses and strains on parent-teenager relationships. Just as parents have trouble understanding and relating to teenagers, teenagers often have difficulty understanding and relating to parents. Teenagers' need for autonomy and freedom conflicts with their need for affirmation and guidance. The mixed signals they send parents usually reflect their own inner confusion as they try to relate to their parents amid all the changes in their lives.

In the same way we as youth workers can help parents understand teenagers, we can help teenagers understand and relate to parents. We can provide opportunities for teenagers to express appreciation for their parents and ask for their parents' support and guidance when needed. We can also help teenagers understand what parents are trying to do through their discipline, rules and restrictions.

• **Relationship with siblings.** Eight out of 10 children grow up with at least one brother or sister.[29] Interestingly, these relationships may cause more stress for teenagers than relationships with parents. When asked how happy they were with various aspects of home life, children and teenagers gave the lowest rank to "relationships with siblings." Only 62 percent said they were happy with these relationships. Moreover, improving relations with brothers and sisters tops the list of things young people say would improve home life.[30]

Actually, brothers and sisters have love-hate relationships. On one hand, siblings compete for attention, privileges, love and power. On the other, they rely on each other's companionship, role modeling and advice. As Jane Norman and Myron Harris write in *The Private Life of the American Teenager*, "Ask any teenager to describe his or her feelings about a sibling and you're sure to hear a barrage of emotions: affection, irritation, excitement, frustration, genuine love, profound hate."[31] Yet when pressed, almost all teenagers said they like their brothers and sisters at least sometimes. Only 3 percent said they don't like them.[32]

What complaints do teenagers have about their siblings? Invasion of privacy tops the list. Forty percent of teenagers say a lack of privacy is a major problem they have with their siblings. Teenagers want their "own space," and invasion of that space is particularly troubling to them. Teenagers' other complaints about siblings include: siblings getting away with things (30 percent), teasing (17 percent) and favoritism (15 percent).[33]

Family therapists Carole Calladine and Andrew Calladine believe sibling relationships are, to a large measure, shaped by parents. They describe three relationship patterns:

1. Heir/heiress—one child is the heir apparent, and other children play a secondary role to this person.

2. Competitors—children learn they can get their parents' attention and affection by outdoing or outsmarting each other.

3. Peers—each child recognizes that he or she is loved and is important to Mom and Dad. So, recognizing they're important to each other, siblings bond together.[34]

Because of these dynamics, parents can greatly influence their children's relationships with each other. Curran believes appropriate modeling is the key. "When parents respect one another and their offspring," she writes, "children tend to respect parents and each other."[35] By respecting each child for his or her uniquenesses, spending time with each child, listening to each child's concerns and refusing to get caught in family squabbles, parents can foster strong relationships among siblings.

Similarly, we as youth workers can strengthen sibling relationships through our own ministry. We can support and educate parents about their roles in their children's relationships. We can open communication channels between brothers and sisters, allowing them to express both their affection and complaints.

Finally, we as youth workers can be aware of the dynamics between brothers and sisters in a youth group and plan accordingly. For instance, if siblings are openly competitive, putting them on the same team in activities can build their cooperation and lessen their competitiveness. If one teenager dominates the other, we can put them in separate discussion groups where the reclusive sibling will feel freer to express himself or herself.

Serious Family Problems

To this point, we've dealt with day-to-day stresses in typical families. However, the stress in many families is more severe than everyday stresses. These families may be dysfunctional—characterized by unhealthy relationships, a lack of harmony, emotional estrangement or suffocating enmeshment. Or they may be confronted with a major crisis such as divorce or teenage pregnancy that puts undue stress on the family's coping mechanisms and relationships.

While it's important that we as youth workers recognize and respond to these problems, we also need to understand our limits. (See Chapter 12 for more about knowing our limits.) Ministering in the midst of major family problems requires special training and skill. Unless we have received special training, we can best serve the families by referring them to specialists who are better equipped to meet their urgent and difficult needs.

Let's briefly look at some of these situations.

• **Divorce.** By its very nature, divorce tears families apart. Though experts now believe divorce is a better alternative for some families than continuing to live in constant tension or violence, the separation is never easy or without long-term consequences. Moreover, most teenagers agree that some parental interactions are more harmful than divorce and separation. Indeed, three out of four teenagers say divorce is justified if parents constantly argue, if physical violence is involved, or if one or both parents is unfaithful.[36]

Because of the prevalence of divorce in our society, few if any youth groups will not be affected by family breakups. We as youth workers and the church can play an important role in helping broken families put the pieces of their lives back together. Ministry may involve individual or family counseling. Or families may need referral to a good lawyer. Or teenagers may need trustworthy adults to turn to when they feel that the most important adults in their lives have let them down.

• **Physical or sexual abuse.** Though we like to think of families as havens, for some people they are hells. Researchers estimate that as many as 1 million children are sexually abused by their parents or caretakers each year.[37] Other studies have found that as many as 43 percent of teenagers have experienced some form of family violence.[38]

Abuse is particularly traumatic for a child or teenager. "Of all the perils of puberty," Elkind writes, "incest or its mere possibility is perhaps the most destructive."[39] Experts have found that victims of abuse often distrust adults and experience sleeping disturbances, eating disorders, anger, withdrawal and guilt. Many develop sexual problems, and many, particularly girls, have low self-esteem. In the end, victims of child abuse frequently become abusers themselves.[40]

As we become involved with families, it's critical that we recognize the signs of abuse and learn to respond appropriately. Often the critical first step is to get the victim out of the home and into a shelter where professionals assess the situation and suggest appropriate actions. When authorities and specialists are involved, they may call on pastors and youth workers to help with the long-term counseling the whole family will need to allow healing to occur.

• **Alcoholic families.** At least 7 million children in the United States live in an alcoholic family—a family where at least one of the parents has a "drinking problem." While the health-care world used to focus its attention on rehabilitating the alcoholic, today it's also working with the alcoholic's whole family. It has discovered that a parent's alcoholism reshapes family dynamics and opens children to a greater risk of emotional, relational and psychological problems. Growing up in an alcoholic home can make children feel guilty, anxious, embarrassed, confused, angry and depressed. It often makes them unable to have close relationships, and children of alcoholics are four times more likely as other children to become alcoholics themselves.[41]

For decades, churches have been strong supporters of organizations such as Alcoholics Anonymous that offer alcoholics a road to recovery. It's now time to expand that ministry to reach out to the silent pain of alcoholic families. If we as youth workers can learn to recognize the signs of alcoholic families, we can work with children of alcoholics to avert more serious problems that develop in adulthood.

• **Troubled teenagers.** Youth minister Greg McKinnon tells the story of a strong Christian family that was devastated by a teenager's problem behaviors. The first two children grew up without any major problems. But everything fell apart when the third child became a teenager. "She got involved in a little bit of everything," he writes in Youthworker, "from sex to drugs to violence to theft. Her parents tried everything, but nothing seemed to work. They prayed, took her to counseling, went to counseling themselves, spent extra time with her. Yet things only got worse."[42]

This family's reality is many families' nightmare. Parents worry that no matter what they do, their child will get involved in all the destructive behaviors they read and hear about in the daily news—alcohol and drug abuse, premarital sex, violence, crime and suicide. When teenagers do get involved it can be devastating, particularly for parents. They say: "Where did we go wrong? What should we have done? If only . . ."

When families experience such calamities, they need the church's support and guidance. Even if we're not qualified as youth workers to counsel families in these crisis situations, we can guide them toward qualified professionals. We can establish support groups where parents can learn to help each other. We can provide resources for parents to help them understand particular problems.

*H*ealthy Families

Often when discussing families, we stop after listing all the problems. As a result, we know what makes some families unhealthy, but we don't really know why others are healthy. Recently, though, researchers have begun looking at healthy families and what makes them work so well. What they discovered is that healthy families have developed a handful of characteristics that protect them from the calamities that strike other families. Here are some of the characteristics of healthy families identified by Nick Stinnett of the University of Nebraska at Lincoln.

• **Appreciation.** In healthy families, members appreciate each other, building a supporting and affirming environment for each other. And because family members respect each other, they also respect one another's privacy and individual concerns.

• **Time.** Even in the midst of many time pressures, members of healthy families make time together an important priority. They regularly share meals together; they do things together; and they recreate together. In other words, they enjoy spending time with one another.

• **Communication.** In healthy families, members learn to communicate in direct, loving and constructive ways. They express their feelings and needs but also listen to those of other family members.

• **Commitment.** Because of their strong sense of togetherness, in healthy families, members are committed to stay together even through crises, difficulties and transitions. Each family member has a sense of mutual trust and shared responsibility. One side effect of this commitment is that healthy families develop strong traditions, and times of celebration have special meaning.

• **Faith.** At their core, healthy families have strong moral and spiritual beliefs. Concern for others and serving God are important to these families. As a result, the families aren't isolated from the world but are involved with other people and their community.

• **Crisis management.** When healthy families are confronted with crisis or pain, they deal with it in positive and constructive ways. Their bonds of interdependence and adaptability give them the strength to cope with crisis—and often make them even stronger as a result.[43]

*H*ealthy Families With Teenagers

In addition to these characteristics of healthy families, Curran has found that families that go through adolescence with less stress have certain characteristics and attitudes that guide them. Despite all the problems with raising a teenager, she writes in her book *Stress and the Healthy Family*, ". . . there are thousands of quiet, unassuming families who seem able to weather these years with a minimum of stress." She found the following characteristics of these healthy families:

• The parents aren't afraid of the teenage years. Rather, they enjoy watching and being with their child as he or she grows from childhood into adulthood.

• The parents understand what's happening inside their teenager. They know their young person is searching for self-identity, and they provide an affirming, loving environment in which to do the searching.

• The parents change their rules and demands as their teenager grows older. They recognize that the changes in maturity and need for independence require different responses at different stages.

• The parents give direct guidance on sexuality. They are comfortable discussing their own and their teenager's sexuality, and they're open with their concerns.

• The parents let their teenager think on his or her own. They accept—even encourage—young people to have opinions different from their own. In doing so, they help their teenager as he or she searches for self-identity.

• The parents only confront their teenager on important issues. While every conflict becomes an explosive confrontation in stress-filled families, parents in healthy families give in on minor issues.

• The parents notice their teenager's friends and other influences. They welcome friends into their home and enjoy getting to know them. When these influences are negative, they deal with the problem in non-confrontational ways.

• The parents spend time individually with their teenager. They go fishing, shopping or to a ball game just so they'll have a chance to talk.

• The parents help their teenager become independent. They help their child look forward to leaving home, and they encourage him or her to make new friends and establish new support systems. This eases the tension between independence and control, and it keeps young people from feeling guilty for leaving.[44]

*H*ealing Families

In ministering to families with teenagers, it's important that we not merely patch up problems in families. Rather, our goal should be to enable families to become strong and healthy so they'll have the inner resources to cope with stresses they'll inevitably face. Effective ministry to families with teenagers seeks to build on each of the characteristics of healthy families.

Such an approach will help not only families, but the church. As Jim Larson writes in his book *A Church Guide for Strengthening Families*: "As families feel loved, supported, and encouraged, their faith will become more practical and meaningful. Whatever strategies the church adopts for strengthening families, its investment of resources will pay rich dividends in terms of both family stability and church growth."[45]

Part 2

*E*lements of a Successful Ministry

Chapter 5
Designing Effective Family Programs

*T*he program was a youth worker's dream. The evening began with a crazy crowdbreaker planned by two parents. Even people who had only scowled during previous activities were laughing and kidding each other.

The short video that followed was a well-chosen discussion starter about self-worth. When the participants broke into parents groups and teenagers groups, they all started to open up about their own positive experiences of affirmation.

Then the program planners put parents together with kids from other families to do role plays. The meeting's message was obviously sinking in as people acted out how negative actions speak louder than positive words.

When families joined together toward the end of the program, the leaders didn't need to give instructions. Families already knew what they needed to do. As parents and teenagers affirmed each other, they shared an important time of family unity.

On the surface, the meeting seemed simple and easy to plan. No one had to give a long speech. There weren't any earthshaking visual aids. In reality, the program took several hours of careful thought and planning to conceive the best way to lead family members to affirm each other.

This chapter offers specific guidelines for designing, scheduling and publicizing programs for families. Taking time to design appropriate and creative family programs can make the difference between a decent meeting and a meeting that leaves a lasting impact on individuals and families.

*D*esigning Family Programs

All too often, the only family-oriented part of church is the ride to and from church. For effective ministry to families with teenagers, plan activities that involve family interaction. While age-specific activities are appropriate at times, plan activities for families together as well. And when you plan family meetings or retreats, give family members plenty of opportunities to interact together.

Many dynamics take place when you bring parents and teenagers together for meetings and other events. Parents and teenagers may not be comfortable with each other. Different families have different shapes. Parents think on a level different from teenagers. Parents and teenagers have different needs and limitations.

Here are some guidelines for designing programs for parents and teenagers:

• **Remember basic programming principles.** Programming for families involves many of the same principles you use in all programming. Diagram 1, "General Programming Guidelines," includes 12 basic programming principles. Photocopy these suggestions for leaders who don't have programming experience. *The Youth Group Meeting Guide* (Group Books) offers additional step-by-step plans for designing meetings for youth groups. Many of the principles and guidelines suggested in this resource apply to all programming.

Diagram 1
General Programming Guidelines

1. Plan ahead. Quality programs take time to develop and plan. Set dates several months in advance and begin thinking about the program. Start a file of notes, ideas, articles and other pertinent information. Last-minute preparation almost always results in missing important details.

2. Be prepared. People can tell when you aren't prepared. It's not enough to have a great personality that attracts kids and parents. If you rely on personality, not preparation, in the long run people will remember you for your lack of preparation, not your charisma.

3. Cover all bases. Be sure someone is responsible for *everything*. Who is in charge of setting up? Who is supplying and serving refreshments? Who will lead singing? Do you have enough name tags? Develop a planning sheet and checklist to help you remember the little details.

4. Vary your teaching strategies. Everyone doesn't learn the same way. Use a variety of strategies to make every meeting different. Use skits, role plays, videos, music, discussions, simulation games, worksheets, creative writing, projects, art or other creative techniques. Variety helps people become active participants in the learning process, not just listeners (or sleepers).

5. Plan too much. When you complete your meeting plan, do you look at it and then pray that you can stretch it to fill time? If so, you haven't planned enough. Plan 90 minutes of programming for every 60-minute meeting. If the meeting moves quickly or if participants don't respond to part of the meeting, you have insurance. Of course, don't feel obligated to use everything you plan if you don't need it.

6. Rehearse. Go over the meeting plan several times with everyone who's involved. Does everyone know what to do and when to do it? This rehearsal is particularly important if you're working with a large group and several leaders.

continued

7. Gather everything and make sure it works. Is all electrical equipment plugged in? Have you assembled all the materials you need? Does everything work? Is there an extra bulb for the projector? These kinds of questions make sure your supplies enhance rather than detract from your program.

8. Start and end on time. If you always start late, people will think it's okay to come late. If you start on time, late comers will soon learn to come on time if they don't want to miss anything. Also, honor your word to end on time. People often have other plans after the program.

9. Pray for the event. Ask God to speak through you, the program and other leaders. Pray that God will guide you and other leaders. And pray that God will open the participants' hearts and minds.

10. Evaluate the program. Ask participants to fill out a brief evaluation form immediately after family programs. Take the results to your next staff meeting to discuss. Note what went well, and brainstorm how to improve.

11. Involve others in the planning. Including participants in the planning process gives them ownership of the programs and adds their insights and ideas. Both parents and teenagers can participate to ensure that the programming addresses their needs and interests.

12. Cover a variety of topics. Surprise participants with a variety of content in your meetings. Focus some meetings on upbeat themes and others on problems. Deal with personal, family, church and social concerns. Be controversial at times. By varying the content, you keep people interested and involved.

• **Focus on common family concerns.** Some families have serious problems that merit special attention. However, in order to reach families, focus your programming on common family concerns such as communication, spiritual growth and conflict resolution. Even healthy families want to improve in these common areas, and many severe family problems relate to these same issues.

Within this foundation of common concern you can address more serious problems as well. For instance, seminars and meetings on self-esteem can address the warning signs and dangers of teenage suicide. Or problems in dysfunctional families can be part of discussions on family relationships and communication. If you discover that certain special needs require additional attention, organize smaller study or support groups to address these issues.

• **Be sensitive to different family situations.** As we discussed in Chapter 2, many teenagers come from non-traditional families. Be sure your programming doesn't leave out any parents and teenagers simply because they don't come from traditional families.

Many different situations arise that require sensitivity and awareness. Walt's church hosts an annual family gym night during which families play two half-court basketball games simultaneously. They used to play a mother-daughter game at one end and a father-son game at the other. But then they realized many boys didn't have fathers to participate, and some girls didn't have mothers involved. To ensure that these young people feel welcome, the families play "the older men versus the younger men" and "the older women versus the younger women." Of course, some people still comment about age insensitivity, but only in jest.

Many false assumptions about families can surface in programming. For instance, do meetings about parent-teenager communication assume two parents are involved? Do meetings about family responsibilities assume that women and men fulfill traditional roles in the family? Does programming make intentional efforts to address the needs of different families? In order for family programs to include all families, such questions should be considered in planning and evaluation.

• **Facilitate family cooperation.** Design activities to help parents and teenagers cooperate, not compete. Avoid putdown games or activities in which one person is the brunt of a joke. Instead, use games and tasks that require families to work together. Then discuss how the activities reflect or teach about life. When you use friendly competition, focus on competition between families, not within them. Similarly, when dividing the group into teams, keep families together.

• **Let families communicate.** Don't do all the talking. Instead, let family members interact with one another during the meeting. Have them discuss tough questions they might feel uncomfortable discussing at home. Sometimes it helps for someone to give a family "permission" to discuss sensitive topics such as sexuality, money or family stress.

• **Begin with non-threatening activities.** Family members must take risks in order to grow stronger in their relationships with each other. But don't force families to take those risks too soon. If honest communication and cooperation don't already occur at home, families probably won't start them during the first parent-teenager meeting you sponsor. Forcing families into uncomfortable discussions too quickly may build resistance and make them stop participating altogether. Ease families into deeper relationships by beginning with non-threatening questions and tasks. As the trust and comfort increase, move into riskier activities.

One useful process is to begin meetings by having parents talk with other parents while teenagers talk with their peers. Then have parents get in groups with teenagers from other families. Finally, at the end of the meeting, bring parents together with their own teenagers. By this time, both generations have had time to relax and open up to each other. They've practiced talking about the topic, and they can now talk together about the risky family issues.

• **Don't let parents dominate.** If parents haven't learned to listen to their teenagers at home, they may inadvertently dominate discussions and activities during parent-teenager meetings and retreats. Don't let this happen. By dealing with this issue from the beginning, you set a pattern for shared dialogue and discussion.

Another way parents sometimes dominate discussions is by believing they have the final word on everything. They use meetings to give their teenagers instructions or to tell their teenagers "what's good for them." While parents sometimes do need to be firm with their teenagers, family meetings aren't the correct times. Meetings should be designed to facilitate two-way communication and mutual understanding.

Develop structures and guidelines for discussions that foster participation of both parents and teenagers. Make conscious efforts to listen to teenagers' questions, ideas and concerns during meetings. Work with leaders to include both generations in small group activities. Ask parents to be aware of this tendency and to make conscious efforts to overcome it.

• **Remember that parents are adults.** Parents meetings shouldn't simply mimic youth group meetings. Parents have different concerns, different perspectives and different thinking processes from adolescents. Remember these differences so your programming for parents will be effective.

Several differences involve personal vulnerability. Adults are less willing to take risks that may embarrass or expose them. They may hesitate to play little-kid games or games their teenagers play in youth group. They may fear that the activities will make them feel stupid. And they may resist discussing personal issues that expose their problems or foibles—particularly in front of teenagers. Therefore, it's essential to begin with low-vulnerability activities.

• **Avoid addressing just one generation.** Imagine a family meeting on discipline in which all the discussion revolves around what parents should do. As important as the topic may be, the approach misses half of the participants, since it doesn't address teenagers' perspectives and concerns. Similarly, a family meeting on school might be useful to teenagers, but unless planned well, it could be a waste for parents.

Whenever you plan intergenerational events, be sure the topic and approach address the needs, perspectives and concerns of both parents and teenagers. Parents shouldn't simply be an audience for a youth meeting, and vice versa.

Most topics can be effectively addressed from both perspectives. For instance, a meeting on discipline could help parents learn their appropriate roles while also allowing teenagers to express their own concerns, needs and ideas. And a meeting on school could help parents and teenagers talk together about expectations and how to support each other.

• **Help each generation respect the other.** Think of how many times you've heard statements like these: "What do they know about it? They're just kids." "Why should we listen to those old folks? Their ideas were outdated before we were born."

Some parents and teenagers perpetuate the "generation gap" with stereotypical remarks about each other. As a result, neither generation learns from the other. Work with parents and teenagers to listen to each other and to respect what each thinks and believes. Without mutual and open respect, parents and teenagers will never build healthy relationships. Help families build this respect by designing programs in which everyone listens to each other openly and respectfully. Use role reversals to help parents and teenagers see issues from each other's perspectives.

• **Be sensitive to participants without their families.** No matter what you program, some parents or teenagers simply won't attend family events. As a result their family members who do come may feel left out if they can't participate fully in the planned activities.

You can deal with this dilemma in at least two ways, depending on the situation. The first approach allows and encourages these young people or parents to participate in family events without the rest of their family. To make them feel comfortable, match them with another family that has agreed to "adopt" the teenager or parent for the evening. This family includes the person in family activities, discussions and sharing times. Such an arrangement offers excellent opportunities for teenagers to get to know active Christian parents and for parents to get to know other teenagers. And hearing from a participant about the fun family event may entice other family members to attend a future event.

Sometimes, though, having an extra "family member" in a family decreases the program's effectiveness for the family. It may inhibit members from openly discussing real problems in the family. For programs that require more openness and vulnerability, specify that the program is a families-only event. Require that at least a parent and a teenager participate together.

Recently Walt's church sponsored a family retreat on communication. Many teenagers wanted to bring friends, but they weren't allowed for two reasons. First, the teenagers most likely would spend most of the retreat time with their friends, not their families.

Second, having other teenagers along without their parents would hinder the communication and interaction necessary for the retreat to be effective.

Whenever you sponsor a families-only event, don't cancel regular youth group programming. Instead, schedule a meeting or event specifically for young people whose parents won't attend church family events.

• **Keep costs down.** Charging individual registration fees for a retreat or special event can make the cost prohibitive for many families, particularly if more than one teenager participates. And single parents with limited incomes may not be able to afford the cost of a simple dinner at church. If possible, plan less expensive events for families. Or consider having a maximum family package so no families will have to pay more than a certain amount to participate. Another option would be to hold fund raisers to eliminate altogether the cost of these events to families.

• **Recognize physical limitations.** For its first family fun night, Walt's family ministry program organized basketball, volleyball and several other high-energy activities for everyone. However, many of the parents couldn't participate because of physical limitations. As a result, these parents didn't really enjoy the evening.

When planning games and activities for meetings or special family events, remember that some parents won't be able to enjoy—or even participate in—many high-energy activities. Plan some activities that require little or no physical skill or exertion such as board games and other table games. Or have families work together to solve riddles or puzzles.

• **Plan for other ages.** Whenever you ask parents to be involved in a meeting or retreat, be sure activities are available for younger children as well. Many parents of teenagers may also have elementary kids (or younger) who can't be left alone for an evening or weekend. Unless you include them in your meeting, make sure other activities or babysitting services are available for them at the church. Or include them on retreats, and plan special activities or crafts for them when the parent-teenager activities aren't appropriate.

• **Relax.** All too often churches plan family retreats as though they are junior high retreats—with activities scheduled for every minute. This approach is unnecessary and even counterproductive for family events. Schedule a lot of free time. Families are weary from a busy week and will appreciate time to relax together. Some families may use the free time to nap or read together. Others may take a family hike.

If you prefer, offer several optional family activities during free time. Design these activities to allow families to spend time together in relaxing and enjoyable ways.

• **Use different leaders.** Step back from always planning and leading meetings and events. Work with a team to plan programs that allow several people to lead in different ways. Use both kids and parents. Ask youth ministry volunteers to participate. Sharing program leadership reminds parents who the leaders are, and it reminds them that they share ownership in the program. Moreover, leaders can practice facilitating large group events and meetings.

Scheduling for Families

Trying to get several family members together in one place at one time can be challenging. Families run in many different directions all the time. There will never be any way to schedule perfectly for all families. However, keep the following guidelines in mind to ensure that the largest number can participate:

• **Program when families can meet.** Plan activities when most families can participate. Use the results from your family survey to determine the best times for family meetings and events. Don't feel obligated to program during traditional times. If families prefer to meet on Saturday mornings, schedule your meetings then.

• **Avoid interfering with youth activities.** Try not to schedule family activities during your traditional youth group times (unless, of course, you're scheduling parents meetings to coincide with a youth group activity). While replacing regular youth activities with family events may seem logical at first, it can make some teenagers feel left out and pushed aside.

One spring Dub's family ministry team hosted a Parent-Youth Oddball Olympic Picnic. The program was set for a Sunday evening when the junior high group usually met. The team thought that since many kids routinely spent Sunday evenings at church, more people would come to the picnic.

It was a fun and successful event in which parents and teenagers shared a picnic and some not-so-common games such as a "Carry the Water Balloon in Your Teeth" three-legged race and "Water Balloon Volleyball." However, despite encouragement from leaders, few teenagers came without their parents. Then it took several weeks to get some of these young people back into the Sunday night fellowship routine.

The leaders later learned that these young people were embarrassed to come to the picnic without their parents. As a result, they felt slighted since their regular program was pre-empted by an event they didn't feel comfortable attending.

Similarly, avoid scheduling family retreats or other special family events to replace youth retreats and programs. Young people still need opportunities to do special activities together with their peers.

• **Avoid over-programming.** Families appreciate useful and insightful programming, but they don't want it every night of the week. Trying to plan too many family activities at church is counterproductive. The result of this approach is that family members spend more time at church than they spend with each other. Instead, schedule your programs carefully. Make sure an event is worth a family's time and effort to attend.

• **Start early and end early.** If your events consistently go late into the evening, you automatically eliminate families with young children who must go to bed early. Begin evening programs early (perhaps with a meal) so these families can participate and still get their younger children to bed on time. Moreover, parents may not want to stay up late, particularly if they have to be at work early the next day.

• **Overlap schedules.** It's often helpful to "piggyback" family meetings with other church activities so that families won't have to take another trip or give up another evening for a church activity. Plan parents meetings in conjunction with youth group meetings and children's meetings so that parents won't have to make another trip to church.

• **Watch the TV schedule.** Whether you admit it or not, many families would prefer to stay home to see their favorite show than to go to a church event. Imagine trying to hold a special workshop on Super Bowl Sunday! When planning an event, examine the TV schedule for any special broadcasts. If there are any, find alternate times for your programming.

• **Watch the calendar.** When planning special events, look carefully at the calendar. Don't set yourself up for failure by planning a special event during the holidays when people go away or get even busier than usual. Avoid planning events during special school events such as graduation and major sports tournaments. By thinking through the timing, you have a better chance of attracting the maximum number of people.

• **Limit time commitments.** Few parents can or will commit to a long series of classes. Limit a series to three or four sessions. Or, perhaps more popular, plan to cover all the material in an intensive one-day workshop. It's better to have two three-week sessions than one six-week session.

• **Duplicate scheduling.** You may find that different groups of parents simply can't meet at the same time. For instance, homemakers may be able to meet on a weekday but not in the evening or on weekends. But on the other hand, working parents may only be able to meet in the evenings or on weekends. In these cases, it may be appropriate to duplicate your programming to reach both groups. Holding each event twice is extra work for the planners, but it may be the only way to meet different families' needs.

• **Don't get discouraged.** Only a few families may show up at first. Programming for families and for parents is novel to most parents, and it may take a few sessions to convince them of the value. Don't give up after your first parenting workshop or family retreat. Instead, work with the parents who do participate and show them you really want to support them and meet their needs. If your sessions are practical and worthwhile, word will get around and your numbers will grow.

*P*ublicizing Family Events

Many important and useful programs are poorly attended because of ineffective publicity. Unless people know about an event, they can't schedule it on their calendars. And if they aren't convinced a particular program will benefit them, they probably won't attend. Thus it's essential to design and distribute quality publicity. Consider these important factors in promoting your family events:

• **Start publicizing early.** Since families are so busy, begin publicizing events weeks in advance so they can plan them into their schedules. Even if you don't have all the details arranged, give families any information available on topic, time and place.

• **Invite everyone.** Be sure to send publicity to everyone who might be interested. Just because parents didn't attend the last five workshops you sponsored doesn't mean they won't be interested in your next topic. And don't assume that a particular family doesn't have a certain need. Sometimes the need may be hidden.

• **Offset parents' fears or apathy.** Many parents—particularly those who aren't involved in the church—may be afraid to attend events because they think they don't know enough about "religion" and will look foolish. Others won't come because they're afraid they'll be given a lot of new responsibilities. Still others may simply be apathetic.

In these cases, focus your publicity on inviting parents to share their needs, experiences and hopes for the family. Invite them to talk about the problems they face in their own homes. By focusing on parents' needs instead of your program's goals, you can attract families who might not participate otherwise.

• **Focus on the positive.** Families are already bombarded with bad news and dire predictions about family life. By focusing publicity on how programs will help them by enriching family life, you attract people who want help to overcome problems.

• **Design attractive publicity.** Even the most dynamic and useful workshop won't attract much attention if advertisements, fliers, posters and other publicity don't catch people's attention. While it may seem quicker to scribble a quick notice, such announcements won't attract people's attention.

Since people subconsciously associate the quality of

a program with the quality of its publicity, these un-professional announcements may actually deter people from attending. By taking the extra effort to type or typeset announcements and to include appropriate graphics, more people will see and respond to the publicity.

When designing publicity, don't give too much information, but tell people what they need to know. Trying to include too much information only clutters the design and detracts from the central message. Always give the event's title, a brief summary of the content, the time, date and place, for whom the event is designed, how much it costs, and whom to contact for more information.

• **Make publicity inclusive.** Unless you're conscious of potential problems, publicity sends unintentional messages that leave some families out. For example, brochures on a family seminar that show a traditional family may leave the impression to single-parent families that the seminar isn't for them. Sending letters to "Dear Parents" implies that two parents will read each letter, while "Dear Parent" or "Dear Parent(s)" tells single parents that they're welcome too.

• **Vary the publicity.** Use different media in publicizing your events. The traditional brochures, fliers and posters are all useful, but don't limit yourself to them. Contact newspapers, radio stations and TV stations that could spread the news about your event either through public service announcements or paid advertising. Use word-of-mouth promotion through telephone chains or door-to-door contacts. Utilize announcement times during worship services to talk about programs or to put on skits that announce special workshops.

When Programs Work

It can be tough to design effective programs for families. Families are so busy that it's sometimes difficult to get them together. Different generations have different needs and interests. Different types of families have different needs. But when your programming works, it has a significant impact on families that participate, making it worth all the effort.

After several months of building family trust through a variety of family programs, Dub's church hosted an intensive six-hour seminar on human sexuality for parents and teenagers led by a certified sex educator in the congregation. The session began with several non-threatening crowdbreakers and group builders. It slowly moved into issues of human sexuality for parents and teenagers.

In the beginning, both generations felt awkward, trying to keep their distance from the subject. But as they shared information, questions and feelings, they began to form a common bond and overcome their awkwardness. Without forfeiting their authority, parents became vulnerable. They discovered that it was okay to express their fears for their children. And they realized they could be honest about not knowing everything about sexuality.

Likewise, teenagers were given permission confidently to seek more information about sexuality. They began asking questions and trusting their parents to affirm their curiosity while also maintaining their appropriate parental protection.

The seminar ended with a brief devotional in which Dub asked participants to do something they probably hadn't done in a long time—if ever. Family members arranged their chairs to face each other. Then they joined hands and looked into each other's eyes while listening to a closing popular song about friendship.

No one could have predicted the tremendous impact the workshop had on participants. Parents and teenagers who cared deeply about each other but never expressed it were saying, in their own ways, that they would "be there" for each other. Few eyes were dry after the song, and most families reached out and embraced each other.

Families want to spend time together. They want to build communication and closeness. But some don't know how, or they haven't been given "permission" to open themselves to each other. Through carefully planned programming, the church can give families the skills and the opportunities to build closeness and express their love. Such programs can be significant catalysts for helping families grow together in Christian love.

Chapter 6
Supporting and Educating Parents

Jane is distressed. In the past six months, her 16-year-old son's behavior and personality have changed dramatically—for the worse. Will used to be compassionate and friendly. But now he's distant and cold. He locks himself in his room for hours at a time. He hangs around with the heavy metal crowd and rattles the house with the loud music he plays on his stereo. Lately Will has started smoking—even at home. His long hair and scruffy clothes reek of marijuana smoke.

Jane doesn't know what to do. "I've tried everything," she tells Walt. "I just don't know what to do next. Can you help me?"

Not all parents of teenagers experience the deep pain Jane is experiencing because of severe problems with their children. But all parents do experience times when they need help and support. When parenting tasks seem insurmountable, parents cry for help. They want to know how to respond to situations, and they want someone by their side as they do.

As youth workers, we often hear parents' cries first. Parents realize we know teenagers and what makes them tick. Parents welcome help from youth workers who offer sound advice and support. If we anticipate these cries for help and are prepared to listen and respond, we can give parents the help and support they need to face problems and issues.

Key Elements of a Parent Education Program

What educational opportunities should the church offer to assist parents? We'll discuss specific programming ideas later in the chapter (see page 112). In order for an educational program to be well-rounded, it should include all of the following elements:

• **Biblical insights for parents.** Many churches sponsor classes for parents of teenagers on Sunday mornings. Sometimes, though, these classes focus exclusively on parents' struggles without ever consulting the Bible or applying its message to parents' particular needs and concerns.

Support groups certainly have their place in the church (see page 114). But the church should provide more for parents than they receive from parenting classes at the local community college or through night-school classes. The church can provide the foundation and framework for understanding the family that other opportunities don't.

There are many ways the Bible sheds light on parenting tasks. Parents can learn more about their Christian responsibilities by studying specific Bible passages on parenting. These passages might include Deuteronomy 6; Ephesians 6; Colossians 3; 1 Timothy 3 or selected passages from Proverbs.

Parents can study stories of Bible families and discuss how these ancient stories illuminate contemporary issues, problems and responsibilities. What does the story of David and Absalom say to parents of a rebellious teenager (2 Samuel 13—19)? What do we learn about sibling rivalry from the story of Joseph and his brothers (Genesis 37—50)? What does Jesus'

relationship with his own family tell us about our
responsibilities to God as families (Matthew 12:46-50;
Luke 2:41-52; and John 7:1-5)? Dozens of Bible stories
could be studied to learn more about parenting and
family relationships.

A third way parents can study scriptures is to examine all the places the Bible uses family imagery to talk
about God, Christ, the church or relationships between believers. What do these passages say about
God? our faith? our families? our responsibilities?
Good Bible concordances point to numerous passages
that draw such parallels. (See page 38 for more about
families in the Bible.)

Just as Sunday school classes should focus on applying scripture to family concerns, other family education programs in the church should flow from a faith
perspective. Without such a perspective, the church
loses its unique contribution to family concerns.

• **Information on adolescent development.** After the junior high meeting on Friday nights, a small
group of eighth-grade girls always congregates in the
parking lot. At the beginning of the year, the girls
glance over their shoulders at the boys who are playing basketball. They giggle and say, "Yuck." Toward
the end of the year, the same group of girls glances at
the same group of guys. But now they giggle and use
words such as "like" and even "love."

Is something wrong? Have the girls inhaled a toxic
chemical that's made them temporarily insane? Of
course not! They're just growing up. Their interests
are changing, and they're noticing boys now. They're
normal eighth-grade girls.

Much of the stress parents experience comes from
sudden and unexpected changes in their kids. "What's
wrong?" they want to know. "Manuel has never acted
like that before." Parents who've never watched a child
become an adult worry that the changes aren't normal.

As youth workers, we see dozens of kids grow up through the years. We watch the changes, and we know that for the most part kids survive them pretty well. As adults who constantly work with teenagers, we're in a position to help parents understand the changes teenagers experience during adolescence. Churches can help parents discover that "Hey! John and Sue are normal!"

Many resources are available that explain adolescence. Classes, books, seminars, films and other resources help communicate information about teenagers' development. Parents want to know about all areas of change—physical, spiritual, emotional, social and intellectual. They want to know what to expect, how to react and what problems could occur. By providing them with this information, we build understanding within the family. We show families we care about them and their concerns.

• **Information on youth culture.** Notice the looks on the faces of middle-age adults when a busload of boisterous church kids pulls up next to their car at a stoplight. As they pull away from the light, they shake their heads and might say: "I don't know what's wrong with kids today. Whatever happened to the good old days?"

Teenagers are a confusing bunch. Styles, fashions, lingo, music, fads and interests change so quickly that it's surprising that kids themselves stay up-to-date. No wonder parents despair of ever staying on top of all the changes!

An effective ministry to parents of teenagers takes the time to understand this confusing and complex youth culture and to educate parents about it. Just because there's a teenager in the house doesn't guarantee that parents know about the latest haircuts, the hottest new albums, the most fashionable clothes and the funniest slang. We can help parents better understand

and relate to their kids by cluing them on what's hot and what's not. Moreover, we can help them analyze trends so they can effectively guide their teenagers through confusing choices.

At a recent meeting with parents, Walt discussed the views of life that different popular rock musicians communicate through their music and stage performances. He found it embarrassing to read to parents the lyrics of songs about sex. But he thought they should know what kids listen to. Then he described a particular group's explicitly sexual appeal both on and off stage.

Needless to say, the parents were shocked. Yet they also were grateful to learn about some of the music kids listen to. What they learned helped them know how to respond appropriately to their kids' music choices.

• **How to prevent and deal with problems.** Too often it takes a crisis for a parent to ask us for help. Most parents believe their kids are immune from the teenage problems they read about in newspapers and watch on television. Parents don't even think about how they would handle those tough situations. "Not my kid," they say.

But then it happens. A daughter gets pregnant. A son is arrested for drunk driving. A teacher says a child is flunking school. Now it's too late.

Thinking through a problem ahead of time sometimes can help prevent it from occurring. Parents need to learn how to deal with situations before they occur.

For instance, many parents are caught off guard when their oldest child begins to date. If the parents and the teenager haven't discussed and agreed to certain rules and guidelines for dating, problems can develop. If parents don't take time to discuss dating *before* their child starts dating, they can't respond appropriately when their teenager unexpectedly introduces his or her first "steady." It's always easier to

address a situation on the basis of previously discussed guidelines rather than scramble at the last
minute to establish a policy—a policy the teenager
will invariably oppose.

Youth workers need to help parents think through a
variety of contemporary problems among teenagers.
These include teenage suicide, substance abuse, delinquency, eating disorders, sexuality, materialism, school
problems and peer pressure. By talking about problems
ahead of time, by learning warning signals and by developing appropriate responses, we can help parents
avert major crises before they occur.

• **Communication skills.** Both parents and teenagers say poor communication is a problem in family
relationships. Husbands and wives have difficulty
communicating with each other effectively. Parents
and teenagers blame one another for not listening and
understanding. Brothers and sisters argue and fight,
solving none of their differences in the process.

Families need to learn to communicate. The church
can provide programs that will help. Chapter 9 is
devoted to ideas for teaching parents and teenagers to
communicate with one another.

• **A variety of resources.** Sometimes the most
helpful training we can give parents is to suggest
resources they can turn to for advice, skill-building
and parent education. We should have a variety of
useful resources available for parents to consult
whenever particular issues, problems or concerns
arise. We can keep a file of articles on parenting and
on teenagers, and we can have books, tapes and
videos available for parents to use. Since some problems call for skills we as youth workers may not have,
we should compile a list of local counselors, specialists and other professionals for parents to use in times
of crisis. (See Chapter 12 for information on when to
seek outside help.)

*K*ey Elements for Supporting Parents

Being a teenager's parent is a lot like learning to ride a bicycle. As kids, we looked at our first two-wheeler and wondered how anyone could possibly balance on those inchwide wheels while speeding down the road. Parents often look at the teenage years with those same feelings. What lies ahead seems like an impossible task.

Just as it's hard to learn to ride a bike on our own, it's tough to face parenting a teenager alone. Parents need the same support a child needs when learning to ride a bike. Before Walt ever climbed on a bike his dad ran him through "ground school"—he explained the bike, how to pedal and steer, and, most importantly, how to stop. Then he spent countless hours going up and down the sidewalk with Walt. Walt wobbled along slowly as his dad held on to the rear fender.

Day after day his dad worked with Walt. Then one evening the boy yelled at his dad to hold on tighter, only to look back to see him half a block behind, grinning and waving. The boy could ride now! Oh, there would be spills and scrapes and bruises. But his dad would always be there to brush Walt off, give him a hug and encourage him to climb back on.

Just as Walt's dad took time to support his son when he was learning to ride a bike, the church should stand by and support parents as they raise their teenagers. Parents want and need help. The church can run behind them and pick them up, give them a hug and encourage them when they fall.

Effective ministries to families with teenagers take time to build support systems for struggling parents. In order for these systems to be effective, they should include each of the following elements:

• **Respect for parents.** Parents need support and encouragement from youth workers. They need to know we respect and support them in their roles as parents. When we compete with parents or question their judgment without first learning all the facts, we destroy the trust we must have in order to offer parents the support they need.

How can we support parents and win their trust? Here are three suggestions:

1. Communicate to them that we understand their God-given role as parents. Let them know we're not there to do their job, but to support them as *they* do it. Even more important, we must make sure our ministry style backs what we say.

2. When teenagers complain about their parents, we should listen carefully but not make judgments without knowing both sides of the issue.

3. We shouldn't get upset when a group member can't attend an event because of a family commitment. As important as youth group is for teenagers, it's even more important for kids to spend time with their families. When the two needs conflict, family should come first.

Walt once confronted the parents of a junior higher because they wouldn't let their daughter come to the weekly dinner before the group meeting. She always arrived just as the meeting was starting. Walt felt she was missing valuable social time with other Christian kids and leaders. But her parents were adamant. They had dinner together as a family every night, and they weren't about to let anything interfere with that important family time.

When they explained their commitment to Walt, he realized they were right and that he had made a mistake. He told them he was excited to hear family mealtimes were important to them. He assured them that their time together was more important than the junior high fellowship meal. After that, it never bothered Walt when Patty came late to meetings.

As youth workers, we spend a great deal of time preparing meetings and events. These are important. But we shouldn't be upset if a family weekend takes precedence over a spring youth retreat. Indeed, we should do whatever we can to respect choices families make to be together.

• **Support from other parents.** Some of the most beneficial support for parents comes from other parents, not the youth worker. Parents need opportunities to meet together to share the problems, ideas, solutions, frustrations and excitement of raising a teenager. To be able to talk and consult with others with similar experiences can be a tremendously helpful outlet for parents. By providing these opportunities, churches help parents help one another in positive and healthy ways.

• **A pat on the back.** All parents sometimes think that either they are failing as parents or their teenager is beyond help. Other times they think they're making wise parenting decisions, but no one affirms this. Like everyone else, parents need to know when they're doing a good job. By recognizing their teenager's positive qualities and achievements and by affirming parents' wise decisions, we can build parents' confidence and reinforce their constructive efforts.

John's parents were distressed because he borrowed the car when he knew he shouldn't. His parents had punished him by taking away his license for a month. John was angry, and his parents thought their punishment might make him rebel. They asked Walt if he thought they had been too harsh. Walt knew John well enough to assure them that his rebellious anger was probably directed more at himself for his poor judgment than at them. Walt affirmed their decision.

When Walt talked with John, he learned that John indeed did respect his parents' decision. He knew he was wrong, and he had learned from his mistake. So

Walt gave John's parents a pat on the back and said: "John really responded well to your decision. Good job!"

Sometimes when parents come to us for advice, they really want affirmation for their job as parents. They want to know if they've responded appropriately to various situations. When we truthfully can tell them, "Good job!" we provide a ministry of affirmation to worried parents.

• **A gentle nudge.** A mother once came to Walt concerned about the company her son kept. After she described her son's friends, Walt agreed that the boy definitely was with the wrong crowd. The mother said she wasn't sure whether she should reinstate a weekend curfew for her son. Walt almost choked. He quickly said he didn't think any 14-year-old kid should be allowed to stay out all night on weekends. Such leniency was asking for trouble.

For some parents, the most helpful support is a gentle nudge or push. In this case, the situation called for Walt to give the mother a little nudge in the right direction. She already knew what she needed to do; now she needed someone to nudge her into action.

When such a situation occurs, we should act with caution. Telling parents what to do isn't our role as youth workers. We should offer advice only when it's requested and when our relationship with the parent assures that our advice will be interpreted as support, not meddling.

• **Spiritual guidance.** The spiritual foundation of our ministry provides important support for parents who aren't part of other support networks. The church is uniquely equipped to be God's voice and hands for parents who deal with problems rooted in sin and who need the comfort and assurance that only God can provide. Youth workers and congregations must become students of the Bible so we can help parents find the guidance and support God offers.

*P*rogramming Ideas

The elements of parent education and support can be addressed in dozens of creative ways. Our challenge as youth workers is to develop programs that capture parents' attention so they'll want to get personally involved. Moreover, each program must be designed to meet the particular needs of the parents we work with.

Though we have separated education and support as distinct goals, the two are interwoven through all our programming for parents. A seminar to teach parents about adolescent sexuality can build mutual support among parents as they struggle with what they learn. An informal support group gives parents opportunities to learn and grow from one another's knowledge and experience.

The possibilities for creative educational and support programming are endless. Here are a few ideas that have worked for churches. They can be adapted, expanded and developed to fit particular situations and needs.

• **Keep a "Parents Only" bulletin board.** Though common, inexpensive and easy-to-keep, a bulletin board is one of the most effective educational tools available. When put in a conspicuous place and kept up-to-date, a creative bulletin board becomes a magnet for parents. Post articles from magazines and newspapers about parenting and teenage issues. Include reviews of good books, movies and videos. If parents themselves are responsible for keeping the board up-to-date, it's bound to be filled with relevant and interesting information.

• **Collect a parents resource library.** If your church already has a library, ask to reserve a special shelf or two for resources for parents of teenagers. If your church doesn't have a library, find a place to build your own. Include as many cassette tapes, videotapes, magazines and books you can find and afford. Purchase as many resources as your budget will allow. Ask parents to donate copies of resources they have found useful. A good place to begin finding resources is the resource list on page 395.

Once your library is established, distribute to parents a list of the available resources. You even can have someone write a review of an especially good resource every month and publish it in the newsletter or worship bulletin, or post it on the bulletin board.

• **Promote a resource of the month.** When parents browse in a bookstore, it's sometimes hard for them to tell which resources are good and which aren't. You can provide a valuable service and save them lots of time and energy by highlighting one particularly good resource each month and making it available for purchase through the church.

Resources could include books, magazines, devotional guides and cassette tapes. By keeping up-to-date with what's available, you can offer the best each month. Or you can ask a parents group to review and recommend appropriate books for other parents.

Print a flier about the resource and include a tear-off order form that parents can return to you with their payment. Collect the orders, and purchase the resource for the parents at the end of the month. If you recommend a book, many Christian bookstores will offer you a discount for a bulk purchase—an added bonus for parents.

• **Use bulletin inserts.** Some parents won't take advantage of educational opportunities. But they might take time to read a bulletin insert on parenting issues while they listen to the organ prelude. You can write and design these yourself, or you can order professionally designed inserts from national organizations. (See resource list on page 395.) Using bulletin inserts not only educates parents but also informs the rest of the congregation about teenage issues.

• **Organize parent support groups.** As you get to know youth group members' parents, you'll undoubtedly discover special needs. Respond to these needs by organizing support groups centered around special situations, interests or problems. A structured parent support group can be one of the most important associations to help parents deal with their particular struggles. In an atmosphere of trust and care, they learn they're not alone, and they find other people who will help and support them.

In his book *Family Survival: Coping With Stress,* Parker Rossman delineates several important benefits of support groups. First, they give members information. Parents learn from other parents how they've successfully dealt with specific situations. Second, these groups renew parents' energy—energy they need to deal with the issues they face. Third, they provide a structure to support parents in times of crisis.[1]

Perhaps some parents have kids who have contemplated or attempted suicide. Others may have kids involved in substance abuse. You may have several single parents in your church or parents struggling to work out relationships in a blended family. Perhaps two-income families are struggling with their time commitments and priorities. Each of these concerns—and many others—might be the focus for parent support groups in your community. Or you can organize more general support groups that deal with a variety of parenting concerns.

Parent support groups can be organized in many ways, depending on the needs of your community and congregation. Whatever the form, support groups should follow these guidelines:

1. Have a focus. The worst scenario for a support group would be for a dozen parents to sit in a circle for an hour without saying anything about their struggles and concerns as parents. If the group gathers "just to share concerns," assertive members will likely dominate the discussion with their own situations.

To prevent groups from becoming nothing more than gripe sessions, focus each session on a specific concern. Be sure all group members understand the group's purpose and stick to it. Printed and video-taped materials are useful discussion springboards, and they also help a group stay focused.

Of course, if a group meets regularly and has developed its own rhythm, a structured agenda becomes less necessary. Coming together regularly often breeds familiarity that, in turn, breeds good discussion.

2. Sign a written covenant. Writing down a group's purpose and members' expectations helps a group stick to its goal. When groups get started, have them collectively write, agree to and sign an agreement or covenant. This gives participants a greater sense of commitment and begins binding parents together as a caring group.

3. Limit the time commitment. With so many time demands on parents, they need to know what's expected of them before they consent to be part of a group. Include meeting times in the group covenant as well as any preparation they'll be expected to do for each meeting.

Also limit the length of time parents commit to the group. For instance, their initial covenant should last no more than eight weeks. If they wish to continue beyond that, they can commit to another eight weeks. Indefinite time commitments discourage many parents from getting involved. If the initial commitment is too long, momentum will diminish and the group may dwindle out.

4. Train leaders. Successful support groups require trained leaders who can effectively facilitate group discussions. A facilitator doesn't dominate the discussion; rather, he or she interjects questions or comments if the conversation flounders or moves off track.

Develop guidelines for leading small groups, and sponsor training sessions where leaders can role play various situations to improve and test their skills.

Groups that focus on critical problems such as chemical use or domestic violence need professionally trained leaders. Family counselors, social workers and psychologists are among those who can provide helpful, skilled leadership.

• **Create a parents newsletter.** A newsletter for parents is a valuable education and networking tool. It can give tips, encouragement and challenges to parents. It can point parents to valuable resources and events. It can give them a forum for getting to know one another. It can keep parents informed about youth and family programming at the church.

A newsletter for parents can cover many topics. Here are some regular features you could include:

1. Teenage trends. This section briefly reports on movies, music, fashions and other influences on teenagers. The column should be primarily informative rather than judgmental. Although some trends should be questioned and challenged, many good things also should be reported.

2. Family corner. Families can use this column to describe creative ways they've spent time with their teenagers. By sharing success stories, families see that the adolescent years can be a special time of rich experiences and memories.

3. Ask an expert. This column can answer parents' questions. An expert in the congregation such as a pastor, psychologist, social worker or professor could volunteer to provide this information. Or a parent could interview an expert about each problem and report the answers.

4. News. Inform parents about upcoming events and report on past activities. Tell parents about youth group activities as well as events for parents and families.

5. Devotional. Offer inspiration and encouragement to parents through a devotional or meditative column. Use biblical references and tell image-filled stories to affirm and challenge parents.

6. Reviews. Have different parents read and review books, videos, movies and magazines that deal with adolescence and family life. This column can help parents find additional resources that address their specific needs.

7. Tips for parents. Watch for practical parenting tips in magazines and newspapers. Condense these tips into short ideas parents can use (be sure to credit the source). If you quote extensively from a source, copyright laws require you to get reprint permission from the publisher.

8. Calendar. Make a calendar for upcoming events that parents can post on their bulletin board or refrigerator. Include youth group, family and church activities. Also include community events or interchurch events that might be interesting and beneficial for parents.

Producing a parents newsletter is an overwhelming task if you try to do it alone. So let parents do it. Find a responsible editor who will oversee the publication. Find writers, typists, layout people, artists and people to help with printing and mailing the newsletter. Not only will parents enjoy the responsibility and challenge, but they'll learn more about parenting and build an important camaraderie as staff. Moreover, they'll be more likely to include information and ideas that will appeal to other parents.

• **Form a parents Sunday school class.** Design a special Sunday school class for parents of teenagers. The class could be ongoing or short-term, depending on parents' needs. Use a standard curriculum or develop one of your own. Plenty of good curricula, books, videos and other resources are available. (See resource list on page 395.)

Invite experts in the church and community to lead discussions on issues such as adolescent development, teenage suicide, substance abuse, parenting skills or conflict resolution. Have class members share leadership by alternating responsibility for leading the class.

Don't feel limited by traditional class structures. A non-traditional class may entice parents who never come to Sunday school to start attending.

• **Sponsor parents seminars.** Set aside an occasional weekday evening or Saturday morning for a parenting workshop. Invite an expert to lead the session, and have resources available for parents to take home. Or show a parenting video and lead a discussion afterward.

Seminars can deal with parenting concerns such as discipline, marriage enrichment or communication. They can focus on teenage issues such as sexuality, adolescent development or rock music. Offer a variety of seminars—some for mothers only, for fathers only and for both parents.

Another option is to encourage parents to attend local or regional parenting workshops sponsored by your denomination or other Christian organizations. Your church also could cosponsor a parenting event with other congregations in your area.

• **Form parent discussion groups.** Week after week kids go to interesting youth group meetings and fellowship while their parents sit at home. Start a Bible study or discussion group for parents that meets simultaneously with a youth group meeting.

A Bible study group can study passages on parenting, stories about families in the Bible or family imagery in the Bible. Or as one parents Bible study group at Walt's church did, the group can study the same passages the senior high kids discuss each week in Sunday school.

Parents can discuss problems and issues they face with their teenagers. You can invite outside speakers to lead the group, or you can show videos and lead topical discussions. In all cases, allow plenty of time for parents to share insights, questions and concerns.

• **Plan parent retreats.** Kids aren't the only people who benefit from a weekend away from home. Intense learning and mutual support among parents can take place during a weekend away from their hectic schedules. Plan a retreat just for parents that includes fellowship, recreation, discussions and learning. Making provisions for the kids who are left behind helps more parents participate. If your youth program has a good support staff, you could even schedule a separate retreat for the kids—at another camp. (See Chapter 18 for a retreat plan for parents.)

• **Design opportunities for single parents.** Many churches mistakenly ignore single parents' unique needs. As a result, these parents lack the support and training they need to deal with special problems and concerns they face. Churches can sponsor a variety of special seminars for these parents. For instance, a divorce-recovery workshop is particularly useful. It often reaches out to unchurched parents and draws them into the body of Christ.

• **Send uplifting notes.** The first pastor Walt worked with told him to start a personal "uplift file." Every time he received a note, card or message of affirmation, he was to put it in that file. Then when he encountered difficult emotional times, he could pull out the file and see that people appreciated him and his gifts.

Parents often feel discouraged and unappreciated. They benefit from an occasional short note of encouragement from the youth worker. Set aside a few minutes each week to write brief notes to parents of youth group members. Compliment parents on something especially nice their teenager did. Encourage them if they're struggling with a specific problem. If appropriate, include an interesting article, poem or scripture to boost their spirits. Even a quick note to let them know you're thinking about them and praying for them is greatly appreciated.

• **Make quick phone calls.** Walt once attended a soccer game in which several youth group kids participated. One of them, Bobby, had been a benchwarmer all year. He hadn't played in any game, yet his mother faithfully attended every match. On this day, though, she couldn't make it to the game. Bobby was called off the bench, and he scored a great goal for the team. After the game, Walt not only congratulated Bobby, but he also called Bobby's parents to describe the goal and say how proud they must be of their son.

Like notes, phone calls take only a minute or two to make. Your time is well-used when you congratulate or affirm parents, when you ask how they're doing or tell them you're thinking of them.

• **Attend special events.** Parents love to know you're behind them. A great way to show support is to attend special events in their teenager's life. Sit with parents at important athletic events, school plays, award ceremonies or music programs. Not only do you show support, but you have a chance to get to know the family better.

• **Use your camera.** A camera is one of a youth worker's best affirmation tools. Many parents have jobs and other responsibilities that keep them from attending after-school activities. But if you or a volunteer camera buff can, attend an event and take lots of snapshots to give parents. Even better, if you have access to a video camera, tape the whole event and drop off the tape that day for parents to see their teenager perform or play. Also take lots of pictures at youth group events, and make the good shots available to both teenagers and parents.

• **Make a Brag Board.** Many group members will get a picture or story in the local or high school newspaper for sports, awards or achievements. Clip these pictures and stories and post them on a family Brag Board. When you take down the clippings, pass them on to parents for their family scrapbook.

• **Sponsor a parent recognition Sunday.** Plan a special program to honor parents of youth group members. Kids can do the work and the honoring. Plan a special dinner and program that includes time for teenagers to honor their parents both publicly and individually. These events can take place on Mother's or Father's Day.

• **Hold an open house.** Sponsor an informal open house to show appreciation to parents. Do it in a home and serve plenty of refreshments. Take time to greet the parents, and personally thank them for their support of the youth program. Affirm and encourage them, and let them know they have your support.

Chapter 7
Building Credibility With Parents

*T*he weekend retreat was a disaster. Tom, a group member, spent the entire weekend disrupting discussions, activities and even prayers. He ruined everything Cathy, the youth worker, had hoped to accomplish through the special event.

But when the group returned to the church, Cathy didn't mention Tom's behavior to his parents. "I just smiled," she recalled, "told them I was glad Tom participated and that I hoped he would come back."

Dub asked her, "Is that how you really felt?"

"Of course not!" she replied. "I was really angry. Tom ruined the retreat for most of the group."

"Why didn't you express your feelings to his parents?" Dub asked. "If the timing was inappropriate right then, you could have scheduled time to meet with them later that week."

"You've got to be kidding," Cathy said. "I'm only 26 years old." She continued: "What could I tell them, anyway? They're Tom's parents, and since I'm not even a parent myself, I don't have any right telling them what to do. Besides, Tom's dad intimidates me. I think he'd much rather have a male youth worker for his son."

• • •

Gary seemed like an ideal youth worker. The kids loved him. He had an excellent education, a sound theology, good organizational skills and creative programming ideas.

Despite his qualifications, the parents in the church drove him out of town. Why? Gary was never credible to the parents. They never learned to trust and respect him. In fact, his relationships with parents were tense at best. No wonder he had to leave the church.

*B*arriers to Parent-Youth Worker Relations

Many youth workers are like Cathy and Gary. They haven't learned to relate to parents. Like Cathy, some feel awkward and intimidated by parents. Others like Gary have good intentions but bad reputations. Why do many youth workers have trouble relating to parents? Sometimes the problem lies with parents' perceptions. But other times the problem results from our own actions, methods and attitudes. While many variables affect each relationship, there are common reasons for our lack of credibility with parents.

• **Lack of respect.** Parents of teenagers are often older than youth workers. In these cases we can be intimidated, feeling inadequate and underqualified. Not only are parents more experienced in life, they have raised children and live with teenagers. As a result, we ask ourselves, "What could I possibly know that parents don't know already?"

Just as we may question our own abilities because of our age, parents may also believe we're too young to be taken seriously as adult peers. Some parents see us as "big kids" who will someday—hopefully soon—grow up and get a "real job." As Darrell Pearson writes in his book *Parents as Partners in Youth Ministry*: "People frequently see youth work as a temporary occupation—something you do until you move on to 'real' ministry. For the volunteer, it's often worse. Some people find it hard to understand why you hang around ninth-graders on your own time."[1]

Unfortunately, we sometimes contribute to this misperception. Recently Dub read some evaluation sheets from a youth group trip sponsored by a neighboring church. Several teenagers said they particularly liked having sponsors who acted just as crazy as the teenagers. One young person wrote, "It was great to have sponsors who were like big kids right along with the rest of us."

Despite the teenagers' enthusiasm, there were serious problems on the trip. Many activities were unsupervised. Teenagers slipped out of their rooms at night. Some went to bars together. A couple even slept together. One teenager said: "I had never tried alcohol before that church trip. That was the last place I had imagined I would take my first drink." When such problems occur because of irresponsible youth workers, it's little wonder that parents doubt our maturity.

• **Unprofessionalism.** When we rely on our youthful looks, natural charisma, speaking ability or athletic prowess to fuel our youth ministry, we can't expect credibility. By depending on these attributes for our success, we neglect important skills such as counseling, scripture study and quality programming. We're never prepared adequately and we hope people will just look at how much fun we are.

Parents expect a youth program to be more than a youth worker's fan club. Parents can see through shallow ministries. Their teenagers tell them why they like the youth program and the youth worker. If this popularity is the only criterion parents have in assessing our performance, we may end up with the undesirable reputation of being an unprofessional goof-off.

• **Mistakes.** No matter how conscientious and thorough we are, we all make mistakes. A new programming idea to reach unchurched kids can bomb. We can alienate families by scheduling a program beyond a group's maturity level. We may give poor guidance during counseling. Or make a rash statement that infuriates parents. Ministry involves taking risks, and those risks sometimes produce failure.

For example, one youth worker decided to host a junior high lock-in as an outreach event. He encouraged group members to invite their friends—particularly those who weren't involved in a church. Not anticipating much outreach, the youth minister recruited only two adult chaperons. Instead of the 20 or so junior highers he expected, 100 kids showed up. He had completely underestimated his group's zeal.

Overwhelmed but undaunted, the youth worker started the planned activities. The first game was "Sardines"—a backward hide-and-seek in which one person hides and everyone else looks for him or her. As each person finds the hider, he or she joins the hider until only one person is left looking. The game seemed to be going well. After 15 minutes, though, the only people who hadn't discovered the hiding place were the adults. The last place they thought to look was the sanctuary. Of course, that was the hiding place.

The moment the adults opened the sanctuary doors, they knew they had trouble. Hymnals, bulletins and offering envelopes were scattered across the floor. The locked organ had been pried open and was still humming. The pulpit had been dragged to the back of the sanctuary and a heart with "JS + BD" was scratched in its front. Topping off the disaster, someone had smuggled in soft drinks and popcorn that had become the ammunition for a glorious food fight.

The youth worker knew he had made a terrible miscalculation—one that would seriously hurt his standing in the church and among parents. As careful as we may be, mistakes will happen. How we handle those mistakes greatly affects our credibility.

• **Misunderstanding roles.** Parents who see youth workers as babysitters don't respect our role as ministers. Those of us who see parents as incompetent build a wall between ourselves and parents. Unless we and parents understand each other and what we are each trying to accomplish, we'll never build mutual respect and affirmation.

• **Lack of communication.** Darrell Pearson tells about a parent confronting him one April about a church activity the previous summer. The mother was upset about the "wet T-shirt contest" he held for the junior high girls. When he heard the complaint, he was also upset. Not only was such an activity inappropriate, it hadn't happened on the retreat at all! As he talked with the mother, he learned that her daughter had come home soaked after a planned water fight on a hot summer day. A misunderstanding brewed for 10 months simply because the parent hadn't expressed her concern earlier.[2]

Parents will never see our ministry as credible if they don't know what we do—or even worse—if they have misperceptions of what we do. Unless we regularly communicate with parents, we'll never change their image of us and our ministry.

Overcoming the Barriers

Though we can't change our age or situations, we can work to change our attitudes and parents' attitudes toward our ministry. By working to overcome the barriers we not only gain support for our efforts, we also open doors to minister to parents as they raise their children. Here are several ways youth workers can develop credibility with parents:

• **Act like adults.** We can't change our age. But
whether we're 20 or 80, we can be mature, responsible, sensible adults in our leadership and relationships.
More than another teenage buddy, young people need
a role model who reflects a healthy maturity. Church
consultant Lyle Schaller once asked a youth group to
think of an adult to whom they could tell their problems. Eleven teenagers named people in their 30s, eight
in their 40s, two in their 20s and three 50 or older.[3]

Sometimes youth workers so zealously seek teenagers' acceptance that they effectively abdicate their
adulthood. Dennis was this way. In his early 20s, Dennis volunteered to join Dub's youth ministry team. He
quickly became a hit with the group members. They
regularly asked him to go to lunch and other activities
with them. He had good rapport with the group members, and he added new excitement to the program.

Then on a weeklong mission trip, Dub sensed
something was coming between himself and Dennis.
And he felt group members acted strangely around
the adult sponsors—except Dennis. So Dub wasn't
surprised when, a couple of weeks after the trip, he
learned that Dennis had secretly arranged with some
of the boys and girls to break the trip covenant by
getting together late each evening in one of the motel
rooms. Moreover, Dennis had let teenagers violate
other rules—as long as it remained "their little secret."

When confronted about his behavior, Dennis was
adamantly defensive. Some of the trip guidelines were
"absolutely ridiculous," he complained, and besides,
"the kids like me better than the other volunteers because I don't parent them."

Dub reminded Dennis that everyone—sponsors, parents and teenagers—had agreed to and signed the
group covenant before the trip. And as a volunteer,
Dennis was expected to be an *adult* chaperon, not a
teenager. Finally, some group members expressed dis-

comfort with Dennis' juvenile behavior. They liked Dennis as a "big brother," but wouldn't trust him if they needed mature counsel and support.

In his book *All Grown Up & No Place to Go*, David Elkind writes about teenagers' need for adults who are comfortable in their role. He notes that authority doesn't mean ". . . being an ogre or a relentless disciplinarian." And it doesn't mean that ". . . we can't play ball with our children or joke with them or have fun with them." Rather, he says, ". . . it means asserting ourselves as adults who have more experience, knowledge, and skill . . . Children and teenagers are young and inexperienced. They very much need and want guidance and instruction from us."[4]

• **Teach parents respect.** In many ways we unconsciously teach people how to treat us. Such seemingly inconsequential things as how we dress, how we keep our office and how we relate to others send messages about how we expect people to relate to us.

These connections are true in our relations with parents. If we always wear the latest teenage fashions and act like a teenager, they'll probably treat us like teenagers. If our office looks like the church dumpster and we have irresponsible work habits, parents won't see us as professionals.

Credibility comes when parents see that we take our job seriously and deserve their respect. The signs of a "professional" in youth ministry are easily communicated and seen.

1. If we take our job seriously, we work hard. By completing every task as efficiently and effectively as possible, we become good stewards of God's gifts. When we use and develop our abilities, and when we recognize our weaknesses and take time to overcome them, we tell parents we're concerned, conscientious professionals.

2. Good preparation marks our professionalism.

Our motto should always be: "No surprises." We should be fully prepared for every activity, meeting, Bible study and retreat where we have leadership responsibility. "Winging it" should never be an option. By learning to manage our time effectively and set priorities, we can ensure that we'll never be caught inadequately prepared.

3. As serious youth workers, we should grow and learn. We must keep up with the times. We should take time to read about adolescence, youth culture and family issues. We can spend time browsing in bookstores, reading teenage magazines, and watching television and movies for another perspective on contemporary culture. We should attend youth and family ministry training events and seminars. And, most important, we should take time to develop our own faith and relationship with God. If we learn and grow, we become a trusted resource for parents.

• **Get to know one another.** One of the best ways to gain credibility with parents is simply to get to know them and let them get to know us. Where do they work? What do they do? What are their interests? What are their concerns? By building personal, caring relationships with parents, we not only come to understand them, we also let them learn about us—our strengths, our dreams, our foibles. These open lines of communication are invaluable when we make mistakes or when conflicts arise.

While we can get to know some parents by occasionally sitting with them at a potluck, we should also intentionally plan specific opportunities to get to know them. We can invite parents to go to dinner with us after church or meet them for breakfast before work. We can drop by during a coffee break to express appreciation for their teenager or to affirm something the parent has done. We can visit them in their home. If we need an "excuse" for the get-together, we can take along information about upcoming events. But we should focus on getting to know parents personally and letting them get to know us.

• **Admit mistakes when they occur.** Teenagers and youth workers get blamed for almost anything that goes wrong in a church. Did someone break a window? "The youth group must have done it." Are the walls dirty? "Those kids . . ." Is the group noisy during Sunday school? "Why can't that youth worker control those kids!"

Sometimes the blame is appropriate. Other times it isn't. Sometimes better planning can short-circuit mistakes and prevent them from occurring. Other times, mistakes or accidents are completely unforeseeable. Sometimes mistakes are a result of the necessary trial-and-error process of youth work.

We should never let ourselves or the youth program become the congregation's scapegoat. But when we do make mistakes, we should admit them, learn from them and move on. Parents (and others) will respect the mature honesty such an approach reflects.

The key is to communicate to parents the youth program's goals and vision. We should tell them the risks we take—and why. When parents understand and share our vision, they'll accept inevitable mistakes and support us in the face of criticism.

• **Know why we do what we do.** Why is the senior high group studying the book of Joel? Why was the last junior high retreat about Christian love? Why doesn't the church have a youth choir? What should group members learn after four years in the high school youth program?

Parents sometimes ask difficult-to-answer questions. Often these questions relate to our basic ministry philosophy. Why do we do certain things with teenagers? What is our ministry's purpose? If we are clear on the reasons for steering the ministry in a particular direction, we can give credible answers to these important questions.

We should think through these issues and develop a written theology and philosophy of youth ministry we can give to interested parents. We should also send parents periodic letters outlining and explaining our strategy for upcoming programming. Parents' confidence increases tremendously when they see the effort, thought and time involved in planning a youth program.

• **Be available and approachable.** Too often we as youth workers subtly communicate that we don't want to be bothered by parents. We are too busy, we don't have time or we don't think it's a priority. Or maybe we're afraid. Whatever the reason, this approach tells parents that we don't care about them or their concerns. Rather than increasing credibility, this avoidance destroys credibility, replacing it with animosity and resentment.

We can build credibility by letting parents know we want to spend time with them, are available and have time for them. Parents must feel they can come to us. Regular verbal invitations during parents meetings and during conversations communicate our willingness. And established, predictable office hours tell parents when we're available for them.

At the same time, we shouldn't wait for parents to come to us. We should schedule time to visit parents; speak to them when visiting group members' homes; sit with parents at school activities; and talk with a parent who answers the phone when we call for his or her teenager. By approaching parents first, we help them feel comfortable approaching us.

• **Develop listening skills.** When talking with parents, it's sometimes tempting to do all the talking and give "the answer" for every problem. However, we're much more likely to win parents' support (and help them) if we learn to listen as they share their problems, dreams and frustrations. When we listen, we communicate care and concern. They, in turn, develop respect and trust in us. By developing reputations as good listeners, we become credible authorities and confidants for parents.

• **Lead interesting meetings.** When we lead parents meetings, we want parents to listen, interact and respond. If our presentations and activities are boring, parents probably will never come to another meeting. But if we hold their interest with well-delivered and prepared talks and creative ideas, we can build enthusiasm, interest and support. (See Chapter 18 for more information on effective programming for parents.)

• **Keep parents informed.** One of the easiest ways to lose credibility with parents is to not keep them informed about youth group activities. Parents want to know what their young people do; what's expected of parents; how much events cost and other pertinent information.

Many of the same channels we use to communicate news to group members can also keep parents informed—fliers, the church bulletin, calendars, youth group hot lines and newsletters. Sending parents letters and copies of brochures about major events (such as trips and retreats) ensures that they hear what they need to know.

Similarly, we should tell parents about schedule changes or cancellations. Nothing makes a parent angrier than to drive five miles through ice and snow for a special youth group concert only to learn it was canceled because of the weather. We should develop phone chains and other ways to tell parents when last-minute changes are necessary.

• **Hold informational parents meetings.** These meetings tell parents what we're doing in our youth program and what we have coming up on the calendar. They're a great way to keep parents informed and help them catch the youth program's ministry vision.

We should plan these meetings at least twice a year and spice them up with crowdbreakers, skits and singing. We should give parents a chance to get to know one another and, of course, allow plenty of time for parents to ask questions and make comments.

During the parents meetings, we can hand out youth group brochures and calendars and spend time reviewing upcoming activities and events. We should explain our program strategy and give parents as much information as possible on dates, costs and other logistics. We can tell parents what we'll discuss at weekly fellowships and Bible studies. We should encourage parents to ask their teenagers questions about their regular youth group meetings. Then at least once a year, we should take time to explain and discuss our youth ministry philosophy.

• **Allow time.** No matter what we do, we can never develop instant rapport and trust with parents. Building trust and friendship is a long process that can't be hurried. When we begin a new position or program, we need to stick with it long enough for parents to get to know us. As Pearson writes: "I've noticed that as my tenure increases, my credibility with the parents of incoming seventh-graders improves. The parents have heard from others about what to expect. Parents who have had older teens in my program already understand what to expect."[5]

Working Together

Building credibility with parents is critical to our efforts to reach out to families with teenagers. Unless parents see us as professionals with important skills and knowledge, they'll have little reason to turn to us for support or education. But when they see us as

competent leaders, we open important doors for
working together with their teenagers.

Dub recalls a time everything seemed to be going
smoothly. Youth group members grew in their faith,
and the youth ministry team was enthusiastic and
well-organized. But then Earl, a concerned parent,
called. "Dub," he began. "What's the deal with this
camping trip next month?"

"What camping trip?" Dub asked.

"That's what I thought," Earl said. Then he explained: "The other night some group members came
to our house after youth fellowship. I overheard them
talking about a camping trip. A former youth volunteer was leading it.

"I thought it was a regularly scheduled trip," he
continued, "until one of the guys said: 'Now remember—don't tell anyone else since we don't want any
other youth group people there. That would mess up
the whole trip. And especially be sure not to tell Dub.'
That's when I decided to check with you about the
excursion," Earl said.

When Dub learned who was leading the trip, he
wasn't surprised. The young man had resigned from
the youth ministry team after Dub expressed concern
about his activities with group members after youth
fellowship. Rather than considering that his behavior
might hurt the group, the young man had accused
Dub of jealousy for his good rapport with group
members. Then he resigned and left. This incident
was the first time Dub had heard about him in months.

"Thanks for calling, Earl," Dub told the father.
"This is certainly not a planned youth group activity,
and some real problems could develop. I appreciate
your willingness to call me about it."

Because of Earl's call, Dub contacted the teenagers
involved and met with them. He explained that the excursion could hurt youth group morale. Dub also said

he was disappointed that they felt they needed to be dishonest with him. And though he had no authority to regulate their activities outside the youth group, their selecting certain group members and presenting the trip to parents as a youth group function was wrong.

When the teenagers heard the problems with their plans, they said they didn't intend for all these issues to come up. They assured Dub they hadn't thought through their plans well enough. They knew they had made a mistake.

Dub told the young people he was going to write a letter to their parents. In it he explained the situation and how he responded to it. Many parents expressed appreciation for his clearing up the issue. They were unaware of the details and uneasy about the unusual veil of secrecy that surrounded the trip.

Dub might never have heard about the camping trip if he hadn't already built credibility with the parents. But since a parent felt he could approach Dub about a concern, a potential disaster for the youth group was averted.

When we establish credibility with parents, they see that we're working with them to help their teenagers. As a result, we can expect them to become our greatest supporters and advocates.

Chapter 8
Reaching Out to Unchurched Parents

Soon after Walt came to his present church, the youth ministry team began assembling information on the family backgrounds of all the teenagers who had attended the junior or senior high groups the past year. The leaders knew that many group members' parents didn't attend the church. But the leaders still were surprised by the statistics they gathered.

First, only 28 percent of the young people were from families in the church. Of those kids, one-fourth of their parents weren't active. Second, 29 percent of the teenagers came from other Protestant congregations, but one-half of their parents weren't active church members. Another 22 percent of the young people were from Catholic families, most of whom didn't attend Mass. The final 21 percent came from unchurched families.

Adding the figures together revealed that 65 percent of the kids' parents weren't active in a church. That percentage translated into 300 unchurched parents. Simply put, the youth program was in the middle of an important mission field. It needed to reach out to parents.

What does it mean to reach out to unchurched parents? It means inviting parents to discover faith in

God, to establish a relationship with him, to learn the importance of the community of faith and to become Christian parents.

Regardless of a group's size, all youth workers inevitably contact kids with unchurched parents. We work hard to help these teenagers become active in the youth group and grow in their faith in God. But we should look beyond the teenagers to their unchurched parents. Because of our relationship with these young people, we have a natural opportunity to reach their parents. By reaching parents, we can teach them to become spiritual guides and nurturers for their children.

Jesus gave us a model for reaching out to others that's appropriate for reaching unchurched parents. He went to people, listened to them, cared for them, loved them, offered himself and let them discover who he was. As Christ's body, the church, we now have the responsibility to carry out this same work using his model. As parents meet us and we meet them, our mission is to allow them to discover Christ in us and through us.

This chapter suggests ways to reach out to unchurched and uninvolved parents. The principles have worked at Walt's church, and with some thought, adaptation and hard work, they can work for you.

*D*iscover One Another

It goes without saying that we can't reach someone we don't know. The first step in reaching unchurched parents is to discover one another. Get to know names and faces. But, even more important, get to know the parent. What are his or her needs, interests, background, abilities and desires?

Likewise, give parents opportunities to get to know you. A healthy relationship can be built if they know the youth worker is concerned and trustworthy and wants to get to know them. Unchurched parents are particularly concerned—and sometimes even worried—about their teenager's church involvement. They have lots of questions. Is this a cult? Will my values be challenged? Will they try to convert my child? Do they burn incense and eat granola at the group meetings? These questions must be addressed, and letting parents get to know you opens doors for asking and answering such questions.

Here are specific steps that will help you discover parents and, at the same time, let them get to know you:

• **Fill out registration cards.** Walt's youth program asks every young person who attends a group meeting or event to fill out a "Who Are You?" card. Leaders start fresh every year to ensure they have up-to-date information on everyone. (For a sample card, see Diagram 2.)

Ask each teenager who visits the group to fill out a card. Every time you meet keep a stack handy along with pencils or pens. Note the date each person first visited the group as well as the name of the person he or she came with if he or she is someone's guest.

One of the most important items on the card is the teenager's parent's or parents' names. The young people record both first and last names, thus giving clues to various family situations. If a young person lists only one parent, the family probably has experienced a death or divorce. Notations of parents with different last names or a last name different from the teenager may indicate a divorce, remarriage, a foster family or another situation.

Thus the information on the card can be a useful introduction to a teenager's family and background. Be careful, though, not to jump to conclusions based on this preliminary information. Parents with different last names may have each kept their family names when they married.

Diagram 2
Who Are You?

Please fill out this card as completely as possible.
Name: _____
Address: _____
Phone number: _____ Age: _____
School: _____
Father's name: _____
Father's address: _____
Father's phone: _____
Mother's name: _____
Mother's address (if different): _____
Mother's phone (if different): _____
Are you a church member?   ☐ Yes   ☐ No
If yes, what church? _____

Permission to photocopy this diagram granted for local church use only. Copyright © 1988 by Dub Ambrose and Walt Mueller. Published by Group Books, Inc., Box 481, Loveland, CO 80539.

• **Send follow-up letters.** Within a week after collecting a new registration card, write two letters. First write a quick, handwritten note to the teenager. Thank him or her for coming to the group and invite him or her to come back. Then write the young person's parents to introduce yourself and to address unspoken concerns they might have about you or the group. Here are some things to include in the letter to parents:

1. Introduce yourself and describe your position at the church.

2. Tell them that you enjoyed meeting their teenager, that you hope he or she enjoyed the event and that you hope he or she will come back.

3. Tell the parents you'd like to meet them, and invite them to call if they want to get together.

4. Explain the nature and purpose of the youth group.

5. List the times and days of your regular youth group meetings as well as special upcoming events.

6. Mention your willingness to answer questions they may have.

7. Give them your home and work phone numbers.

8. Include an up-to-date youth group brochure and a current youth group calendar.

It might be tempting to save time by mass-producing these letters. Don't! A personalized letter makes a more positive impression, and the extra time spent will pay off. If you have access to a computer, you can keep the basic letter in the computer and adapt it for each parent.

• **Use the Six-P Plan.** Once you and the parents have met, get to know one another beyond just names and faces. The following "Six-P Plan" lists ways to build a relationship and establish trust between a youth worker and parents. Since you don't see un-churched parents on Sunday mornings, contact them in each of these six ways as often as possible.

Six-P Plan

1. Parking lot. The best way to make face-to-face contact with unchurched parents is to be in the parking lot before and after youth group meetings. Try to greet as many parents as possible who drop off and pick up their teenagers. While many teenagers may drive themselves to meetings, others rely on their parents for transportation. These simple hellos can turn into lengthy and meaningful conversations.

2. Postal service. Unchurched parents won't read church bulletins or the bulletin board on Sunday mornings. So mail them everything you print—fliers, brochures or announcements—to help them get to know you and the youth program. If you sponsor a special program they might be interested in, jot them a personal invitation to attend.

3. Phone. An occasional phone call to invite parents to an event or to ask how they're doing can help you get to know unchurched parents. Whenever you call a teenager and a parent answers, identify yourself and carry on a brief conversation.

You can begin to get to know parents over the phone. Walt has seen one unchurched mother only two or three times. But whenever he calls her daughter, the mother answers the phone. Walt has had some great conversations with her. By taking time to talk with her, Walt has become acquainted with someone he would hardly know otherwise.

4. Personal visits. Just as you can learn a lot about teenagers by seeing their rooms, you can also learn about parents by visiting their homes. Nothing can replace a personal home visit as an important contact with unchurched parents. By visiting them in their home you not only show that you're interested in them, but you have an ideal opportunity to get to know them one-on-one. Many youth workers intentionally visit each group member's family at least once or twice a year.

You don't need a formal agenda for your visits. Dropping by to say "hi" is usually adequate. If, however, you feel too uncomfortable to just drop by, find a reason to go. With all the plans and publicity involved in youth work, you can always find something to take along to make yourself feel more comfortable.

5. Programs. Unchurched parents often go to special youth programs. Walt's youth group makes special efforts to invite unchurched families to its regular family potluck suppers, which are usually well-attended.

Many educational events are good times to reach out to unchurched parents. Non-threatening programs on parenting concerns, youth culture and other important topics to parents can spark their interest and bring them to church. Also, by offering educational services to the community, churches can reach out to unchurched families and bring them into the fellowship.

When parents show up for events, talk to them, get to know them and make them feel welcome. Concentrate on making these visitors feel welcome rather than just visiting with people you already know. Also encourage other families to reach out to the new-comers by asking them to join them for dinner or to join their discussion group.

6. Parent information form. Filling out a parent information form helps you learn a wealth of information about parents. It can tell you their marital status, occupation, hobbies, interests, skills, needs and other important information to help you get to know and reach out to them. (For a sample form, see Diagram 3.)

Fill out the form during a personal visit two months after a teenager's first visit to the youth group. Waiting two months gives parents time to get acquainted with you and to be comfortable with their young person's youth group involvement.

*I*ntercession

As youth workers, we sometimes mistakenly believe that hard work, well-packaged programming and strong persuasive skills can change sinners into saints. But they can't. While we must be responsible in our ministries to offer attractive programs, we must constantly remember we're dependent on God for results. We don't have the power to change hearts. Only God through his Holy Spirit can reshape people's lives.

Understanding our dependence on God in reaching unchurched parents underscores the importance of prayer for our ministry. Once we discover unchurched parents, we should begin praying for them—even if we just know their names. Here are some suggestions

Diagram 3
Parent Information Form

Young person's name (last name first):_____

Mother's name: _____

Father's name: _____

Guardian's name (if applicable):_____

Other siblings' names and ages: _____

Street address: _____

City: _____ ZIP code: _____ Phone: _____

Mother's occupation:_____

Place of employment: _____ Phone: _____

Father's occupation: _____

Place of employment: _____ Phone: _____

Mother's hobbies, interests, sports: _____

_____

Father's hobbies, interests, sports:_____

_____

Marital status: ____ Married   ____ Separated

____ Divorced   ____ Widowed

Address and phone of non-custodial parent (if applicable):_____

_____

List special skills or talents that either parent might be willing to share with young people:

What do the parent(s) expect the church's youth ministry to do for their children?

What do the parent(s) need from the church's youth ministry?

Comments:

Permission to photocopy this diagram granted for local church use only. Condensed from *Fast Forms for Youth Ministry.* Copyright © 1987 by Group Books, Inc., Box 481, Loveland, CO 80539.

for how to pray for unchurched parents.

• **Pray for them daily.** Make time every day to pray for unchurched parents. If you have trouble developing a consistent daily prayer life, try these simple steps: First, be realistic about how much time you'll spend praying for parents. If you set your goal too high, you're setting yourself up for failure. Second, find a place to pray that allows you to concentrate. Some people need absolute silence, while others can pray in the shower or while driving through rush-hour traffic. Pray where you know you can pray. Finally, set aside the same block of time each day to pray, and hold to it. Once you find a time and place to pray daily for unchurched parents, it won't be long before you've developed a great habit.

• **Keep a prayer notebook.** An easy way to remember who and what to pray for is to keep a prayer notebook. Use a small notebook that fits in your pocket, purse, backpack or briefcase. Carry it at all times so you can pull it out during free moments to pray or when someone mentions a prayer concern.

Walt divides his notebook into two main sections. The first section lists concerns he prays about daily. The second section is divided into the seven days of the week. Each day he prays for different parents. By the end of each week he has prayed for all of them—both churched and unchurched.

• **Invite others to pray.** Invite parents who are active in the church to pray for unchurched parents. Organize a monthly prayer meeting for the youth group. Give parents the names of unchurched parents to use in that meeting and in their own prayer times. Or set up special prayer times with the youth group members to pray for their parents.

• **Let parents know you're praying for them.** When unchurched parents involve you in situations where knowledge of your prayers would reassure them, it's appropriate to mention that you're praying for them. For example, if someone in the family is ill, facing a crisis or in trouble, tell the parents you're praying for them. If they at least think prayer can't hurt, they'll appreciate the care and concern you offer.

However, be sensitive and discerning in mentioning your prayer support. You'll alienate families if you corner them and say: "Hey, I just want you to know that we're praying for you and your family. We've got kids, leaders and other parents praying that you'll see the light."

Communicating With Unchurched Parents

Communicating with unchurched parents is different from communicating with parents in the church. Since unchurched parents aren't in church week after week, they won't hear about events and activities. They probably won't share your vision and understanding of youth ministry. They'll also wonder what happens at youth group meetings.

Our job is to impart that vision, communicate with them about events and help them understand what the youth group is all about. A parent with a clear picture will more likely support the program and get involved. Here are some specific ways to communicate with unchurched parents:

• **Communicate everything.** In order for parents to understand and support what you do, they need information about everything. By giving them complete information, you'll ease their fears and build their interest.

Communicate to unchurched parents all information in as many attractive ways as possible. Information that is easy to read, is attractive and communicates essentials will appeal to them. It will enhance their interest and increase your credibility.

• **Sponsor a parents meeting.** If there's any single event to encourage parents to attend, this is it. Parents meetings are particularly important for unchurched parents. The goals are to meet parents face-to-face, to allow them to meet other parents and to communicate about the youth program.

Make sure parents receive both a written invitation and personal phone call inviting them to the meeting. Then create a relaxing atmosphere in which everyone can get acquainted. Use the time to communicate your philosophy of youth ministry. Challenge unchurched parents by explaining what it means for the teenager to be a Christian. This explanation may be the first time many of the parents hear the gospel.

• **Hold a parents night at youth group.** Give parents a taste of a normal youth group meeting. Invite all parents—both churched and unchurched—to a weekly fellowship meeting. When they come, don't let them sit in the back of the room as observers. Rather, get them involved in games, skits, discussion groups and other activities. Both the kids and parents will love it.

After the meeting serve light refreshments and mingle with the parents. Get to know them and answer their questions.

Assimilating Unchurched Parents

The ultimate goal of reaching out to unchurched parents is to see them form a relationship with God and his church. Though their first contact with the church is through the youth program, they should be drawn into the church fellowship.

Each church assimilates parents into its structure and programming in its own unique ways. However, here are two basic steps you can take to get the process going:

• **Involve parents as youth program volunteers.** Some youth workers believe you shouldn't ask unchurched parents to help with the youth program. These youth workers say that asking these parents to help only makes them feel uncomfortable. However, such fears are unfounded.

Bill's son first came to Walt's senior high youth group in the ninth-grade. Bill was a rough-looking guy who you'd think would just want to sit at home and watch football games. He certainly didn't seem to be the most promising candidate for a youth group volunteer. But Walt discovered Bill was a licensed bus driver, so he asked Bill to drive the bus to a youth group retreat. Walt was a little hesitant to ask since he knew Bill hadn't had time for church in the past. Walt couldn't believe Bill's enthusiastic response to the request. He was delighted to help! Today Bill is the youth group's most reliable driver. He loves the kids and tries to get to know them individually.

Bill's story typifies the response of many unchurched parents when asked to help with the youth program. Often parents with the least commitment to church will help the youth program the most. They may have needs in their lives that prompt them to serve, or they just may want to fit in somewhere. Whatever the reason, parents like Bill need to be asked. Their willingness may surprise you.

• **Involve them in the congregation.** Once parents have been absorbed in the youth program, they must come to see the importance of being involved in the life of the congregation as a whole.

Once again, Bill's family is a perfect example. After getting involved in the youth program, Bill and his wife began to see the importance of church involvement and faith in God. Before long they began attending Sunday worship. Eventually they joined the church and became active members.

Getting parents involved in the congregation reaches beyond the youth worker's responsibility. Churches should create channels to welcome unchurched parents. As youth workers, we should communicate to the church as a whole who these parents are and then rely on the congregation to follow up in the many ways churches reach out to others. These methods may include personal visits by pastors and laypeople, invitations to adult education classes, invitations to men's and women's groups, and holding a special visitors Sunday when everyone invites someone new to worship. If churches don't have an established outreach process, youth workers can challenge them to begin such a process by first assimilating the unchurched parents who have become involved in the youth program.

*H*elping Everyone

Reaching out to unchurched parents isn't a traditional role of youth ministries. But because parents are concerned about their teenagers, youth programs are a natural bridge between the church and these parents.

Walt's church has seen many families join the church because of outreach through the youth program. Each family comes with different needs, different gifts, and different levels of spiritual maturity and commitment. Families have become excited about their involvement and, as a result, they have enthusiastically invited other families to get involved. But even more important, these families are growing in their faith and seeking to apply that faith to their everyday concerns and problems. They're learning their responsibilities to one another, the church and the world. They're learning what it means to be Christian families.

Chapter 9
*H*elping Families Communicate

*T*he quiet Sunday afternoon at home is interrupted by another phone call. When Walt picks it up, a weeping mother of a ninth-grade girl is on the other end. "We don't know what to do," Mrs. Davis cries. "Sarah is causing so many problems. Can you help us?"

As Walt listens, he learns that Sarah has lied to her parents, and now the family is arguing over her punishment. Sarah thinks her parents are being unfair, and they wonder if they've been too lenient. "Sarah just doesn't listen to us anymore," Mrs. Davis says. "If she would only listen, she might understand."

Five minutes after this rather lengthy conversation, the phone rings again. This time it's Sarah—also crying. Between tears she explains how unfair her parents have been with her. "If only they would listen to me," she says, "they'd understand."

The Davises are experiencing the normal tensions of having a teenager in the family. As Sarah tries to loosen her ties with her parents, they feel like they're losing their little girl. The Davises don't understand their daughter, and Sarah doesn't understand her parents.

In one survey, 34 percent of teenagers said, "Communication between my parents and me is a real problem."[1] Another survey asked teenagers what

would make home life better. The top items they
mentioned were "being treated more as an adult" (44
percent) and "being able to talk openly with parents"
(40 percent). At the same time, teenagers want their
parents to give them freedom and privacy. Twenty-two
percent of the teenagers said home life would be better if parents were less involved in their personal lives.
The survey concluded: "Teenagers appear to be sending a message to their parents to find the delicate
balance between responsibility and privileges of adulthood, on the one hand, and unrealistic expectations
on the other; between open communication and the
need for privacy."[2]

Ways to Help

If families want so much to communicate, why
don't they? Search Institute researchers found four
primary reasons parents and young people don't communicate. Each reason suggests specific ways we as
youth workers can help families communicate.

• **Skills.** Neither parents nor teenagers have the
skills they need to talk about important subjects
without hurting each other.

• **At-home diplomacy.** They don't know how to
be diplomatic or to negotiate solutions when they
have conflicts or difficulties.

• **Trigger event.** Nothing or no one ever brings up
the important subjects. When they do come up, it's
usually in the middle of a crisis or conflict, making
healthy communication difficult, if not impossible.

• **Courage.** Talking about many important subjects
requires courage and energy. It's risky to bring up a
subject that could make you hear things you don't
want to hear or that could make you say things that
would hurt or offend someone.[3]

Skills to Build

Churches provide an important ministry to families when they help them overcome these obstacles. In his book *Planning Family Ministry: A Guide for a Teaching Church*, Joe Leonard Jr. writes: "Fulfilling family relationships obviously depends upon the ability of family members to communicate clearly with one another . . . Probably no aspect of family life education is so important and so practical."

Leonard suggests churches should teach families six skills to improve communication among family members. Our programs for families should model, encourage and teach each of these skills.

• **To speak for themselves.** The first step in building family communication is to help all family members learn to speak for themselves. Too often people say what they think others want them to say rather than what they themselves believe. As a result, families don't take their members' real concerns or desires into account when making decisions.

• **To express feelings, thoughts, intentions and behavior.** How many times do family members misunderstand each other because they don't express what they really feel? No one can know a parent's or teenager's needs or concerns unless they're expressed. The church should help family members learn to value one another's opinions and thoughts. When people know they won't be ridiculed, criticized or reprimanded for what they think, they're more likely to express their thoughts and thus open the way for clear and constructive communication.

• **To listen effectively.** Expressing thoughts, feelings and needs is only half the equation in effective family communication. The other half is listening. Unless family members learn to hear what others say, think and feel, communication can never be complete.

Thus teaching listening skills is critical.

• **To clarify what others say and mean.** Family members may express themselves and others may listen. But they still can misunderstand one another. This is particularly true in communication between parents and teenagers, since the two generations don't always understand each other's "language." It's important that listeners make sure they understand what a person is trying to say and mean. Otherwise misunderstanding is inevitable. We, as youth workers who live and work with both generations, can help translate for one generation what the other means when it says something.

• **To negotiate solutions.** While conflict and disagreement are normal in families, families don't have to be torn apart by these problems. Churches can teach parents and teenagers to negotiate mutually satisfactory solutions to their conflicts. By learning to express the needs, fears and desires behind their conflicts, families can develop creative solutions that meet everyone's real needs behind the conflicts.

• **To build self-esteem and mutual respect.** Healthy communication depends on a person's self-esteem and respect for others. Unless family members feel good about themselves, they're unlikely to express what they think and feel. And they're more likely to let others have their way, while anger and resentment build inside. Similarly, respect for others allows family members to value another person's feelings, thoughts and beliefs—even if they disagree with them. By teaching family members to see themselves and others as children of God, the church can help build mutual respect within families.[4]

*I*deas and Guidelines

Each of these basic skills should guide our efforts to

improve family communication. We can work toward all the goals simultaneously through a variety of programs and opportunities. Here are ideas and guidelines for helping parents and teenagers understand and communicate with each other more effectively.

• **Model effective communication.** Families will never learn to communicate effectively if they don't see models of effective communication. In our programming, counseling and other work with families, we should model skills and principles. Do we allow group members to speak for themselves and express their own thoughts and feelings without being condemned? Do we listen attentively and seek to clarify what people say? Do we work with people to negotiate creative solutions to conflict, or do we insist on having "our way"? Do we foster self-esteem and mutual respect in the way we treat others and expect them to treat each other? By living out these principles, we give families a model to watch as they work on their own skills.

• **Lead them into each other's world.** One reason for misunderstanding between parents and teenagers is that they live in different cultures. Tony wants money for stylish clothes, but his parents think the money would be better spent on a "normal" haircut. Annette is embarrassed when friends stop by during her mother's garden club meeting, while her mother feels out of place and awkward as a chaperon for the school dance.

The two generations are, indeed, quite different. But recognizing the difference doesn't necessarily lead to conflict. Rather, each generation must learn to understand, accept and respect the other on its own terms. Teenagers and parents must learn to step out of their own cultural boundaries and into the other's world.

As youth workers we should lead regular seminars for parents on adolescent development and culture.

Likewise, we should teach kids to appreciate things that are important to their parents. Values, priorities, styles and interests all change. We need to help parents understand their kids' world, and we need to help teenagers see the world from their parents' perspective.

There are dozens of ways to facilitate such understanding. Encourage families to schedule family activities in which they experience things that are important to both parents and teenagers. Plan special family activities that bridge the generations. Sponsor a Golden Oldies party where parents introduce their teenagers to their favorite music. Then invite parents to a Top 40 party where teenagers introduce their favorites. Or sponsor a Past-and-Present fashion show where parents model the hottest fashions from their high school days while teenagers model theirs. In the midst of the laughter, parents and teenagers can ask questions and tell stories that help them understand each other better.

● **Help parents and teenagers see each other's perspective.** Brian doesn't understand that his criticism of his mom's cooking really hurts. Gloria thinks her parents don't like her because they punish her. The Joneses don't understand why Tom won't go out for the track team. After all, his dad was a big star.

Both parents and teenagers sometimes have trouble seeing the world from the other's perspective. Teenagers aren't aware of the pressures their parents face at work or the financial strain of supporting teenagers. Parents get tired of kids' moods and wish they'd "get their act together and do something constructive."

As youth workers, we can help both parents and teenagers see issues, problems and stresses from the other's viewpoint. Simulation games, role plays and other fun activities can help people see things from someone else's perspective. When teenagers or parents come to us for advice in the midst of a conflict, we can ask questions that help them think about why other people do what they do.

Once parents and teenagers understand what the other is experiencing, they're more likely to be sympathetic—not confrontational. Moreover, as parents and teenagers begin to see issues and problems from the other's perspective, they'll also grow in their respect for each other.

• **Create opportunities for families to be together.** One reason families don't talk is because they don't have much to talk about. Family members rarely share experiences with one another. By creating opportunities for families to be together, we give them common experiences they can talk about, laugh about and relive—together. These experiences also give families opportunities just to talk.

Schedule several intergenerational activities each year to bring families together. Family suppers, special programs, concerts, workshops, workdays, mission projects, retreats, game nights and movie extravaganzas can be effective vehicles for bringing families together.

Family activities are particularly effective when family members interact in one or more specific ways. Use "conversation kickers"—simple, non-threatening questions that families have fun thinking about. These questions can help them remember past experiences. They can help people share what they think, believe or value. Or they can be zany questions that bring out laughs and creativity. For example: What was the best vacation your family ever took? What TV characters do family members remind you of? Why? If you had a million dollars, what would you do with it? If you were an animal, what would you be?

Have families play games together. A family olympics in which each family represents a different country can be great fun. Or bring families together for cooperative tasks such as building things out of glue, paper and string; figuring out a puzzle; or solving a problem. These kinds of activities build communication, cooperation and shared experiences.

• **Challenge families to spend time together.** Many families simply don't spend time together. As Search Institute researchers write: "Too often, household routines, school schedules, the family's comings and goings, and television's mesmerizing distractions carry parents and children along, week after week, until suddenly the children are graduating from high school, and all the things they meant some day to talk about—and the right times to do it—have vanished."[5]

Families need to learn that having healthy family relationships is far more important than being involved in all the outside activities. We as youth workers should teach families the importance of letting go of outside activities and commitments—including those at church—in order to make time for family.

• **Teach families to listen.** Several years ago, two teenagers in Walt's community spent a night at the top of a quarry getting drunk and listening to music. Shortly after daybreak, the boys tied themselves together at the wrist, ran toward the quarry and jumped several hundred feet to their deaths.

Many questions would have remained unanswered if the boys hadn't purposely kept a tape recorder running during their last few hours of life. Their final words revealed hatred of and disgust with people who never took time to listen to them. They cursed their parents for giving advice without ever listening. The tape revealed a sense of helplessness. The last sounds on the tape were those of running feet and the boys' screams as they leapt to their deaths.

Those teenagers had severe problems and needed professional help. But they also might have been helped if someone had just listened to their needs, their fears, their loneliness.

Many times teenagers and parents aren't heard because no one's really listening. We can help in many ways. Schedule meetings, seminars, classes and retreats on developing good listening skills. Allow parents and teenagers to practice those skills together. Help young people use active listening skills in youth group meetings—skills they can take home. And actively listen when talking and counseling with parents and teenagers.

• **Teach families how to ask questions.**
"Did you have fun?"
"Yeah."
"Do anything interesting?"
"Nope."
"Meet anyone interesting?"
"Uh-uh."
"Anything else happen?"
"Nope . . . gotta go."

Such conversations take place in almost every family with teenagers. Parents who are interested in their teenager's life give up on trying to learn anything. Every question they ask receives only one word or a grunt in response. Teenagers get tired of just a "yes" or an "of course not" from parents who are too busy reading the newspaper to carry on a conversation.

Communication would increase dramatically if families knew how to ask questions. Good questions require more than a yes or no response. They lead people to open up and express feelings, emotions and experiences. Good questions communicate that the questioner really wants to know what the other person has to say.

A great way to train families to ask good questions is to prepare lists of questions about the weekly youth group meetings for families to use at mealtimes—some questions addressed to parents and others to young people. Some questions should ask for opinions, while others should focus on facts. All questions should be designed to stimulate discussion. When sent home with group members each week, these discussion guides not only facilitate discussion, they reinforce in teenagers' minds what they learned and also teach parents.

• **Teach parents and teenagers to admit mistakes.** Parents who are "always right" teach their children that they, too, always have to be right. But everyone makes mistakes, and unless we admit those mistakes, we can't be open and honest with each other. Churches need to teach families to share God's grace with each other. It's okay to fail. It's okay to make mistakes. God still loves us, and we still love each other. The best way to bounce back from failure is to admit the mistake and then work together to overcome the problem.

• **Deal with all aspects of communication.** Talking isn't the same as communicating. Spending time together isn't the same as communicating. Sharing information isn't the same as communicating. While each of these elements is an important part of communication, none of them alone is enough.

When helping families improve their communication, deal with all dimensions of communication. Families must learn that effective communication involves spending time together, using appropriate communication styles, and being honest and vulnerable with each other.[6]

Families must also learn to notice non-verbal communication. A University of Pennsylvania study found that when one person speaks to another, 70 percent of his or her message is in body language, 23 percent is communicated through voice tone and inflection, and only 7 percent is from the specific spoken words.[7] As youth workers, we need to help families pay attention to these non-verbal signals.

Communication Builds Healthy Families

Good communication is critical for healthy family relationships. Through communication, parents and teenagers learn to understand each other and each other's needs. They develop common experiences, interests and values through communicating their own thoughts openly and honestly.

However, good communication isn't simple to develop or maintain. Family counselor Judson Swihart says: "Strong families do not automatically have a good communication system. They have to desire it, work at it, re-evaluate it and consistently maintain it. Communication requires a constant watchful eye and large doses of nurturing."[8] As youth workers we can play an important role in helping parents and teenagers develop the skills and attitudes they need for effective communication. In the process, we provide them with an important tool for keeping their families strong and healthy.

Chapter 10
*H*elping Families Through Conflict

*A*ll teenagers experience conflict with their parents at one time or another. For some the conflict is minor. For others it's major. Some conflicts are resolved quickly, while others become a downward spiral of tension and anger. Some conflicts lead family members to deepen their relationships with one another. Other conflicts cause rifts that sometimes lead to abuse, running away from home or suicide attempts.

Family conflict is inevitable. But families can learn to deal with conflict constructively, not destructively. As Dolores Curran writes in her book *Stress and the Healthy Family*: "No matter how well the family communicates, there are bound to be confrontations over friends, school, work, appearance, and behavior. In highly stressed families, every issue evolves into an explosive confrontation."[1]

*A*reas of Parent-Teenager Conflict

A study in the Journal of Psychology found that the most common areas for parent-teenager conflict are home responsibilities and spending money. The third area of conflict with mothers is clothes selection and with fathers, using the phone.[2] In his book *Counsel-*

ing Teenagers, G. Keith Olson identifies the following six areas where parent-teenager conflict is potentially the most explosive.[3]

• **Selection of friends.** As teenagers grow older, their parents' influence decreases while their friends' influence increases. Parents feel they're losing their teenager, and they may react by criticizing friends. Or parents may feel their teenager is "getting mixed up with the wrong crowd." In both cases, attacking the teenager will only exacerbate the problem.

Olson suggests several alternate approaches. First, he says, parents should concentrate on building a healthy self-esteem in their children, since people tend to choose friends who reflect the image they have of themselves. Second, by supporting teenagers in their search for friends and by welcoming those friends into their home, parents can learn more about their child's friends and, as a result, ease some of their own fears.

Third, before criticizing a teenager's friends, parents should draw from the teenager his or her own feelings, attitudes and thoughts about the friends. Finally, parents should avoid outright attacks on friends such as "You're not allowed to see him any more" or "She's a bad influence on you." Such attacks, Olson says, only "produce more rage, defensiveness or passive withdrawal."[4]

• **Dating and sexual activity.** Teenage dating can provide enjoyable and profitable interaction for parents and teenagers. Teenagers can learn from and laugh about their parents' dating experiences, and parents can share an important and exciting part of their teenager's life. But too often dating and sex become battlegrounds between disapproving parents and independent teenagers. In fact, 66 percent of teenagers surveyed said that even the most understanding parent wouldn't understand if they talked with him or her about sex—the highest score of any issue on the survey.[5]

Olson points out several reasons for conflict over

dating and sexuality. First, he says, parents often burden their children by reacting to their own dating experiences. For instance, they may overcompensate by pushing teenagers too quickly into relationships. Or they may be overprotective out of fear of the "danger" of teenage dating.

Second, parents and teenagers disagree over the timing of dating freedom and limits. Teenagers need limits and structures, but these must change as a teenager becomes more mature and independent. Finally, the issues of sexual involvement create conflict in some families. Parents worry that their kids will "go too far," and teenagers may feel their parents are too restrictive.

By instilling self-esteem and moral values in their young children, parents can limit the need for restrictions and confrontation during adolescence. Olson writes:

> *Open communication with adolescent children is usually the result of an ongoing pattern of healthy interaction between parent and child. It is a pattern of mutual trust, respect and openness that has been reinforced many times in the child's life . . . Healthy young people really do want to do what is right for themselves and their dating partners. They do wish to please their parents and other valued adults. But offsetting these wishes are their sometimes overwhelming impulses for sexual release and pleasure, the joy of feeling valued and desired and the craving for an intimate relationship.*[6]

• **Alcohol and other drugs.** Parents who hear and read stories about widespread drug use in high schools are understandably concerned about their teenager. Then when a young person does get involved, tension in the family can explode.

Teenagers begin using drugs for many reasons. In a

survey of high school seniors, the most common reason mentioned for drinking alcohol was "to have a good time with friends" (75 percent). Other top reasons included: "to feel good or get high" (50 percent), "because it tastes good" (47 percent) and "to experiment—to see what it's like" (43 percent).[7]

When conflict between parents and teenagers erupts over drug use, it's important that parents deal constructively with the issue rather than alienate their teenager through anger and rage. It's also important to discover the reasons behind the drug experimentation or use so that the real issues can be dealt with. If drug use becomes chronic, parents must overcome their denial of the situation and seek professional help.

Many of the same defenses against other problems also prevent drug abuse. Keys to avoiding drug use are ethical beliefs, a strong self-image, and personal moral and ethical beliefs teenagers learn from their parents. Parents must also guard against inconsistencies in their own attitudes toward drugs, since young people will rebel against perceived hypocrisy. For example, do parents tell their children to avoid drugs, while they themselves have lost control of their own drinking habits?

• **Money.** Surveys have repeatedly shown that money concerns are the greatest stresses on families. This stress can be intensified by the costs of being a teenager—the latest fashions, a new car, an active social life and so forth. Moreover, as teenagers begin working and managing their own finances, parents and teenagers can clash over values, priorities and responsibilities.

Conflict between parents and teenagers over money generally erupts for several reasons: families don't develop policies on handling finances; parents change policies without adequately consulting teenagers; or parents establish an excessive, burdensome policy for teenagers. It follows, therefore, that the best way to avoid conflict is to establish a mutually agreed-upon policy on how teenagers will use money. As teenagers mature, parents can work with them to develop an understanding of budgeting, saving, tithing, gift-giving, investing and other important financial values.

• **School.** Academic performance is a common area of conflict between teenagers and their parents. A Group Publishing survey of parents found that school problems are the most common problems parents confront with their teenagers.[8] Other surveys have found that grades are one of the top two teenage concerns for senior high students, junior high students and parents.[9]

Parents obviously want their children to do well in school, and teenagers want to please their parents. Parents feel proud when their child does well, and they're embarrassed and frustrated when he or she does poorly. When the load gets too heavy, or when a young person simply doesn't have the ability to do better in school, anger, discouragement and resentment build between parents and teenagers.

• **Disinterest in church.** Many young people lose interest in church during their teenage years. The most common time for people leaving church is during the teenage years. When asked why they left, teenagers most often said, "I got involved in other things" (26 percent), "I was put off by hypocrites" (20 percent), and "church was dull, boring" (17 percent).[10]

When parents want teenagers to stay active in church after they've lost interest, serious conflict can erupt. The problem presents serious dilemmas to parents and youth workers who believe that participation in church is an important part of faith development.

When a teenager begins to lose interest, parents shouldn't confront the teenager, demanding that he or she attend church. Such a response only builds resistance and resentment. Instead, Olson suggests, parents should try to understand why a teenager doesn't want to attend. Is it boredom? Are youth group members making fun of him or her? Is there a personality conflict between the teenager and youth leader? Are there spiritual problems underlying the reluctance? Once the underlying cause of the disinterest has been discovered, appropriate solutions can be negotiated.

*H*elping Families Resolve Conflict

Youth workers can serve three important roles in helping families deal with parent-teenager conflicts. First, we can help parents and teenagers deal with the underlying issues that lead to conflicts. For instance, we can offer educational opportunities to help parents develop healthy parenting styles that pre-empt possible conflicts. Second, we can work with families to resolve conflicts in healthy ways. Third, we can refer parents and teenagers to qualified specialists when family conflicts result from serious problems. (See Chapter 12 for more on this third point.)

As youth workers, we become involved in family conflicts in several ways. In some situations, families come to us asking for help and guidance. In these cases, the conflict is usually severe and requires skilled counseling. Other times we find it necessary to initiate contact with the family and challenge family members to resolve issues in constructive and healthy ways. No matter how our involvement develops, though, we should keep the following guidelines in mind:

• **Focus on preventing problems.** As we have seen in the discussion on areas of conflict, most parent-teenager confrontations result from long-term problems—low self-esteem, poor parenting styles, poor communication and lack of personal values. Conversely, families without these basic problems tend to have fewer and less severe conflicts. It follows, therefore, that our most important role as youth workers in preventing family conflicts is to help families deal with these issues before they become major confrontations.

• **Be a good listener.** The best way to help people resolve conflicts is to listen, giving them our undivided attention. As youth workers, we should study and practice listening skills so we're prepared to hear what others say.

Good listeners aren't quick to offer advice. Rather, they listen closely to what people say and how they say it. Don't spend time preparing questions while people communicate information. Wait until they've completed their thoughts, and then show them that you listened by responding with a related question or comment. Ask questions that lead them to clarify their own feelings and outlook on the situation.

• **Challenge families to live their faith.** Some family conflicts result from misunderstandings, personality clashes or conflicting needs. Others come from unchristian behaviors or attitudes. In both kinds of conflict, families should be challenged to resolve conflict in a Christlike manner.

How do family members' beliefs influence how they respond to conflict? How does the Bible speak to each person's role in the family? How does family members' Christian love for one another influence their solutions for resolving conflict? If Jesus were in the family, what would he do? By helping family members ask these and other faith-related questions, we help them grow in their faith together and apply their beliefs to an aspect of their daily lives.

• **Listen to both sides.** Brian says his mother nags him about cleaning his room. He tells Walt how unfair it is that she makes so many demands on his time. After all, he's already busy with school, homework and basketball.

In situations like Brian's, many youth workers almost immediately accept the teenager's story without hearing the other side. There's almost always another side.

By speaking with Brian's mother, Walt discovers that Brian's room is, indeed, a mess. Even more important, though, he learns that Brian's mom is trying to help her son become more responsible about cleanliness around the house. She explains that Brian habitually ignores her efforts to keep the house clean. He leaves clothes strewn wherever he pleases, and he carelessly tracks mud across clean floors.

As youth workers helping families deal with conflicts, we must always listen to both sides of issues before making judgments. This need is particularly strong with teenagers who tend to exaggerate stories or who see only a small part of the big picture. By hearing both sides, youth workers can understand everyone's perspective and then help resolve the underlying issues satisfactorily.

• **Don't take sides.** It's always tempting in a conflict to act like a judge, pronouncing the guilty and not-guilty verdicts. Granted, a few situations may demand judgment calls. In most cases, though, youth workers should avoid passing judgment. Rather, we should help parents and teenagers rethink the situation to discover their own mistakes. They'll be more open to resolving the conflict if they aren't put on the defense by being told they're wrong.

Occasionally parents or teenagers will call a youth worker to talk about a family conflict. In the midst of the conversation, they often will say: "I've tried to make sense to her, but she just won't listen to me. She respects you. Would you just tell her what I'm trying to say so she'll see that I'm right?"

When this happens, tell the person you'd be glad to help, but you won't take sides. You can help family members clarify their messages, but the family must come to its own agreement.

• **Serve as a mediator.** When parents and teenagers are embroiled in a conflict, it's sometimes difficult for them to see the real issues involved. They bog down in trying to hold their positions and to win the battle. In this situation, we can serve best as mediators. By asking questions that clarify issues, we lead family members to understand the problem, to isolate the causes of the conflict and to work together to create a solution.

Many youth workers offer help by moderating family meetings. The youth worker guides the discussion, making sure each person follows basic, mutually agreed-upon rules for speaking and listening. In this way we help families negotiate their own solutions to their conflict and give them a model they can use for resolving future conflicts as well.

One Sunday night Dub was greeting junior highers before their regular fellowship meeting. When he asked David how he was doing, the usually cheerful eighth-grader mumbled, "Okay, I guess." Recognizing that something was wrong, Dub invited the boy into his office.

"David, you seem really down about something," Dub began as David slumped into the chair. "What's going on?"

After an awkward silence, David began crying. "My parents don't trust me," he complained. "They just don't understand." He went on to say that he had lied to his parents after coming home late last night. They found out what he'd really done and grounded him for a month. It seemed so unfair.

Dub and David talked for about 15 minutes. Dub tried to help David think about what he could've done instead of lying to his parents. He asked David to think about the importance of taking responsibility for his own decisions and their consequences.

By the end of the conversation, David had developed a better understanding of what his parents had done. As he was leaving, Dub said that if David's parents wanted to, he'd be glad to talk more with them and David about the situation. The next day David's father called. David had told his parents about his conversation with Dub, and now the family wanted to get together.

That afternoon Dub talked with the family for an hour. Each person described how the incident made him or her feel. Dub guided the family to practice active listening by having each person clarify what he or she heard each other saying. Then the members discussed how to avoid this kind of situation in the future.

In that meeting, David and his parents learned how to listen to one another. They learned that each other's actions grew out of genuine love and concern. They also clarified family expectations. As a result, they left the meeting with a greater respect for one another and a renewed feeling that they were all on the same team.

• **Lead parents and teenagers to practical solutions.** Once the problems and issues have been identified, families must agree on a solution. Youth workers can suggest specific steps families can take to resolve their conflicts such as writing contracts, developing action plans and assigning specific tasks to each family member. Be creative and practical so families will not only be willing to work on the solution but will be able to resolve the conflict as quickly as possible.

• **Be direct if necessary.** Many counselors practice non-directive counseling in which they don't offer guidance or suggest direction. However, when working with family conflicts, it's sometimes necessary to step beyond this model and be direct. Parents and teenagers want to solve their conflicts. If they're unable to see possible resolutions to disputes, don't hesitate to offer suggestions and direction that might result in a more expedient and complete solution to the problem.

• **Develop a follow-up plan.** Include in the solution a plan for a checking and evaluating process. Set a meeting for checking progress, assignments and feelings about the process. If problems have developed or if no recognizable progress has occurred, take steps to change the plan, to meet again or to re-evaluate the problem.

*I*nevitable, Not Insurmountable

Family conflict is inevitable. Different personalities, ages, needs and perspectives that each person brings to a family invariably lead to conflict. But "conflict" doesn't necessarily mean "crisis." Healthy families learn to negotiate differences in ways that satisfy and benefit each family member. By dealing with conflict before it becomes a crisis, families grow stronger as they learn how better to live together.

As youth workers, we have valuable opportunities to help families learn to deal with conflict. We can teach them the skills they need to successfully negotiate solutions themselves. We can work with families to resolve conflicts that have become crises. We can help them discover how their faith applies to their everyday problems and disagreements. In the process, we can help families grow stronger together in Christian love.

Chapter 11
Involving Parents as Youth Ministry Volunteers

*R*emember our excitement (when we were teenagers) when the youth director announced the dates for the next youth retreat? With information and registration forms in hand, we'd leave the meeting talking excitedly about all the fun we'd have together in the mountains. Who would be in our cabin? How late could we stay up? Would the ice be thick enough to skate on? Would we get snowed in and miss a day of school? What pranks could we pull without getting caught?

But there was always a kink, wasn't there? In the midst of our excited anticipation, we knew that two or three of our parents would go along as chaperons. Oh, how we dreaded that thought! If our own parents went, the weekend would be ruined.

The generation gap plagued the '60s and '70s. It wasn't "cool" to be seen anywhere in public with your parents. Family vacations were a necessary but painful duty. You never, ever wanted to get caught kissing Mom.

Though this same generation gap still exists to some extent—and always will—many parents' and teenagers' attitudes have changed. Today parents and teenagers long for a refreshing pause in our hurried, impersonal world. They know they need each other, and they want to spend time together. Even when they have no idea how to communicate, they want to be together and get along.

As a result, many kids and parents are becoming more willing to be together in the church youth program. Fewer kids fear the idea of having their parents along for a winter retreat or summer camp. It's no longer "uncool" to have Mom or Dad around during youth group meetings. Even kids who don't want parents involved can learn that it can be fun to be with their parents.

Why Parents Should Get Involved

Many of us never think about including parents as volunteers in our youth ministry program. Others think about it but never get around to it. Perhaps a fear of parents or a desire to do everything alone causes us to avoid this tremendous opportunity to improve our program by utilizing parents' gifts.

Regardless of the reasons we list for not including parents as volunteers, the advantages of involving them far outweigh any disadvantages. Here are some specific benefits we reap from having parents join our youth ministry team.

• **Parents learn more about working with teenagers.** When parents drop kids off before the youth group meeting and pick them up afterward, they have no idea what happens in between. As a result, they develop misperceptions about the meetings and how to treat teenagers. "I don't know what you do with them," they say, "but I don't envy you at all." They picture a youth worker as some kind of rancher who rides in circles around a herd of wild horses making sure no one's hurt and nothing's broken. While our job may feel that way sometimes, it's not an accurate picture of youth ministry.

By getting involved in the youth program, parents can see what youth ministry really is. They can develop a deeper understanding of adolescence, its unique problems and how to meet kids' needs.

• **Parent-youth worker communication and understanding improve.** The most common tension between parents and youth workers results from parents and youth workers not understanding each other. Youth workers can have distorted images of parents based on colorful misinformation from teenagers. Parents often hear bits and pieces about the youth worker that also leave false impressions. By working together, though, parents and youth workers develop a mutual understanding that reduces or eliminates this tension.

We want parents to know that we're professionals (not big kids who goof off with teenagers) who love our jobs and take them seriously. Likewise, parents want us to know that they, too, take their jobs as parents seriously, that they love their kids and want to do what's best for them. Working together in ministry with the kids encourages and facilitates this type of mutual understanding. Parents can watch our youth ministry team struggle, succeed, fail and rejoice. We can see parents' strengths, weaknesses, struggles and joys.

• **Parent-youth worker teamwork develops.** Parents and youth workers need to remember that they're working toward the same goal: to help young people grow into strong, mature Christians. By joining together in the youth program, we learn to cooperate with each other and develop a unified team.

When kids notice that moms, dads and the youth worker support one another, they respond positively. Our affirmation of parents may encourage teenagers to affirm their parents also. And parents' affirmation of our work can give us added credibility in teenagers' eyes.

● **Kids are exposed to more adult role models.**
A professional youth worker can't be *the* only significant adult role model for all youth group members.
By involving parents in the youth ministry, we give
kids a chance to get to know, respect and even like
other adults who are their parents' age.

With parents on our youth ministry team, kids are
involved with other adults in a variety of situations
and activities. Teenagers discover that adults are
"okay" after all. Indeed, they'll often turn to these
adults for counsel and advice. During a time parents
sometimes feel they're the only people trying to influence their kids for the good, they find it reassuring
that the church also provides positive adult role models for their teenagers.

Providing positive adult role models is particularly
useful for kids from dysfunctional or single-parent
families. The role models help provide the stability
that some homes can't or don't provide. Several boys
in Walt's youth group are from single-parent families.
Their mothers constantly express their appreciation
for the interest the men who work with the youth
group have in their sons' lives.

● **Our resource network expands.** Do you ever
feel like your creativity is drying up? You can't think
of programming ideas. Every problem stumps you. Or
have you ever been unable to figure out a particular
kid in the group?

Involving parents in your planning and leadership
might solve these kinds of problems. Parents know
kids in ways youth workers never can. They intimate-
ly know their teenagers and understand their background and experiences. Parents' insights from their
own experience can shed valuable light on how to
minister more effectively to all teenagers.

Some parents are also good at creating programming ideas. They know their kids' real needs and have ideas for how to meet those needs. Sure, some ideas from their own youth group experiences might be dated now. But some ideas are good.

Less than a month after Dub joined the staff of a metropolitan church, he met with parents and teenagers. Their goal was to review the past year and start planning the next year. In the midst of brainstorming ideas, one mom asked, "How 'bout a square dance?"

No one said anything and Dub didn't know what to say. This wasn't the small-town church he had just left. This church was supposed to be sophisticated.

Then the mom's son spoke up. "Come on, Mom," he said. "Square dances are for squares."

Mom was undaunted. "But I remember getting together with my high school friends each month at church for some rousing 'swing-your-partner' fun," she said. "We joked about it, but we loved it! Your youth group would too."

No one seemed completely convinced. So the mother threw out another idea. "I have a friend who calls square dances on weekends," she said. "I'm sure he'd call your dance. Why not try it? What do you say?"

With the mother's prodding, everyone seemed willing to try a square dance—even though they thought it'd certainly bomb. So the group started planning and promoting the event. Every high schooler who heard about it said: "A square dance? You've got to be kidding." Yet more and more people signed up. In the end, about twice as many young people showed up for the event as any previous fellowship.

The evening of the dance Dub was anxious. He'd been on staff only a few months, and the group was already sponsoring an event he had doubts about. After this failure, he thought, it would take years to get the kids to come to another event. But he kept his composure and acted as excited and positive as he could.

The caller went to the microphone. Without any introduction or explanation, he spun a record and called an entire dance. No one moved. The dance floor remained empty as teenagers stood around with cups in their hands, trying to figure out the caller's mumblings.

So no one was ready for the next surprise. After the danceless dance, the caller said: "All right, everybody. Now that you know how real square dance music sounds, let's dance! Grab a partner and form a circle around the room." Suddenly the teenagers were grabbing any nearby friend. And it didn't matter that there were more girls than guys. Some girls grabbed a girlfriend and joined the fun.

The caller walked the group through some basic steps and led it through a "grand march." By the end, everyone was in a square. And everyone was laughing. As the music and dancing continued, the enthusiasm skyrocketed. Kids mingled with people they never talked with at meetings. Now they were dancing, talking and laughing together.

After two-and-a-half hours, the caller was hoarse and the teenagers were dripping with perspiration. No one wanted to stop dancing. Before they left, the teenagers decided to make the "Square Dance Jamboree" an annual youth group affair.

• **Parents learn to use their gifts.** By including parents in youth ministry work, we help them discover the gifts and abilities God gave them. Then we encourage them to use those gifts in service. Some parents' gifts may be more obvious and easier to use than others'. In fact, it may sometimes seem impossible to use some parents' gifts in youth ministry. But a little work and creativity usually uncover an important and appropriate ministry for any interested parent. Some parents might be best suited to pray for the youth group. Others make great bus drivers. Others can serve as kitchen hands, phone callers, administrators or discussion leaders.

Darlene was a quiet parent. But she seemed to be relatively organized. So Dub asked her daughter Maria if it'd be okay to ask her mom to coordinate the group's summer Mystery Ramble—a parent planned trip where the group members don't know where they're going or what they'll do from one day to the next. The excited daughter assured Dub that her mom was, indeed, "the organized type."

Dub contacted Darlene, and within a week she set an appointment for an initial meeting. She arrived with notebook and pen in hand, as well as a purseload of maps and fliers about recreational possibilities in surrounding states. Within 45 minutes, Darlene had worked with Dub to identify a route, estimate costs, compile a list of potential sponsors, divide the details into seven categories and structure a planning time line.

After this impressive beginning, Darlene continued to invest herself and her skills in making that summer's Mystery Ramble a phenomenal success. Although the teenagers had no idea where they were going or what they would do when they left the church, all parents and trip sponsors had detailed agendas with schedules, addresses, contact people and phone numbers. Darlene even organized a phone chain (in which parents call each other) in case the sponsors needed to contact all parents quickly.

When Dub asked Darlene to help organize the trip, he had no idea that this quiet, unassuming person would meet the challenge in such grand fashion. But he saw a potential gift in her and asked her to use it. Since then Darlene has become a primary youth group resource for assuring that detail work is efficiently and accurately completed.

• **Young people learn about the body of Christ.** In many churches with large youth programs, young people aren't involved in worship and other churchwide programs. As a result, they sometimes equate "church" with "youth group." Many different forces are to blame for this narrowness. Some churches don't give teenagers opportunities for meaningful involvement outside youth group. Some youth workers don't encourage members to participate in the larger church.

Regardless of the causes, one way to overcome the division is to help kids get to know parents and other adults who volunteer in the youth program. In this way, parents and teenagers learn how to appreciate each other's unique qualities and gifts. In the process, everyone gains a more realistic and healthy picture of the body of Christ.

• **Parents get to know each other.** When Walt began involving parents in the youth program, many volunteers had never even met. Some who weren't part of the church at the time didn't know anyone at all.

But as parents worked together, they began to develop friendships among themselves—just like the kids were growing closer as a group. The parent volunteers began socializing after events and in each other's homes. Christian fellowship developed from their youth work, and they initiated their own Bible study and support groups. Moreover, several unchurched families became committed Christians because of their exposure to this Christian fellowship.

Including parents in youth ministry leadership gives them opportunities to meet other adults facing many of the same concerns and questions. As a result, their needs for fellowship, friends and support from other adults are all addressed through their involvement with youth ministry.

Guidelines for Involving Parents

Parents can be valuable additions to our youth ministry team. Yet our efforts to involve parents will end in disappointment or even disaster if we don't follow some basic guidelines. Let's look now at guidelines that guarantee success for your efforts to include parents as youth ministry volunteers.

• **Communicate needs.** Many parents don't get involved in the youth program simply because they don't know what's needed. Let parents know their help can improve the youth program for their teenagers. Communicate every need in the youth program; there's a good chance a parent has the gifts, abilities, resources or desire to fill that need.

Communicate needs through all available methods: newsletters, "parent want ads," the church bulletin, letters and announcements. Tell parents what time, effort, money and skills are needed. Some parents don't volunteer because they assume jobs require time or skills they don't have. Most parents are surprised to discover they can help more than they ever expected. Let them know that all parents can contribute, regardless of their gifts, abilities or interests.

• **Invite *all* parents to get involved.** "I would've been glad to help, but no one ever asked me." That line is all too common in the church. Sometimes we blame the person using it for not taking the initiative. After all, we asked for volunteers, didn't we? Why didn't he or she step forward? But trying to place blame doesn't solve the problem. A much more constructive way to use our time is to invite parents to volunteer—all of them. Every parent needs to know he or she can contribute.

The proverbial wisdom in the church is that 10 percent of the members do 90 percent of the work. They're always asked to help, so they end up doing everything. If this pattern develops with parents in your youth group, figure out who is and who isn't involved. Then personally invite those who aren't involved to discover the joy of contributing to the youth ministry.

Of all the parents in the church, Maryanne seemed the least likely to relate to teenagers. She was shy, plain and somewhat out of style in what she wore, said and did. So Dub had misgivings when Maryanne volunteered to be a sponsor for the upcoming spring retreat. He knew she wouldn't cause any problems, but he didn't think she'd make much difference. However, he needed volunteers, so he agreed.

Throughout the retreat, Dub never noticed Maryanne. But a week after the retreat, a parent called Dub. "I just want to thank you for recruiting such a super group of parents for the retreat," she said. "I'm especially grateful that Maryanne went along."

Somewhat puzzled, Dub asked, "Why?"

"Oh, didn't you know?" she began. "Maryanne really helped my daughter Sally. Sally said the first day was tough for her. She went to bed that night and sobbed in her pillow. She felt so alone and like no one cared about her. She wished she could be back home.

"Apparently Maryanne was awake and heard Sally. So she got up, went over to Sally and knelt by her bunk. As she gently stroked Sally's hair, she asked what was wrong. The question made Sally burst into tears.

"Of course, Sally's crying woke everyone up. Before long all the girls surrounded Sally's bunk, listening as she described how lonely she felt. When the girls heard her, they apologized. They didn't mean to ignore her, but had gotten so wrapped up in the activities they forgot to include everyone. They assured Sally that she was important to them, and everyone gave her a warm hug."

Sally's mother concluded: "At that moment, Sally told me, she felt she was really part of the youth group for the first time ever. At last she felt like the other girls cared about her. If Maryanne hadn't been there, I don't know if Sally would've ever come back to the youth group. Now I know she will."

After he hung up the phone, Dub thanked God for Maryanne and others like her. Since then, he has resisted drawing conclusions about parents' limitations. As a result, he has repeatedly seen significant ministry occur through the presence and offerings of many unlikely ministers.

• **Expect all parents to be involved.** Don't feel guilty for asking parents to volunteer. Avoid the attitude that says: "Youth ministry is *my* job and, besides, parents are already too busy." Even if you were supposed to do youth ministry alone, you could never do it by yourself. If you try to do everything, you're setting yourself up for failure and depriving parents of important opportunities to serve. Instead, have an attitude that expects parents to be involved and then holds them accountable.

Wendy was desperate. She was taking 22 high schoolers on a ski retreat the next day, and only two adults had agreed to chaperon. She knew she didn't have enough adult supervisors, and she didn't know what to do. What if something happened? Half the kids weren't from her church, and she'd be risking all their parents' respect and trust. So much for trying to reach out to them!

She needed to call the parents and explain that the retreat would be postponed if she couldn't find more chaperons. She didn't want to change plans, but she had to be responsible for the kids' safety.

This approach did three things. First, it showed parents honesty. Straightforward communication let parents know what was happening and why. It built trust and cut off possible misunderstanding. Second, it told the parents Wendy needed their help and expected their cooperation. They needed to take responsibility for helping with this ministry to their teenagers. No one else could do it. Third, it invited parents to spend quality, fun time with their kids. This spur-of-the-moment offer could open the door for long-term volunteer commitments once parents learned how fun the activities could be.

• **Encourage teenagers to get their parents involved.** Most parents will consent when they find their son or daughter actually wants them around for a youth group activity.

Two types of young people need encouragement to get their parents involved. First, encourage those teenagers who desperately want their parents to participate but whose moms and dads aren't interested. You can help by personally inviting these parents and planning low-vulnerability activities that expose parents to the program. Plugging into such activities may overcome their hesitancy to get involved.

Second, encourage kids who don't want their parents to be involved at all. In most cases, these young people are apprehensive about having a parent on their own turf. After all, many group members see youth group as a place to escape from parents, brothers and sisters.

This is the same kind of fear you experience the first time you get on and off a ski lift. Actually doing it eliminates the fear. Encourage these teenagers to let their mom or dad come once—even for a behind-the-scenes job. Once the parent is there most kids adapt quickly, and parents make significant contributions to the youth program.

When a teenager doesn't want his or her parents at youth group events, we must deal with the problem sensitively. It's often appropriate to nudge teenagers to accept parental involvement since it can open the door to dealing with deeper issues of family relationships.

If serious problems about parent participation do

develop, talk with the parent and teenager together. Have them reach a mutual agreement about parents' participation in the youth program. If this approach doesn't work, it might be better for the parent to keep a low profile for a while.

There may be times, of course, when a teenager is adamant about not wanting his or her parent to be involved in the youth program. Then the best option is to respect the young person's wishes. There are other church activities to reach and include parents without alienating a young person from the youth program.

One final word of caution: Before pushing a young person too hard to bring his or her parents to meetings, be sure you know about any severe family problems a teenager might hide behind his or her reluctance. These could include marital problems, sexual abuse, alcoholism or a disability. One church asked a family to help lead an Advent celebration only to learn— during the reading—that the father was functionally illiterate. In encouraging kids, be sensitive to hidden issues that lead to embarrassment and resentment.

• **Use parents wisely.** While it's important to invite parents to participate, don't let adult volunteers overwhelm the group members. One church was so successful in getting parents involved that more sponsors than kids attended meetings. When involving parents in youth ministry, keep a ratio of one parent to eight kids or so during meetings. Use other volunteers in behind-the-scenes responsibilities.

• **Communicate expectations.** It's terribly embarrassing for 10 parents to show up to help with an event only to have eight of them say afterward: "Hey, that was a great program! But why did you need me? You guys handled everything; I didn't do anything."

Never ask parents to volunteer without giving them specific suggestions and guidelines for what they'll do. If they're expected to accomplish something, they'll feel useful and will probably volunteer again. But if they don't do anything, they'll see that volunteering for the youth program is a waste of their precious time. So they won't volunteer anymore.

An opposite problem is asking a parent to help with a small project only to have it mushroom into a full-time job. How many times have parents volunteered to make snacks for a youth meeting—only to find themselves leading the meeting a month later? A few experiences like that make even the most concerned parent reluctant to volunteer for anything.

Communicate your expectations in two ways. First, write parents a job description with task guidelines. You can have several standard job descriptions for chaperons, discussion leaders, drivers or kitchen helpers. A week or more before an event, mail appropriate job descriptions to each volunteer. Not only does this prepare them in advance, it reminds volunteers of their commitment and tells them you're counting on them.

While job descriptions communicate general guidelines, you also need to explain specific responsibilities for a specific meeting or event. Have volunteers meet with you for 15 minutes (or longer) before the event. Explain what will happen during the meeting or event, and give them specific instructions. They'll be comfortable knowing what to do and you can stop fretting about details, knowing the parents will carry out their duties.

• **Avoid burning parents out.** Dave was a youth worker's dream of the perfect parent. When he began helping with Walt's youth group, he signed up to help with everything. He was enthusiastic, energetic, and the kids loved him. If Dave wanted to be involved all the time, Walt thought, they'd put him to work.

What a mistake! Before long, Dave began wearing out. His enthusiasm and energy levels dropped quickly, and he became completely unreliable. He burned out. Eventually he dropped out completely.

In many congregations, the same people do everything all the time. At first they're enthusiastic. But after a while those enjoyable opportunities for service become boring chores of obligation. And if these people continue to serve, their lack of enthusiasm permeates the group and changes the ministry's tone.

Use parents wisely. Even if they want to do everything, don't let them. Tell them you appreciate their interest but you want to give other parents opportunities to help. Add that you don't want them to burn out. They're too valuable to the youth program to let that happen. At the same time, don't discourage their involvement. Rather, encourage them to pick responsibilities that maximize their gifts and maintain their enthusiasm.

• **Take care in involving parents in retreats and other major events.** Since major events get young people away from their usual patterns in order to grow spiritually, take special care in inviting parents to help with these events. When planning retreats, trips, conferences and other major events, ask teenagers before inviting their parents to be leaders or chaperons. Many young people may prefer not having their parents along; they might feel inhibited by their parents and not participate freely. Honor and respect these feelings.

When a young person gives permission for you to invite his or her parent and the parent agrees to help, be sure to communicate that the parent is going as an adult leader, not a parent. This guideline is critical. Parents must let their children participate and act like every other group member—with no added restrictions or leniency. Also make them understand that you handle any problems that arise with their children in the same way you handle problems with other group members.

If a parent constantly watches and corrects his or her child during the event, friction is bound to develop. The teenager may never want his or her parent along again.

Getting Parents Involved

Using parents as youth program volunteers may seem logical, but how do you get started? How do you know where parents can help? And how do you know which parents can best fulfill which needs?

The following six-step plan for recruiting and involving parents can dramatically increase the effectiveness of your youth ministry. Adapt it to your own situation.

• **Step one: Plan the program.** Advance planning is essential. If your only advance planning begins one hour before the youth group meeting, you'll never succeed in involving parents as volunteers. If you want to involve parents, you must know when and where you need them. With all the advance dates on the calendar, parents can plan to get involved. A good rule of thumb is to plan special events at least four months in advance.

• **Step two: Recruit parents.** Once you've planned the program, decide when and where you need what type of help. Then recruit parents to meet those needs. Two elements are vital for a successful recruitment drive.

1. Parents letter. Send a letter to parents asking them to be involved in the program. Mention a variety of specific needs and explain any changes in the youth program or special events that require extra help. Finally, ask parents to fill out and return a parent involvement sheet.

2. Parent involvement sheet. Use the "Family Ministry Involvement Card" (Diagram 19) or explain

your specific needs by designing a "Parent Involvement Sheet" (Diagram 4). Give parents a deadline for
returning the sheet and allow space for additional
suggestions. Send separate forms to each parent.

Try to get all parents in your group to fill out this
sheet. Give them an opportunity to indicate they
don't want to be contacted to help with the youth
program. This option will save you from making fruit-
less phone calls when they don't return their sheet.

• **Step three: Follow-up.** You probably won't
receive many completed parent involvement sheets
before your deadline passes. Don't give up. In order
to get the forms returned and tell parents you want
their help, start calling them. Give family ministry
team members a list of every parent who hasn't
responded to your letter. Be sure all parents who
haven't responded receive a call. Ask them to send in
their sheet right away, and use the conversation to
build relationships with uninvolved parents.

• **Step four: Coordinate results.** Once parents
have returned their involvement sheets, give the
sheets to the parent coordinators, who recruit and organize volunteers for the youth program. They can
coordinate the responses and let parents know exactly where they're needed. If, by chance, fewer parents
than you need express interest in a particular event,
invite parents who aren't doing much or parents of
new members who didn't receive the sheet to fill in
where needed.

• **Step five: Send out job descriptions and reminders.** Two weeks before each event, call all the
parents who will help with the event—or send them
a short note. Remind them about the event, and tell
them when and where to meet before the event to
discuss logistics. Also send them a short job description listing guidelines, expectations and responsibilities. Parent coordinators can take responsibility for

Diagram 4
Parent Involvement Sheet (Sample)

Please fill out . . .

Name: _____   Home phone: _____

Address: _____   Work phone: _____

We're trying to find volunteers for upcoming events in the youth program at Supplee Presbyterian Church. Please fill out this form and return it to the church by December 15.

Here are the upcoming special events. Please check any event you would like to help with. We'll contact you about your specific assignments.

I'm willing to help with the following special events:

January 11: Family Potluck
               ☐ Set up   ☐ Help in kitchen

January 19: Ski Trip
               ☐ Drive bus   ☐ Drive van   ☐ Chaperon

January 30: Family Fun Night at Lakeside
               ☐ Drive bus

February 13: Junior High Skating Party
               ☐ Drive bus   ☐ Drive van   ☐ Chaperon

February 20: Christian Music Concert
               ☐ Drive bus   ☐ Drive van   ☐ Chaperon

March 6: The Wild, Wacky and Wonderful Wakeover and Spaghetti Explosion
               ☐ Drive bus   ☐ Drive van   ☐ Chaperon
               ☐ Cook

April 10: Junior High Backward Progressive Dinner
               ☐ Drive bus   ☐ Drive van   ☐ Chaperon
               ☐ Host a course

April 15: Friendship Lunch
               ☐ Help in kitchen

April 26: Senior High Progressive Dinner
               ☐ Drive bus   ☐ Drive van   ☐ Host a course

May 1: Junior High Shopping Mall Derby
               ☐ Drive bus   ☐ Drive van   ☐ Chaperon

continued

May 9:   Junior High Mystery Trip
            ☐ Drive bus   ☐ Drive van   ☐ Chaperon

May 17:   Family Picnic
            ☐ Set up   ☐ Help barbecue ☐ Clean up

June 5:   Phillies Game
            ☐ Drive bus   ☐ Drive van   ☐ Chaperon

June 7:   Senior Banquet
            ☐ Kitchen help

Sign me up for the following:
_____ To serve and clean up for the junior high dinner once during the next three months.
_____ To serve on the youth committee.
_____ To help lead youth group discussions.
_____ To pray daily for the youth ministry.
_____ To chaperon youth group events.
_____ To assist with administrative tasks in the youth program.
_____ To host youth programs at my home.
_____ To drive a bus or van for the youth group.
_____ To help with special projects.
_____ Other: _____

If you don't want to be contacted about helping, check here: ☐

Ideas or comments:_____
_____
_____
_____
_____
_____
_____
_____
_____
_____
_____
_____

these contacts. (See Diagram 5 for a sample job description.)

• **Step six: Thank parents for their help.** Don't let parents' efforts go unnoticed. After every meeting and event, write personal thank-you notes to parents who helped. Then follow the notes with a personal word of thanks next time you see the parents.

Occasionally some parents will expend extra effort for the youth program. They might take time off work to chaperon a trip, or they might organize a special event on their own. Or perhaps they provide some sort of ongoing assistance. Use the church newsletter, worship bulletin and announcements to express your thanks publicly. Or give a small, inexpensive gift as a token of the group's appreciation.

What Parents Can Do

Like all volunteers, parents can get involved in the youth ministry program in many different ways. Although different skills are needed for each job, communicate that every single job is necessary and important. Let parents know they're an important part of the ministry team. The mother who drives young people to the ice-skating party is just as important as the father who teaches the junior high Sunday school class.

Think about your own church, youth program and ministry style. What are the group members' parents like? What are their needs? their gifts and abilities? As you recall each parent, think of creative, meaningful ways he or she could enhance your ministry.

Here are 13 ideas for using parent volunteers in a typical youth program. Adapt and change the ideas to fit your own situation and needs. Come up with your own ideas for involving parents as volunteers in your youth program.

• **Parent coordinators.** Parents can make the job of involving parents much easier for you as the youth worker. Ask a parent or a couple to serve as parent coordinators. They can lead efforts to include parents in the youth program, match parents' gifts with specific needs, and ensure that volunteers fulfill their responsibilities. By recruiting responsible, enthusiastic parents to coordinate other parents' involvement, you save yourself time and energy. And you give parents responsibility and ownership in the youth program.

• **Discussion leaders.** Many parents have the gifts and abilities to lead a good discussion. Teenagers respect parents and listen to them. If parents know how to ask the right questions, the discussion will be great.

Recruit parents who are good listeners and who can guide the discussion appropriately. Put together a short list of suggestions on how to lead discussions and give it to these parents. Or hold an evening training session on leading discussions. Not only will parents add to your ministry team, they'll also get to know and understand teenagers better.

• **Program helpers.** Youth ministry involves mountains of administrative details—paperwork, meeting setups, arranging transportation and other tasks. One person can't and shouldn't take care of them all. But many parents who'd never lead a discussion would gladly help set up a room, prepare and serve a meal, or coordinate cleanup after an event.

Walt's church has developed an "army" of parents to take on these kinds of responsibilities. As a result, the youth ministry staff can spend time with the kids while these parents work behind the scenes.

Jobs that are a youth worker's nightmare can be a parent's dream. For example, the senior high group at Walt's church sponsors an annual outreach event called "The Wild, Wacky and Wonderful Wakeover and Spaghetti Explosion." Every year parents come and stay up all night, setting up, tearing down, cooking and serving a 5 a.m. spaghetti dinner for the kids. The parents love it! They enjoy serving the kids, and they have a great time getting to know one another.

• **Youth ministry team members.** Some parents make great group sponsors. They have their own kids, and they have experience with teenagers. If their kids don't object, invite these parents to join the youth ministry team. Train them and supervise them as you would any other team member.

• **Youth ministry committee members.** Some parents should be part of the committee that guides the youth ministry program. With them on the committee we can hear parents' concerns, share ideas with them, and listen to their insights. Sometimes they hear things from their teenagers that young people would never say to a youth worker. Also, by giving parents ownership of the youth program, they become enthusiastic and willing to recruit other parents.

• **Sunday school teachers.** Parents who are particularly concerned that their children get a good Christian education are sometimes excellent Sunday school teachers themselves. Moreover, they're likely to take extra time to prepare and do a good job. If, however, the parent has a child in the class, be sure both parent and teenager enthusiastically agree to the arrangement.

• **Special speakers.** The mother of a teenager in Walt's youth group goes to Jamaica twice a year for a short-term mission project. One year she came to the youth group meeting before the trip and told the group about her plans and how they could support her with their prayers. When she returned, she came back to the group armed with photos, slides and music from her experience. It was an inspiring presentation on missions.

Many parents have experience, skills and expertise

that are helpful and interesting to teenagers. A doctor or nurse can speak on issues of sexuality and health. A funeral director can help teenagers learn about and discuss death and dying. A business person can speak on living his or her faith in the marketplace. Or an artist can talk about seeing God through creative work. Indeed, most parents have interesting personal stories and insightful information for teenagers. They're a valuable resource for planning interesting meetings.

● **Special project leaders.** Sometimes youth groups want to do projects beyond your own areas of expertise. But chances are good that a parent has the knowledge to head up the project. Parents who can't commit to an ongoing responsibility might be able to contribute significantly through a short-term ministry.

For instance, if the group wants to do home repair service projects, a woodworking buff or construction worker can provide the expertise to guarantee a successful ministry. Or maybe you have an actor or drama teacher who can provide necessary skills for the group to produce an impressive play or musical.

● **Hosts.** Many families have large yards or recreation rooms they'd love to open up for youth group parties or socials. Parents are usually delighted to host one course of a progressive dinner, offer their living room for a youth group Bible study, lend their back yard for a cookout or make their pool available for a swim party. Some parents have vacation homes they might offer for small group lock-ins or retreats. Let parents know what you need, and give them the opportunity to respond.

● **Chaperons.** Being a chaperon is a great, non-threatening way for parents to get to know kids, see you in action, have some fun and develop an understanding of youth ministry. Be sure parents know that being a chaperon isn't being a babysitter. Rather, they're an important part of the youth ministry team as they build relationships with kids and keep problems from disrupting significant ministries.

• **Drivers.** Recruit and train parents to drive cars, vans or buses for the youth group. It may sound silly to say parents need training to drive, but anyone who drives a carload of excited junior highers to a retreat wants as much help as possible. (See Diagram 5 for a job description.)

Organization is the key to transporting group members as safely as possible in a car, van or bus. Parents will appreciate your attention to detail. Walt once took a vanload of teenagers from Pennsylvania on a 24-hour marathon trip to south Florida. In the middle of the night the group took a rest stop in North Carolina. Two hours later—well into South Carolina—someone in the back yelled, "Where's Sherri?" With horror, the group realized she was still in North Carolina, and they had to go back to get her.

• **Prayer supporters.** All parents can pray for youth ministry concerns. Keep parents informed of concerns through a parents newsletter or a prayer bulletin. Ask them to pray for group members, staff, volunteers, other families and the program.

Two specific programs can encourage parents to pray for the youth ministry. First, publish a monthly prayer calendar with names and concerns written for each day. Second, start a parents prayer chain with one parent as the contact person. If a family has a concern, they can contact this person who will quickly mobilize the chain.

• **Financial supporters.** Offer parents opportunities to contribute financially to the church's youth ministry above and beyond their tithe to the church. Since many teenagers in Walt's group come from unchurched families, the youth program intentionally invites these parents' financial contributions—especially for special projects. The church has found that these

Diagram 5
Drivers Job Description

1. Your responsibility is to drive the young people in your vehicle safely to and from the destination. You're responsible for the young people while they're in the vehicle with you.

2. Be cautious in all your driving decisions. Take no risks whatsoever. Safety is imperative.

3. Arrive at the church 30 minutes before departure to discuss the event and trip.

4. Secure maps and directions from the youth leader.

5. Be sure your vehicle is full of gas and oil and in good operating condition.

6. Don't leave until the youth leader gives the signal.

7. Be sure you know how many kids are in your vehicle and who they are. These same teenagers should travel back with you.

8. Remember you're part of the youth ministry team. Get to know the kids and have lots of fun.

9. If you have any problems, you're in charge. Tell the youth leader if anyone causes trouble.

10. Obey all speed limits and other traffic laws. Always wear your seat belt, and require young people to wear seat belts.

11. Check your vehicle after the event to see if the young people have removed all their belongings. Make sure they clean up trash too.

parents are delighted to support a program that means so much to their teenagers. One year Walt's youth ministry committee said "thanks" to six volunteers by raising money to send them to a national weeklong youth ministry training event.

*R*eady and Willing

As youth workers, we sometimes think that no one wants to help. We develop "martyr complexes"—"I'll do it for the group, since I know no one else will." However, believing that no one will help becomes a self-fulfilling prophecy. We don't ask anyone to help, so they don't!

Parents are often delighted to help with the youth program. If we make our needs known, take time to plan in advance and then recruit parents, not only can we improve our ministries, we also give parents opportunities to minister themselves.

Chapter 12

Letting Go: When Should You Refer?

When Allison first came to the junior high group, Walt immediately knew something was wrong. She wasn't a typical, giggly seventh-grader. In fact, as soon as Walt enthusiastically introduced himself to her, Allison turned away. Through the entire meeting she faced the wall. She wouldn't participate, talk or even look at anyone.

After the meeting, Walt intercepted Allison's mom and introduced himself. He mentioned that Allison seemed uncomfortable in the youth group. "Oh, no!" her mother insisted. "She really wants to come." Then Allison and her mom turned around and headed home.

Walt's puzzlement grew as Allison showed up week after week without speaking to or looking at anyone. Eventually she began looking at some people, but it still was clear that something was severely wrong.

Out of concern, Walt tried to discover the problem so he possibly could help her. Before long he learned that Allison had recently been sexually abused by her father. The incident had devastated the family, and Allison's mom had brought Allison to the youth group hoping the church could help.

As Walt learned more about the situation, he realized the family needed more help than he could offer.

In order to minister most effectively to this family, Walt decided to refer the family to experts in abuse counseling. He knew they had the skills and training needed to begin healing this hurting family.

When to Refer

As shocking as they may be, cases like Allison's are not uncommon. In Chapter 4 we examined the extent of some major problems in families today. As youth workers who reach out to families, we inevitably will encounter families and individuals who need specialized help. As families begin to trust us for counsel and advice, they inevitably will turn to us for help with a variety of problems.

Quite honestly, it's nice to know families are comfortable turning to us for counsel. And we may want to minister to their problems. But just because families turn to us and we're willing to help doesn't mean we're necessarily qualified and able to offer the specific help they need.

Sometimes the best ministry we can provide to families is to refer them to a specialist who is better qualified to address their needs. As Christian family therapist G. Keith Olson writes in his book *Counseling Teenagers*, "Just because someone comes to a counselor for help does not imply that that counselor is the best source of care for the particular counselee."[1]

It's sometimes difficult for us to admit that we can't deal with a particular problem. However, we must keep families' needs foremost in mind. Sometimes our reluctance to refer families to specialists grows out of our own needs rather than what's best for the family. "It is important that the counselor not feel competitive, chagrined or self-condemning when he or she recognizes the need to refer," Olson writes. "People who are caring individuals and who gain a sense of

personal satisfaction from being able to help others
are susceptible to the 'messiah complex.' This malady
inflicts us with the false and unrealistic expectation
that we ought to be able to help everyone."[2] The
counselor suggests that, just as everyone is unique, his
or her problems "are just as intricate, complex and
widely variant as are their owners. It is totally unreasonable to expect that any one person could effectively meet all of these varieties of needs."[3]

As youth workers, we must recognize our limits and
not feel as though we fail when we can't handle every
case that comes to us. God has given each person
different gifts and abilities. Some of us can deal with
certain situations, while others are equipped to deal
with other situations. By working together with other
specialists, we can better minister to families' needs.

How do we decide when to work with families ourselves and when to refer them to other specialists?
Here are several questions to ask about each situation:

• **What are the family's real needs?** A family's
problems aren't necessarily the same as its needs.
Sometimes the problems are symptoms of deeper
needs. A teenager's delinquent behavior may signal
neglect at home. Sexual promiscuity may be a warning of sexual abuse. Constant arguments may point to
serious marital problems.

Unless we know the underlying causes of outward
behaviors, we may do more harm than good in our
attempts to help a family. If Walt had concluded that
Allison was just naturally shy, he might have tried to
pull her out of her shell in ways that only would've
alienated or hurt her. By discovering the problem behind her behavior, he knew what issues needed to be
confronted and whether he could meet her needs.

• **Am I qualified to meet the needs?** One week,
three different families came to Walt for help with
three different major problems. One daughter had

tried to take her life for the second time. A son who had been struggling with depression had finally snapped and was incoherent and unmanageable. A third teenager had been arrested for sexual assault.

Walt was the first person each family turned to. Despite his willingness to help, he knew he wasn't the right person to offer the appropriate help. Instead, he ministered to the families by helping them find appropriate specialists. He also offered spiritual counsel and advice, and he worked alongside the other professionals in counseling. But it would've been irresponsible to intervene and counsel alone.

In each case, Walt had to decide whether or not he was qualified to deal with the problem. He realized he did have a role to play in spiritual counseling, but he also relied on other specialists—psychiatrists, lawyers and doctors—to meet each family's complex needs.

Dealing effectively with severe family problems requires specialized training. Unless we have such specific training, we can minister to families best by learning the warning signs of severe problems and then referring families to specialists when we encounter or suspect such problems. These problems include sexual and physical abuse, running away, alcoholism, suicide, depression, eating disorders, sexuality disorders, substance abuse, crime, mental problems, legal questions and divorce. Of course, we can play a role in each of these and other family problems by providing support and spiritual counseling. But we also should turn to other professionals who are better equipped to meet these families' complex needs.

• **Can I afford the time commitment?** This question may seem crass. "Of course I have time!" you argue. "These families need me! What kind of minister am I if I don't take time to help?" Of course as youth workers we feel called to help people in need. But dealing with many family problems would require ex-

tensive time commitments. Unless we realistically can
make these commitments, we will only hurt the families by not providing them with the help they need.

When we encounter a situation that requires extensive counseling and therapy, we should ask ourselves,
"Can I give enough time to resolve this problem adequately?" If our answer is no, we should refer the
family to other professionals who can make such a
commitment.

• **Are legal questions involved?** Many family
problems have legal ramifications. A family going
through an ugly divorce faces loopholes in the law
that could greatly affect its future. A family's economic crisis may involve foreclosure, bankruptcy and
other legal matters. Incest or rape opens a host of
difficult legal and ethical questions.

While youth workers can provide valuable support
and care, we shouldn't deal with these situations
alone. We should refer families to a competent lawyer
when legal questions arise. Laws are extremely complicated, and trying to play Perry Mason can get us
into trouble—and it certainly won't help the family.

• **Do I get along with the family?** Even though
we have the knowledge and expertise to handle a particular situation, a personality conflict may make us an
inappropriate person to resolve the problem. If our
relationship with a counselee is strained, the tension
between us will interfere with the issue at hand. In
this case, we should send the person to someone who
won't have to deal with personality barriers.

Many times, one family member won't like us, while
everyone else will think we're the best person to help.
But since one person's resistance may prevent healing,
we should refer the family to someone else.

• **Am I liked _too_ much?** When teenagers and parents experience conflict and discord at home, it's easy
for them to be physically attracted to a loving and car-

ing youth worker of the opposite sex. Beware of this tendency. If you suspect that someone is inappropriately attracted to you, or if you find yourself attracted to a client, ask someone else to take over for you. It's better to terminate the relationship than risk the danger of compromise.

• **Am I the best person to help the family?** This question should be our primary concern in deciding whether to refer a family to other professionals. If our goal in ministry is to resolve problems—not to build our own client lists—then we should focus on the best ways to meet a family's needs.

In some cases we will be the best person. We may have developed a close relationship with the family and know its interests, concerns and dynamics. We may have special skills in the type of counseling the family members need. If so, our ministry actually may be to help the family resolve the problem. But if the problems are complex, requiring special skills we haven't developed, then our most effective and important ministry is to refer the family to other professionals.

Develop a Referral List

When a crisis or conflict reaches the youth worker's office, it's usually too late to think through all the options and then read several books on how to deal with it. Sometimes people become irrational, or they may be on the verge of hurting themselves. They've finally asked for help, and they need it immediately.

As youth workers, we can become trusted helpers if we're prepared to deal with various situations. One way to prepare is to develop a referral list of who to go to in specific crisis situations. While we can never develop the expertise needed to deal with every situation, we can connect families with organizations and with individuals who do have the needed training.

Frantically flipping through the phone book isn't an effective way to find trusted professionals. Take time to develop a list of trustworthy and reliable people and organizations to call on in various situations. Discover these resources by asking pastors and other youth workers in your area whom they would recommend. You may have competent professionals in the congregation who would gladly give their time as a part of their personal stewardship.

Visit the professionals you learn about. Ask them questions, and get to know them and their abilities. Visit community organizations, and collect information, ask questions and learn about their methods, philosophy, staff and reputation. As you visit professionals and organizations, don't be afraid to ask tough questions. Remember, when you refer families to them you entrust those families to their care and integrity.

Here are some types of people and organizations to include in your search:

• **Psychiatrists.** Contact Christian psychiatrists in your area who have developed a qualified and competent reputation. Check their philosophy, educational background, years of experience, certification and faith perspective.

• **Psychologists.** Find Christian psychologists in your area who specialize in problems of families and teenagers. Again, carefully check their qualifications, skills and perspective.

• **Doctors.** Teenagers and families may come to you with questions that require expert medical opinion or attention. Don't try to answer these questions yourself. Have one or two doctors to contact in times of crisis. Find doctors who will answer questions that might arise during counseling. Cases of domestic violence may require immediate medical attention. Teenagers with eating disorders and girls who become pregnant will need medical care.

• **Lawyers.** Cases of abuse, incest and broken families all have legal ramifications. Families who deal with these problems need a trusted lawyer to guide them. You may occasionally need to consult a lawyer for a legal opinion. Work with skilled and compassionate lawyers who are willing to help in times of stress and need.

• **Support groups.** Discover support groups in your community that are available to help people with special needs. Divorce recovery groups, Alcoholics Anonymous, Alateen, Al-Anon, battered spouse groups, compulsive eater groups and many others provide support, encouragement, direction and help for people struggling with specific problems. Many groups meet in churches, and many can provide troubled families with a supportive network of Christians. (See Chapter 6 for ideas for forming support groups in your congregation.)

• **Marriage and family counselors.** Many counselors specialize in marriage and family concerns. Several probably serve your community. Find one or two to whom you'd feel comfortable referring families for intensive counseling in cases of marital discord and internal family conflict.

• **Law enforcement officers.** Get to know the police officers in your community. It's helpful to have a good working relationship with them when problems occur in the congregation that require police intervention. These could include domestic violence, running away or substance abuse. An excellent way to build rapport is to serve as a volunteer chaplain.

• **Social service agencies.** Most communities have numerous public and private agencies that help families, parents and teenagers with a variety of problems. These agencies include food pantries for emergency needs, shelters for battered spouses and organizations dedicated to helping with unplanned pregnancies.

Each can be a valuable contact in a crisis.

• **Counseling centers.** Locate counseling centers in your area. Many churches, church coalitions and other religious groups have Christian counseling centers to deal with problems from a distinctly Christian perspective. Many require only minimal fees for financially strapped families. These centers can be particularly valuable references for families needing long-term counseling.

• **Hospitals and medical facilities.** Many communities have public and private treatment centers that deal with a variety of specific problems. Compile a list of treatment centers for drug abuse, eating disorders, delinquency, running away, domestic abuse and other serious problems. Also contact hospitals with inpatient and outpatient treatment facilities and clinics that deal with specific problems.

• **Hot lines.** Publish a list of numbers for hot lines in your area as well as national toll-free hot lines. Dozens of hot lines are available for problems such as suicide, running away, sexual abuse, domestic violence, alcoholism and drug abuse. Trained, anonymous counselors can be lifesavers in times of crisis when individuals or families can't reach anyone else or when they're afraid to admit their problem publicly.

• **Other ministers.** Many times it's appropriate to refer a family or teenager to another minister in your church or another church if he or she has particular insight or expertise related to the problem. Survey the ministers in your community to discover who has special training or gifts. Other ministers are also important referrals when you have a personality clash with a family member.

• **Other families.** One of the greatest sources of help and support in a time of conflict or crisis can be another family that has experienced a similar problem. Give families opportunities to minister to others by sharing their experience, knowledge and empathy. A large church in Texas has developed a computer data base of its entire membership that lists all the major life events each family has experienced such as the death of a child, the death of a spouse, divorce and suicide. When a family experiences a crisis, the church can link the members with another family that has lived through a similar experience.

Sharing the Load

Sometimes the variety and volume of family problems can be overwhelming. How can we ever learn enough to help everyone? How can we find the time to meet everyone's needs? These questions may make it seem hopeless to minister effectively to families.

But in today's world of specialization and diverse services, we don't have to minister alone. Other professionals—doctors, lawyers, counselors, social workers, psychiatrists, psychologists and others—can share the load, allowing us to minister more effectively as a team.

As youth workers who minister to families with teenagers, we will be approached for counsel in many situations. If we can't provide the best help, we shouldn't hesitate to seek assistance from others who have the experience and training we don't have. Our job is to assure families the best help possible for their problem or conflict. If we lead them to the help they need, then we truly minister to them.

Part 3

*B*uilding a Ministry to Families With Teenagers

Chapter 13
Deciding to Build: Sharing the Ministry Vision

Dub knew he had to do something. He had just returned from a youth ministry conference. Search Institute president, Peter Benson, had reported on the organization's major research study of teenagers and their parents. He had discussed teenagers' needs, concerns and problems. He also had noted that the 10,000 parents in the study were crying out for better understanding of themselves and their teenagers. Not only did parents want new programs, but they in a sense were standing in line at their church's doors waiting for opportunities for support and learning.

Dub's initial reaction was excitement. What a wonderful opportunity for ministry! Imagine the impact the church could have by addressing the needs of families with teenagers.

His next reaction was: "Where should we start? Statistics point to many needs and concerns. There's no way one church—much less one youth worker— can do everything that needs to be done."

One way to begin would be to write a few fun ideas on the calendar. If the response is good, add more. While this approach may seem easy, it's not effective. In order to develop an effective and well-rounded ministry to families with teenagers, we must build it from the foundation up. Like a contractor constructing a house, we must work in an orderly way to ensure that in the end the ministry structure we build is solid and useful.

The four chapters in this section are a builders guide to ministering to families with teenagers. Each chapter includes a complete meeting to help the planning task force of parents and teenagers coordinate the building process. The meetings' length and content can be adapted to fit your needs. Schedule one meeting per week (90 minutes to two hours per meeting) or combine all meetings during a weekend retreat. The planning task force meets for this short-term commitment to form the basic ideas and structure for the family ministry. The process includes the following steps:

- **Deciding to Build.** How to convince the congregation of the need for the ministry. How to enlist a planning task force.
- **Surveying the Land.** How to assess family needs in the congregation and community. How to conduct surveys and analyze the data.
- **From Blueprint to Building.** How to build a ministry on a solid foundation. How to design a committee structure based on your mission statement. How to begin developing programs based on your objectives.
- **The Housewarming Party.** How to throw a fun and enticing party to introduce your ministry to the congregation and community. How to establish a family ministry team to coordinate the ongoing program.

This chapter on deciding to build a family ministry is divided into the following sections:

- Convincing the Congregation
- Hiring the Construction Crew

• Task Force Meeting #1: Catching the Vision

Convincing the Congregation

As you read the first 12 chapters of this book, you probably became convinced of the needs and opportunities in your congregation to minister to families with teenagers. However, unless others in the congregation share your vision and enthusiasm, your dream for a ministry to families will turn into a nightmare of frustration and burnout. So before you begin any work, spread your vision and enlist other people's support. If you garner support, you'll be prepared to build a strong and useful structure. If you don't, you'll be left hammering a structure that no one really wants. While you may be able to ramrod a program and get it started on your own, it will eventually fail without broad support.

Every congregation has its own process for conceiving, approving and implementing new programs or emphases. Be sure to follow the procedures for your own congregation. As cumbersome as it sometimes may seem, following these procedures ensures that you'll have the leadership's support for the programs you implement.

At this point you haven't gathered any specific survey information, and you haven't developed a specific structure. Resist any pressure to take these steps too early. Explain that you need to have congregational support for the ministry before the survey. Otherwise the survey will raise people's hopes for the ministry— hopes that might alienate families if no program is developed. Explain that the specifics of the program can be worked out only once you've carefully studied the specific needs in the congregation and community.

As you discuss your dream with various people and groups, be sure to clarify your reasoning for the program. Your purpose is to strengthen and nurture families, not to bring more families to the pews (though the latter may be a byproduct). Unless everyone shares a similar vision, friction will develop and you'll lose support for the program.

Here are some people you may need to share your dream with:

• **The senior pastor.** Congregations usually look to the senior pastor for leadership and direction. Getting him or her to support your plan is a critical step in developing congregational support. Personally talk with the senior pastor. Share your dream and why you think it's important. Explain how a family emphasis will help the youth program and congregation.

• **Other church staff people.** If you work in a multiple-staff church, explain your ideas to other staff members. Explain how this program will fit in with other programs in the church. Show its importance to the youth program and to congregational life in general. Get staff members' ideas of who to include in the planning, and work through their concerns.

• **The youth committee.** Since outreach to families with teenagers is an extension of youth ministry, be sure to work with the youth committee in planning and implementing your proposal. Explain how this program would augment—not take away from—the current youth program. Listen to the committee's concerns, and ask if any members want to become part of the planning task force.

• **The youth group.** Youth group members may be skeptical about your plans, particularly if their parents aren't active in church. Explain to them what you're planning and why. Assure them that they'll be an active part of the ministry and that the program will help them relate better to their parents. Include a short article in the youth group newsletter about the vision. Answer any questions or concerns youth group members may have. Find out if any group members want to help with the planning.

• **The church council.** The church council (or similar body) will be the group you'll rely on for support—including a budget—once you begin your ministry to families. It's imperative that this group understands and shares your vision. Bring your idea to a church council meeting, and listen to members' suggestions and concerns. Explain as much as you can, but don't make promises you can't fulfill. Give the council your proposed schedule for implementing the program, including the steps you plan to take. Ask if any council members would like to be part of the family ministry planning task force.

• **Youth group parents.** In order for parents to feel ownership and leadership in the ministry to families, it's important that they share the dream and help make it become a reality. Send letters to parents explaining the idea, and ask them for their feedback and support. Talk individually with influential parents who will honestly share other parents' concerns with you. Ask them to help promote the idea with their peers.

• **The congregation.** Developing a ministry to families with teenagers will be a visible and an important change. If the congregation as a whole resists this change, your efforts could prove ineffective. Therefore, keep the congregation informed about the idea, its progress and its timetable. Give members opportunities to express their concerns and support. Include a sheet in the worship bulletin that lets them give their feedback on the idea. Talk about the plans in congregational meetings, and take time to answer members' questions. If the senior pastor strongly supports your initiative, ask him or her to preach about families and the church's responsibilities to families.

*H*iring the Construction Crew

In planning a ministry to families with teenagers, it's important to work with a family ministry task force from the very beginning. This approach not only spreads the work among many people, but it also gives teenagers, parents and other leaders ownership and responsibility for their own program.

Since you're just beginning to build a ministry to families, you can start by forming a temporary planning task force to oversee and implement the process. Then when specific programs are agreed to, you can form an ongoing family ministry team in which members commit to specific responsibilities and longer appointments.

• **Choosing task force coordinators.** As a youth worker, you shouldn't be responsible for organizing the ministry to families. Find a capable person (or couple) and a youth group member to coordinate the planning. Work through your congregation's committee structure to select the people who can coordinate the ministry. They could be people who have expressed interest in such a program. They could be leaders in the congregation or dedicated youth ministry volunteers.

Ask a young person also to serve as a coordinator. This person should be mature and should relate well to adults. Including a responsible leader from the youth group will help the teenagers claim ownership of the new initiative. The teenager can be an elected youth group member, a youth group leader or someone who expresses particular interest in the ministry to families.

Have these coordinators work together throughout the rest of your planning. They can work with you to oversee the program as it develops and to select other people to work on the task force.

• **Designing the task force.** Your family ministry task force can take many different shapes, depending on your community and the size of your church. Your team could consist of parents and teenagers as well as other interested people in the congregation and community.

Here are a few guidelines to use in building your task force that will ensure balance and effectiveness:

1. Include people from different kinds of families. Single-parent families have concerns different from two-career families. Blended families face issues different from traditional families. Therefore it's important to represent different family structures on your family ministry team. The give-and-take of different people's perspectives will guarantee that all types of families are considered in your planning.

2. Include both parents and teenagers. Parents will enjoy some programs that teenagers will hate—and vice versa. Bringing both together helps you plan to meet everyone's needs. However, if parents are reluctant to share their concerns about teenagers in these planning meetings, form a subgroup of parents to discuss their specific concerns. Do the same with teenagers. If you're uncomfortable having a young person head an area, team a young person with an adult for each responsibility. But be sure that the adults don't dominate the teenagers. Help them develop teamwork.

3. Include experts if possible. If you have family experts in the congregation, ask them to join the task force. These experts might include psychologists, social workers, school counselors or professors. Their advice and perspective can help your program stay on track. If they're too busy to work in the nitty-gritty of planning the program, ask them to serve as consultants. There may be experts in the community who don't belong to your church who also might provide valuable insight.

4. Limit the task force's size. With all the different family structures and people involved, it's easy for your family ministry task force to become so large that it can't be effective. Including more than eight people limits effective group discussion and coordination. Therefore choose the core people carefully, then ask others to serve in other roles once the ministry has started.

5. Limit members' commitments. Few people will commit to an open-ended responsibility. It's important, therefore, to tell task force members what specifically is expected and how long they'll serve in this capacity.

• **Recruiting task force members.** Recruit task force members the same way you enlist volunteers for other programs. Begin by sending a letter to parents of youth group members. Explain the vision of the ministry and ask them if they're interested in helping make the vision become a reality. Invite them to your first planning meeting, or suggest that they call you if they're interested.

Talk with leaders in the youth ministry and the congregation about who would be good to include on the family ministry task force. If a personnel committee oversees appointments in the church, work with this committee. Talk to the pastor about who he or she thinks would be a valuable addition to the task force. Keep in mind the need for including a mix of family types on the task force. Once you've gathered the names, call or visit them to explain the vision and to ask if they're interested in getting involved. Also talk with responsible youth group members who you think could contribute to the family ministry task force.

Once you've gathered the list of interested task force members, send a follow-up letter. Again describe the vision of the ministry and why you think they could contribute to the task force. Explain the group's role and responsibilities.

Invite those people who are interested in joining the task force to attend the initial meeting. Schedule it several weeks in advance so they can plan for it. Explain that they're under no long-term obligation. If they decide after the first meeting that they aren't interested or don't have the time to invest, they'll have the opportunity to withdraw.

Several days after mailing the letter, call the people you contacted to gauge their interest. Answer any questions they have about the plans and responsibilities. If several people say they don't want to participate, you may want to contact other people to attend the initial meeting.

Finally, about a week before the meeting, send all the participants an agenda for the meeting so they'll know what to expect. In order to prepare them for the meeting, ask them to think about the needs and concerns they see in families in the church and community.

*T*ask Force Meeting #1: Catching the Vision

People will come to your first planning meeting full of anticipation, enthusiasm and personal agendas. Set the stage for your entire planning process by being well-prepared, open to ideas and comments, and ready to work. Have the chosen task force coordinators lead the meetings. It's important that families understand that the ministry will be *their* ministry, not the youth worker's.

• **Objectives.** The meeting is designed to:
1. Help task force members get acquainted.
2. Share the dream of the ministry with participants.
3. Begin assessing current programming for families.
4. Enlist help for conducting surveys.

• **Preparation.** Contact parents, teenagers and other interested people as suggested in the section on recruiting task force members (page 215). Ask someone to take minutes from the meeting to distribute to participants.

Work with the task force coordinators to determine the best way to conduct surveys in your congregation and community. (See Chapter 14 for more information.)

Gather name tags, newsprint, markers and pencils. Collect enough newspaper articles and other statistics about family needs and trends for each person to have one for the "Sharing the vision" section. Include statistics from Chapters 2 and 4.. Summarize the information on separate 3×5 cards (one trend or problem per card). Cover a variety of family trends such as single parenting, divorce, discipline, money, busyness and domestic violence.

Make copies for each participant of the "Family Needs" worksheet (Diagram 6) and the "Should We Do Family Ministry?" worksheet (Diagram 7).

• **Opening.** As participants arrive, ask them each to write only their first name on a name tag. When it's time to begin, tell them to pair up with someone they don't know well. Tell them to find out three things about that person that have nothing to do with family. After two or three minutes, take a vote on how much they've learned about the other person. Tally the number of those who say "a lot," "some" and "not much."

Now have each person add his or her last name to the name tag. Have participants find someone else they don't know well. This time tell them to find out three things about the person that are related to family. Then ask them how much they've learned about this person: "a lot," "some" or "not much."

Ask the group to compare the two scores and what the difference says about the importance of families. Then have each person briefly introduce his or her

Diagram 6
Family Needs

Trend or Problem	Very Important	Somewhat Important	Not Important
1.			
2.			
3.			
4.			
5.			
6.			
7.			
8.			
9.			
10.			
11.			
12.			

Diagram 7
Should We Do Family Ministry?

Following are 10 important questions to address before launching a ministry to families with teenagers. As a group, discuss the question, developing your own responses to each one.

1. Does our church see a need to improve family life in the congregation and community? Explain.

2. Is our congregation ready to help meet this need? Why or why not?

3. Why should we minister to families with teenagers? Are these reasons adequate and appropriate? Explain.

4. What does our church believe the Bible says about its responsibilities to families? Are families important from a theological or biblical perspective?

5. Are our congregation leaders committed to improving family life in the congregation? Am I personally committed?

6. What kind of family ministry do I anticipate?

7. With this family ministry do I want to reach people in our church? unchurched families? both? healthy families? stressed families?

8. Are other churches and organizations in the community already providing this ministry? Would our ministry duplicate what others are already doing?

9. What resources would our church need to fulfill this ministry? Would our church need personnel? funding? facilities? other resources? Are these available or possible?

10. Who will plan and run the program? Will families? parents? church staff? others?

partner to the whole group.

• **Sharing the vision.** Give each participant one of the 3×5 family trend cards. Also distribute copies of the "Family Needs" worksheet (Diagram 6). One by one, have each participant read the information on his or her card, and have all the other participants mark on their worksheets how important that need is for families in your church and community. Continue around the group until all cards have been read.

Once participants have begun to think about these family needs, brainstorm other needs of families in the church and community. What problems do they have? What stresses do they face? Without commenting on or critiquing the ideas, list participants' ideas on newsprint.

When the group begins to run out of ideas, move the sheet of newsprint aside and label a new sheet: "How is our church doing?" Ask the group to think about how well—or poorly—the church is meeting family needs. Write the comments on the newsprint. Include programs you already have for families as well as programs that may interfere with family life. List any issues the church has overlooked or ignored. Encourage the group to be honest. Remind participants that the purpose of critiquing past programs is to help develop a more effective and faithful ministry.

Finally, on another sheet of newsprint write: "Our dreams for ministering to families." Have participants compare the first two lists and think of ways the church could be more effective in reaching and supporting families. Write all their ideas on this third sheet of newsprint. What does the task force hope to accomplish? What needs would it like to meet? What does it see as the purpose of beginning a ministry to families with teenagers? Asking these questions will help all participants begin to understand and share a common vision.

● **Can we do it?** Divide the group into teams of three or four people. Distribute a copy of the "Should **We** Do Family Ministry?" worksheet (Diagram 7) to each person. Have each team think through and answer each question. Allow plenty of time since this step becomes a foundation for each member's commitment and shared ownership in the vision.

When the teams are finished, bring everyone back together. Discuss each question as a large group. Come to a consensus on how to respond to each question.

● **Assigning responsibilities.** Explain to the group that the previous exercise is useful to get ideas going and to establish a foundation. But it isn't an adequate way to discover specific needs in the congregation and community. Explain the need for conducting a survey and interviews. Describe the steps needed to develop a target ministry. Tell how long you think the process will take. Answer any questions that participants have.

Now ask for volunteers to help with specific tasks in surveying the church and community. Each person is to complete the task and report the results to the group. In some cases, a person will work with a team of people to complete a larger task (such as conducting the phone survey). The task force coordinators should take primary responsibility for coordinating the major surveys.

Depending on the survey methods you choose, the tasks could include:

1. Analyzing, adapting and revising the survey to fit your congregation and community.

2. Examining church records to learn more about families.

3. Contacting community and government organizations for information on families in the community.

4. Conducting the survey.

5. Tabulating and analyzing survey results.

6. Interviewing families in the community.

7. Helping with a phone survey.

8. Interviewing experts in the community about family needs and reporting to the group.

Once everyone who wants to volunteer has done so, set a time for the next meeting. Decide which tasks should be completed by that time, and ask the responsible people to report to the group at the next meeting.

• **Closing.** By the end of this meeting, participants will feel excited, challenged and overwhelmed. Conclude the meeting by reminding participants of the importance of the church ministering to families. Ask participants to think back to the beginning of the meeting when they described their families to one another. What did that exercise tell them about the importance of the family?

Read Romans 15:5-6, where Paul encourages the church in Rome. Suggest that participants listen to Paul's words as if he were encouraging them in their new and challenging ministry.

Finally, close the meeting with prayer, thanking God for each person's support and asking God for guidance as your church seeks to minister to families with teenagers.

Chapter 14
Surveying the Land: Assessing Families' Needs

*I*f all churches and people were the same, we could specify a program that would fit everyone's needs—like a kit from a mail-order catalog. We could tell you exactly what programs to initiate, what to emphasize and how to schedule the next three years. All you'd have to do is connect one part to the next and you'd have a perfect ministry.

However, each church, community, family and person is different. Therefore each congregation has a slightly different terrain to build on. Before you start building, it's critical to pull out your surveyor's instruments to discover what kind of structure you need to minister to families in your church and community. This chapter takes you through the steps of gathering and analyzing information about families in your church and community. It's divided into the following sections:

- What to Look For
- Tools to Use
- Gathering the Information
- Task Force Meeting #2: Assessing Needs

What to Look For

When land surveyors begin examining a new site, they have specific goals and needs in mind. They don't look at flowers and birds through their surveyor's level; rather, they check topography, dimensions and property lines.

Similarly, when you begin discovering families' needs in your community, you should look for specific types of information. Here are four critical areas in which to gather information.

• **Demographics.** What kinds of households and families are in the congregation and community? How large are families? What is their income level? What are their racial and ethnic backgrounds? How old are family members? What kinds of transportation do they have?

These and other questions can influence the eventual shape and emphases in your ministry. For example, an outreach to single-parent families might be futile if there are few such families in the community. Or charging admission for workshops could be counterproductive if many families in the community have limited incomes.

• **State of families.** What are families' needs, concerns, interests and attitudes? How do families feel about themselves? What are they struggling with? By asking these questions, you uncover specific issues to address in your programming.

• **Resources.** Surveys within the congregation and community can help you locate potential resources and experts for your family ministry programming. You may discover experts in family concerns who would be delighted to work with the church to strengthen families. Or you may discover organizations and other resources in the area that can provide contacts and referrals for your ministry.

• **Faith commitments.** When a congregation seeks to reach out into its community, it must recognize the faith commitments—or lack of them—of people in the community. Are families active in other Christian congregations? Are they adherents to another faith? Are they inactive Christians? Or are they non-religious?

Such questions can shape several elements of your family ministry program. If most people in the community are active in churches, you could offer joint family workshops and seminars to avoid competition between like-minded congregations. On the other hand, if the community has nominally Christian or unchurched families, evangelism may need to be an important part of the family ministry program. These questions also indicate whether many families would be open to participating in church-sponsored family workshops and other events.

*T*ools to Use

Several different surveyor's tools are available. Each gives a slightly different perspective. Some are more precise than others, and some fit specific youth programs better than others. Decide which approach is best for your group, or scope the land with several different tools. Indeed, using several methods together can provide the most thorough look at families with teenagers in your church and community.

• **Church records.** You may have a great deal of information already to help you plan your ministry to families with teenagers. If you keep attendance records with information about families, look through these to discover the shape of families in your congregation. Make a checklist like "Families in the Congregation" (Diagram 8) to determine the number of youth group members who come from various types of families.

If you haven't kept such records, design a simple attendance form that asks for family background information. Ask everyone who attends youth group activities to fill one out. The form should ask:

1. The teenager's name, address, phone number, age and grade

2. The name and address of each parent (or guardian)

3. Parent(s)' marital status

4. Parent(s)' occupation(s)

This information is a valuable starting point for your outreach to families. It can help you several ways.

1. It gives you hints about needs in your congregation, since families in the same situation often have similar needs. If you have a large number of single-parent families, your program needs to differ from one for mainly traditional families.

2. It ensures that you balance the needs of different families in your family ministry leadership and program. For instance, a leadership team consisting of only people from traditional families is less likely to see and address the needs of two-career families or single-parent families.

3. Once you've gathered information about your community, you can compare your church's makeup to the community's to determine whether your church is reaching a cross section of people in the neighborhood.

• **Community and government agency information.** Before taking a survey of your community, contact community and government agencies that might have already conducted such a survey. These include health facilities, political organizations, schools, law enforcement agencies and food banks. Some of their information may be more thorough and scientific than you can compile. Moreover, people in these agencies can share their valuable insights and perspectives on community needs, concerns and problems.

• **Written surveys.** If properly constructed and ad-

Diagram 8
Families in the Congregation

Make a mark for each family in the youth group that falls under each category. If families fit more than one category, mark them each time. Tally the total number in each situation in the right column. (For a description of each family type, see pages 30-37.)

Type	Tally	Total
Traditional families		
Two-career families		
Single-mother families		
Single-father families		
Blended families		
Others		

ministered, a written survey is the most accurate, specific and comprehensive information-gathering tool available to a church. Not only does it provide background information on families, it can uncover families' needs and limitations.

Survey several different groups in order to get a well-rounded picture of the families and needs in the congregation and community. These groups should include parents, teenagers, church members and unchurched community members.

Design one survey to give to all groups that speaks to each group's specific needs. Or design slightly different surveys for each group. If you take the latter approach, be sure that each survey asks similar kinds of questions. This way you can compare the responses of different groups.

We've designed a "Family Survey" (Diagram 9) you can use or adapt in your congregation. If you choose to design your own survey or adapt the sample, here are some guidelines.

1. Keep it anonymous. There will be plenty of opportunities to find out who needs what kind of help. At this point it's important that you guarantee people that their responses are anonymous and that no one will contact them about their responses. This way you have a better chance of people filling out the survey with complete honesty. It also allows you to ask tough questions. Since anonymity prevents you from gathering information on resources and talents, use other methods to gather this information.

2. Vary the format. Don't just ask yes-or-no questions, and don't just ask essay questions. Both are appropriate, but neither is adequate in itself. Simple questions help you gather precise statistics on specific questions. But they don't allow respondents to express themselves in other areas. Open-ended questions help you discover needs you hadn't thought about,

Diagram 9
Family Survey

Dear Friends:

The family ministry planning task force at ___(church name)___ wants to help meet the needs of families with teenagers in the church and community. Please fill out the following survey as completely as possible so we can better understand you and your needs in order to serve you better. Have each parent and teenager complete the survey individually.

Be completely honest in your responses. This survey is totally confidential. Do not put your name or other identification on the survey. The information from numerous families will be summarized in one report. We'll send you a copy of the summary, if you like.

Thank you for your cooperation and help. We hope this survey will help us better meet your needs.

General Information
Please check (✔) the appropriate box:
1. Are you: ☐ a teenager's mother   ☐ a teenager's father
☐ a teenager's stepmother ☐ a teenager's stepfather
☐ a teenager   ☐ other: _____
2. What is your age?
☐ 10 to 17 years   ☐ 40 to 49 years
☐ 18 to 29 years   ☐ 50 to 59 years
☐ 30 to 39 years   ☐ older than 60
3. What type of transportation do you rely on?_____

Family Life
4. How would you characterize the quality of your home life?
☐ excellent   ☐ good   ☐ fair   ☐ poor
5. Which of the following would improve your home life? Rank them from most important (1) to least important (5).
_____ to talk more openly with my parent(s)/teenager(s).
_____ to spend more time together as a family.
_____ to get along better with my parent(s)/teenager(s).
_____ to have more money in the family.
_____ to share more responsibilities at home.
_____ other: _____
6. Which of the following do you believe your family really needs to work on? (Check all that apply.)
☐ communication   ☐ privacy
☐ fun times   ☐ trust
☐ religious life   ☐ expectations of family members
☐ discipline   ☐ getting along together
☐ other: _____

continued

7. Below are problems some families face. Please indicate how much you deal with each problem in your family.

	very often	often	occasion- ally	never	not applicable
lack of communication	☐	☐	☐	☐	☐
financial problems	☐	☐	☐	☐	☐
alcohol abuse	☐	☐	☐	☐	☐
disagreements over religion	☐	☐	☐	☐	☐
parent-teenager arguments	☐	☐	☐	☐	☐
arguments between parents	☐	☐	☐	☐	☐
drug abuse	☐	☐	☐	☐	☐
sibling relationships	☐	☐	☐	☐	☐
stress at home	☐	☐	☐	☐	☐

other:_____

8. Sometimes families or individuals need special support, encouragement, counseling or other services. Below are possible types of services. Check (✔) any services that would benefit someone in your family or one of your neighbors.

☐ marriage counseling
☐ drug abuse therapy and treatment
☐ dealing with domestic violence
☐ recovering from rape
☐ personal counseling
☐ coping with unemployment
☐ coping with alcoholism
☐ coping with a disability
☐ counseling for unwed mothers
☐ suicide hot line
☐ food and clothing assistance
☐ divorce recovery support group

☐ other: _____

9. How would you characterize your family's economic status?
  ☐ low income   ☐ middle income   ☐ high income

You and the Church

10. What is your religious affiliation, if any?
  ☐ a member of this church
  ☐ a regular participant in this church
  ☐ a member or regular participant in another church
  ☐ a Christian who doesn't regularly attend church
  ☐ a member of another faith (specify: _____)
  ☐ not religious

11. How important is your faith and church involvement to your family life?
  ☐ very important ☐ somewhat important ☐ not important

12. How often do you attend church activities?
  ☐ at least once a week   ☐ occasionally   ☐ never
  ☐ at least once a month   ☐ rarely

13. To the best of your knowledge, how well does the church's current programming meet your family's needs?
  ☐ very well   ☐ okay   ☐ poorly   ☐ don't know

continued

14. If the church sponsored a program dealing with each of the following topics, which ones would you consider attending? (Mark as many as you like.)

☐ parent-teenager relationships ☐ suicide prevention
☐ family money management ☐ drug and alcohol abuse
☐ teaching values ☐ communication
☐ discipline ☐ sharing responsibilities
☐ time management ☐ human sexuality
☐ single-parent families ☐ divorce
☐ family conflict ☐ stepfamily relationships
☐ dealing with stress ☐ family worship
☐ other: _____
_____

☐ I would not attend church-sponsored activities

15. Which of the following family activities would you consider attending if the church sponsored them? (Mark as many as you like.)

☐ picnic ☐ game night
☐ movie night ☐ overnight retreat
☐ talent show ☐ crazy olympics
☐ mystery dinner ☐ worship service
☐ skit night ☐ '50s dance
☐ other: _____
_____

☐ I would not attend church-sponsored activities

16. When is the best time for you to attend activities and workshops?

☐ weekdays during the day (which days: _____)
☐ weekday evening (which days: _____)
☐ Saturday morning ☐ Sunday morning
☐ Saturday afternoon ☐ Sunday afternoon
☐ Saturday evening ☐ Sunday evening

17. How often would you be interested in meeting for family-related activities or workshops?

☐ once a week ☐ once a month
☐ every other week ☐ only occasionally

18. If you could ask for one thing from the church to help your family, what would it be? _____
_____

For Parents Only
Questions 19-25 are for adults only. Teenagers proceed to #26.

19. What is your marital status?

☐ married ☐ remarried ☐ single (never married)
☐ single (divorced) ☐ single (widowed) ☐ other: _____

20. What is your occupation?

☐ homemaker ☐ self-employed ☐ retired
☐ skilled trade ☐ semi-skilled worker
☐ professional ☐ unemployed

continued

21. How many hours do you spend on your job in an average week? _____

22. Check the appropriate box:
   ☐ My spouse works outside the home.
   ☐ My spouse doesn't work outside the home.
   ☐ I don't have a spouse.

23. How many children do you have? _____
   What are their ages? _____

24. What is the biggest problem you face with your teenager(s)? __
   _____

25. What do you like most about your teenager(s)? _____
   _____

For Teenagers Only
Questions 26-30 are for teenagers only. Parents proceed to #31.

26. What grade are you in?
   ☐ 6th   ☐ 8th   ☐ 10th   ☐ 12th
   ☐ 7th   ☐ 9th   ☐ 11th   ☐ other: _____

27. What is your parent(s)' marital status?
   Father: ☐ married ☐ single ☐ remarried ☐ deceased
   Mother: ☐ married ☐ single ☐ remarried ☐ deceased

28. Whom do you live with?
   ☐ both parents   ☐ my mother and stepfather
   ☐ my mother   ☐ my father and stepmother
   ☐ my father   ☐ brothers (how many) _____
   ☐ a guardian   ☐ sisters (how many) _____
   ☐ other: _____

29. What is the biggest problem you face with your parent(s)? ___
   _____

30. What do you like most about your parent(s)? _____
   _____

Comments

31. If you have any suggestions or comments about family ministry, write them here: _____
   _____
   _____

Thank you for your cooperation in completing this survey. It will help us better serve you and other families in the community and church.

Sincerely,

Family Ministry Task Force Coordinators

but they are more difficult to analyze and compile. Moreover, some people who might check off boxes may not take time to answer longer questions.

3. Don't make the survey too long. Unless your respondents are dedicated, they won't fill out a long survey. Therefore, precisely design a questionnaire to gather the information you need in a short space.

4. Don't make the survey too short. While people won't respond to a survey that's too long, you won't get the information you need if it's too short. So you'll end up going through the whole process again.

5. Share the results. Anyone who participates in a survey is probably curious about what you'll learn. Keep track of the families you survey so you can contact them again. When you've compiled the results, send them to the families that participated as a way of thanking them for their participation.

There are many different ways to conduct a survey. Each has advantages and disadvantages, depending on your own situation. We discuss these differences in detail in the section on "Gathering the Information" (page 238).

• **Personal interviews.** Personal interviews provide valuable information beyond what you can gather through a written survey.

Together with other qualified leaders in the family ministry task force, choose a cross section of families in the congregation and community to interview about their family concerns. If possible, send the interviewers out in teams of one man and one woman.

Carefully train each interviewer by explaining what to do and what not to do. Explain various problems they may encounter. Urge them to be courteous, open and non-judgmental in people's homes. Give them opportunities to practice interviewing each other before they go into the neighborhood.

Arrange the interviews ahead of time so that entire

families can participate. Then ask them a series of questions about their concerns, their needs and what they would like the church to provide. Give them plenty of time to answer each question and ask follow-up questions when appropriate. Allow each parent and teenager to respond as he or she wishes.

Begin with simple, non-threatening questions and gradually move to more personal questions. However, you won't be able to ask many personal questions without offending the family. Be sensitive to the unspoken messages the family sends during the interview. Often it helps to ask families if they know any neighbors with various problems or that need various services. They may be more open in sharing their own needs—and those of their neighbors—in this indirect manner.

Keep notes on families' responses and the interviewer's impressions. A sample "Neighborhood Interview Form" is provided in Diagram 10. Have each interview team fill out one form for each house they visit.

• **Expert consultation.** Family therapists, social workers, school guidance counselors, pastors, professors and other experts in your area can give valuable insights into the needs of families in your community. Indeed, they may have conducted surveys themselves that they would share with you.

Arrange for each expert to meet with your family ministry planning task force to discuss the demographics and needs of families in your community. Ask them to share their perceptions, and ask them specific questions you have uncovered through surveys or other research. Ask them to compare your community to national averages, suggest additional resources and tell you about any unique characteristics of your area.

• **Brainstorming.** Teenagers, parents, leaders and other congregation members may have great ideas for

Diagram 10
Neighborhood Interview Form

Ask each family you interview the following questions. Give the members plenty of time to answer each question. Allow all parents and teenagers to respond as they wish. Keep detailed notes on their responses. Fill out one of these forms for each person you interview. Some questions may not be necessary or appropriate for all family members. Use good judgment.

General information
Address: _____ Date and time: _____
Type of dwelling: ☐ single-family home ☐ duplex ☐ apartment
☐ other:_____

Questions
1. What is your family size? How many people live at home? What are the ages of any children living at home?

2. Do you work outside the home? If so, what is your occupation? How many hours do you work in an average week?

3. Are you a member of a church or synagogue? If yes, which one?

4. If provided free of charge, what types of services would benefit your family or neighbors?

☐ marriage counseling
☐ drug abuse therapy and treatment
☐ dealing with domestic violence
☐ recovering from rape
☐ personal counseling
☐ coping with unemployment

☐ coping with alcoholism
☐ coping with a disability
☐ counseling for unwed mothers
☐ suicide hot line
☐ food and clothing assistance
☐ divorce recovery support group

5. What types of family activities would you consider participating in if they were provided?

☐ workshops on family issues
☐ fun family activities
☐ family Bible study and worship
☐ workshops on drug abuse or other problems

☐ marriage enrichment opportunities
☐ workshops on parenting teenagers
☐ workshops on teenage issues

6. When would it be most convenient for you to participate in church-sponsored activities?

continued

After the interview
Record general impressions from the interview:

What church literature, if any, did you leave with the family?

If any follow-up seems appropriate, what kind?

your ministry to families with teenagers. Announce a meeting to brainstorm ideas. You could even conduct a short meeting after church or during a regularly scheduled church meeting time.

Begin the meeting with a fun, get-to-know-you crowdbreaker. Explain to the group your plans for a ministry to families with teenagers. Tell them you want to meet real needs in the community and congregation, and you need their help to find those needs. Then mention a few guidelines for brainstorming:

1. There aren't any right, wrong, good or bad answers. Say whatever comes to mind.

2. All ideas are okay for now. There will be time to critique later on. Right now, no one should criticize an idea.

3. Think as quickly and creatively as possible.

4. Don't be shy. Speak up if something comes to mind.

Divide the discussion into different parts: Who are the families with teenagers? What are their needs? How can we help them? Put each of these questions at the top of a sheet of newsprint and post them on the wall. Begin with the first question and spend time on each one individually. Jot down all responses on the newsprint. These will be valuable prompters when you design your program.

When the group members finish brainstorming, spend time discussing what they've done and answering any questions they have. Tell them how you plan to use the material they've provided and give them a specific timetable for when they can expect to see results. Thank them for their help and close with a short devotional about families.

Gathering the Information

Gathering data in your congregation and community may seem like an overwhelming task. And it can be—if you don't plan carefully or spread the responsibilities among several people. However, if the planning task force takes time to organize the process, it will go smoothly. Here are steps to gather your information.

• **Examine survey methods.** There are several ways to administer a formal survey. Each has its advantages and disadvantages.

1. Mail surveys. Mail the survey to families in the congregation and community around the church. Include a cover letter with the survey explaining who you are and what you're doing. (See "Sample Cover Letter," Diagram 11.) Ask families to fill out the survey and return it to the church. Include a self-addressed, stamped envelope.

This survey is perhaps the easiest to conduct. And it has the potential of reaching the largest number of people. However, there are several disadvantages.

First, few people take the trouble to fill out a survey they receive in the mail. So your number of responses probably will be low, particularly from the community. Second, it doesn't allow different family members to complete a survey, thus limiting the perspectives. (One way to deal with this problem is to design surveys with spaces for several people to respond.) Third, it can be expensive, since you have to pay double postage. Fourth, it can be difficult—and expensive—to get a mailing list of people in the community who aren't connected with the church. Finally, it limits your personal contact with families—contact that could be important later in your programming.

Because of its disadvantages, use this approach only if you have a large mailing list for both the congregation and community. Otherwise, other approaches are more effective.

2. Telephone surveys. Using the telephone may be the best way to hear from the largest number of people. And by using a pool of volunteers to make the calls, it can be less time-consuming and less expensive to conduct than a mail survey.

Design a simple questionnaire that volunteers can use to ask questions over the phone. Train the volunteers to introduce themselves, explain what they're doing and ask the questions appropriately. Have volunteers call everyone involved in the church and people in the surrounding community.

While it's easy to reach a large number of people with a telephone survey, this format also has disadvantages. First, the questionnaire has to be shorter than a written questionnaire. People won't take time to answer too many questions over the phone. Second, people will feel uncomfortable answering personal questions over the phone. It's much more difficult to believe your answers will remain anonymous when someone else hears you say them. Third, you may have difficulty getting phone numbers of people in the community. Finally, though it can be inexpensive, a telephone survey requires lots of volunteer work and coordination.

3. Group surveys. An easy way to gather information is to distribute surveys when groups gather. This method is particularly useful in surveying church members. Distribute surveys before a worship service, during Sunday school or during a fellowship meal. Or pass out surveys at a community festival or block party. Ask people to fill them out immediately and return them while you wait.

This survey is perhaps the easiest to conduct. And you're likely to get a high return from people with the "while-you-wait" formula. However, it has disadvantages. First, it limits your audience. While you can find out about active church people in Sunday school, you won't get any information about unchurched families. Second, your setting sometimes limits the quality of your response. Conducting a serious survey in the midst of a carnival colors the thoughtfulness of the responses. Third, people won't fill out a long, detailed survey when they're in a hurry to do something else. So you have to keep the questionnaire short.

You could try to gather a large, representative group specifically to complete the survey. This approach can have excellent results but can be difficult to coordinate and plan.

4. Neighborhood canvassing. Old-fashioned, door-to-door canvassing is a particularly effective way to contact families, discover needs, conduct a survey and introduce the church and the ministry program to unchurched families. Moreover, you don't have to buy expensive mailing or phone lists to find families; you just have to knock on doors.

Design a list of questions that volunteer canvassers can ask families, or a survey they can give families to fill out themselves. Gather a team of volunteers to spend a Saturday or two blitzing the neighborhood asking questions.

Once again, this approach has disadvantages. First, it's sometimes difficult to find people who will volunteer for door-to-door canvassing. Second, some residents feel threatened by visitors and refuse to let them in. Third, you won't be able to ask difficult questions in person without offending people. Finally, an unannounced door-to-door survey can be frustrating for volunteers who don't find anyone home on the blocks they canvass.

Obviously, each type of survey has advantages and drawbacks. Choose the method most likely to gather the specific information you need. Or use a combination of methods to ensure complete results.

• **Find help.** Regardless of the methods you use for gathering information, ask several people on the planning task force to take responsibility for planning and organizing the surveys. These people can, in turn, ask other interested parents and teenagers to assist with the legwork involved in gathering information.

Several survey methods are much easier to conduct if you have a large number of volunteers. Recruit people during Sunday school, through the church newsletter and during announcement times. Many parents and teenagers may help with the survey, even though they can't commit to the ongoing planning process.

When you've decided how to gather your information, calculate how many people you need to conduct the survey efficiently. This number depends on the size of the congregation and community involved. Some methods require more volunteers than others. For example, a mail survey just requires people to prepare and mail the survey and then tabulate the results. But a phone survey requires many volunteers to make the calls. And neighborhood interviews require teams of two people who can devote time visiting in the community.

After you determine how many people you need to conduct the survey, recruit people for specific jobs during specific times. If you have difficulty recruiting the number of people you need, you may want to reassess the survey method to be realistic. Otherwise a few hardy volunteers could end up overloaded with a job that should be spread among many people.

• **Answer basic questions.** Before you gather information, the family ministry planning task force needs to answer some basic questions. In his book *Ministering to Families: A Positive Plan of Action*, Royce Money delineates several issues to resolve before gathering information:

1. What does the planning task force believe about

families? These preconceptions will color the types of questions the group asks and how the group interprets the data it gathers. Numerous factors influence these beliefs, including personal biases, biblical insights and the church's attitude. By discussing these issues up front, you reduce misunderstanding and miscommunication on the planning task force.

2. What is the context? Do you want to minister only to families in the congregation? Or do you want to reach out to the community? Just surveying the congregation hardly gathers the information you need if you want to reach out to the community. But if you want to focus on the congregation, surveying the community wastes lots of time and energy.

3. Can you meet expectations you raise? Whenever you gather information, you raise people's expectations. Will the questions you ask give people the impression you will provide more services than you can realistically deliver? If not, people will be disappointed, making it difficult to reach them with the ministries you can provide. Keep your information-gathering techniques consistent with the type of commitment you can make to the ministry. Thus, if your congregation is small and your resources limited, you may not want to conduct an extensive survey.

4. How will you use the information? There are literally hundreds of pieces of information you can gather about families. But there's no reason to gather the information unless you can use it to form relevant ministries to families with teenagers.

5. What method will best gather the information? We have suggested several options for gathering information. Each has advantages and disadvantages. Discuss the various options with the family ministry planning task force. Weigh the pros and cons of each method for your particular situation.

Several factors may affect your choices. For instance,

if your congregation keeps accurate, detailed records about its membership, analyzing church records can provide a wealth of valuable material. If your congregation is small, a detailed survey may be inappropriate. If you are in a college town, you may have access to several insightful experts. Most likely, the best options involve a combination of several survey techniques. You may adapt a method to fit your particular situation.

Regardless of your final choice, don't choose a particular method because it's the easiest to do. Some methods provide more accurate and thorough results than others. For instance, the easiest information-gathering method for most churches is a brainstorming session. While this approach may yield valuable insights, it certainly isn't systematic. And the results will likely reflect the biases and concerns of the participants much more than the needs in the community.[1]

• **Customize the survey.** As you discuss the types of information you'd like to gather, decide what questions will elicit that information most effectively. Look through the sample "Family Survey" (Diagram 9) and the "Neighborhood Interview Form" (Diagram 10) to find the most appropriate questions for your congregation and community. Don't include questions you won't use, and add other useful questions.

You may also discover that you need to ask different questions of different people. For instance, you might ask church members questions that might be inappropriate to ask people in the community. In these cases, design slightly different surveys for each distinct group. However, when possible ask similar questions of different groups so you can compare their responses.

When customizing your survey, remember that few churches have the resources or energy to conduct extensive, thorough, scientific research. Moreover, such research isn't necessary for planning purposes. Your goal is to find focus and direction for ministry, not to learn all the details and dynamics of family life in your community.

• **Publicize the survey.** The best way to ensure interest and cooperation as you gather information in the congregation and community is to tell people what you're doing. Put announcements in the church bulletin and newsletter. Contact the local newspaper. Distribute fliers in the church and community. Briefly explain your vision for the ministry. Tell people that they can help shape that ministry to meet their particular needs. Then tell them how and when you will gather the information.

By being forward and open about your process, you accomplish several things. You overcome any suspicion people have about your motives or plans. You begin building interest for the ministry you're developing. And you tell people that their concerns, interests and needs are important to the church.

• **Gather supplies.** When you determine your information-gathering methods, gather all the supplies you need such as copies of the survey, pencils, phone lists and address labels. Write a letter of introduction and explanation to families that participate. (See "Sample Cover Letter," Diagram 11.) This letter will help them overcome any reluctance or suspicion they have. Attach the letter to surveys you mail or distribute. People who conduct interviews can give copies of the letter to people they contact.

If you conduct a written survey, neatly type (or make a computer printout) and photocopy a survey for all family members, and provide pencils for everyone. If volunteers conduct interviews in the community, photocopy plenty of interview forms for them, and supply pencils and extra paper.

• **Train volunteers.** Volunteers involved in the sur-

Diagram 11
Sample Cover Letter

Dear Friends:

Families are the building blocks of our community. They give the community its stability and character. But families aren't perfect, and they face many pressures and stresses in today's world.

Broad Street Church recognizes the importance of families and the pressures families face. So it has begun to find ways to help families with teenagers in the community. To do this, we need your help. We are surveying and interviewing families with teenagers throughout the community to determine who they are and what services the church could provide for them.

We would like all parents and teenagers in your family to take a short survey. All your answers are completely confidential. The survey asks the following types of questions:

- What is your family's size and makeup?
- What is life like in your family?
- What kinds of services could the church provide your family?
- What are your family's religious commitments?

You do not need to be a church member to participate. The church is not asking you to commit to any programs or give any money to support a program. We are simply gathering information so we can serve our community more effectively.

Thank you for your cooperation and interest. If you have any questions, please call Joanne Schmidt, Family Ministry Planning Task Force Coordinator, at 555-1234.

Sincerely,

Joanne

Family Ministry Planning Task Force
Broad Street Church

vey process need to be trained to ensure that they gather appropriate information in appropriate ways. The amount of training varies among survey methods. For instance, people involved in door-to-door canvassing or neighborhood interviews need more training than those who help with mail surveys.

Most training can take place just before you conduct the survey. Ask volunteers to come an hour or so before you conduct the survey. Explain what they'll do, what's expected of them and how you'll use the information they gather. Make sure they understand the process so they can answer questions congregation and community people have.

Give volunteers opportunities to practice their jobs. Role playing works particularly well for interviewers and telephone surveyors. Make sure volunteers feel confident and comfortable in their roles before you send them out on their own.

● **Gather the information.** When you've spent time designing, planning and publicizing your survey, actually gathering the information is easy and fun. If you have gathered all your supplies in advance and trained your volunteers, the process should go smoothly.

Use the information-gathering process to build community among your volunteers and interest among families. If you survey large groups, plan activities and refreshments to help people relax and enjoy themselves. If volunteers survey or interview the community, have a debriefing meeting and party afterward. People will want to talk about their experiences— some of which may make hilarious stories.

● **Tabulate and summarize results.** You don't need a sophisticated computer program to analyze the data you collect from the congregation and community. You need to compile two different types of information:

1. Survey data. You can summarize answers to some questions you ask with simple percentage calculations. Find people in the congregation who are adept with numbers and ask them to help figure percentages for each response. In some cases, simply adding up total responses to different questions points out specific trends and needs.

Separate the responses of different groups in order to compare their needs and interests. For example, separate parents and teenagers. Also separate church members from people in the community.

For more information on tabulating and analyzing surveys, see *Determining Needs in Your Youth Ministry* (Group Books). This resource has a complete survey, tabulation sheets you can adapt, and suggestions and cautions for analyzing information.

When you compile all the information, pick out the highlights and surprises. Compile these on one sheet to distribute to the planning task force at the planning meeting. You may also want to distribute some of the more interesting results to people in the congregation and community who participated in the survey.

2. Open-ended questions. Questions that require written responses can't be summarized with percentages. However, you can sort through the responses and group them in categories. For example, several people may answer the question: "If you could ask for one thing from the church to help your family, what would it be?" with similar responses. By grouping these together, you may reveal critical needs.

Gather all the responses and type them onto a master sheet. But don't distribute all the information to everyone. It will overwhelm most people. Instead, work with your leaders to pick out highlights, surprises and insightful comments to summarize on one sheet for the planning task force.

*T*ask Force Meeting #2: Assessing Needs

When you've gathered and summarized the data from families in the congregation and community, the planning task force must decide what the results mean. What kinds of families are in the community? What are their needs? How can the church respond to those situations and needs? This meeting brings the task force together to address these questions.

• **Objectives.** This meeting is designed to:

1. Share the data you've gathered with the whole planning task force and "listen" to families through that data.

2. Assess how well current programs in the church and community meet families' needs.

3. Begin discussing the data's implications for the shape of your ministry.

• **Preparation.** Most of the preparation for this meeting involves gathering, tabulating and summarizing the results of your surveys. Make copies of the summaries for each planning task force member to distribute at the meeting.

Make copies for each participant of the "My Priorities" handout (Diagram 13), a blank copy of your survey, and the "Current Programs Assessment" sheet (Diagram 12). Bring newsprint and markers.

• **Opening.** Open the meeting with a brief prayer, asking God to open your eyes to the true needs of those families you are called to serve. Pray for guidance and direction as you begin shaping your ministry to families with teenagers.

Lead planning task force members in the following exercise, designed to help them see what it's like for someone else to say what they need without ever asking. Distribute a "My Priorities" handout (Diagram 13) to each planning task force member. Ask members to

list the top three priorities in their lives right now
from the list. Then have them pair up with someone
in the group they don't know well. Have each person
guess what his or her partner chose as top priorities.

When both people have guessed what their partner
wrote, have them discuss:

1. How accurately did your partner guess your top
priorities?

2. How did it feel for someone to tell you what you
"need" without asking you?

3. How would you have felt if your partner had
asked you to tell him or her your priorities instead?

4. What does this activity say to us as we try to assess the needs of families with teenagers in the
community?

• **Sharing survey data.** Distribute blank copies of
the survey to each planning task force member. Ask
members to fill out the form to reflect their perceptions of the responses you received when you conducted the survey. Thus, they would, for instance,
estimate the percentage of traditional families and
single-parent families. And they would rank the different family needs. If you surveyed both the church
and community, have half the group think about how
the church would respond and half think about the
community.

When planning task force members work through
the survey on their own, have them compare their
perceptions with the actual survey results. Look at
each section of the survey separately. What surprises
do they see? What do the results say about families in
the community and church? List observations on
newsprint.

Keep the discussion moving and on track. Focus on
listening to the data; don't start thinking how to
respond until you complete this exercise. Moreover,
don't pass judgments on the data or what it says

Diagram 12
Current Programs Assessment

Use a separate sheet for each problem you analyze.

Problem, concern or need: _____

Answer the following questions concerning this issue.
1. What existing church programs address (or could address) this
need? _____
_____
_____
_____

2. How well do these programs meet the need? _____
_____
_____
_____

3. Are other community agencies already dealing with this issue?
If so, are they addressing it effectively? Explain. _____
_____
_____
_____

4. How well are other congregations dealing with this concern?
_____
_____
_____
_____

5. Would the church unnecessarily duplicate other programs by
addressing this need? Explain. _____
_____
_____
_____

6. What are some ways the church could begin addressing this issue? _____
_____
_____
_____

Diagram 13
My Priorities

From the list below, choose the top three priorities for you right now. Rank the things you need or want in order. DON'T SHARE YOUR RESPONSES WITH ANYONE IN THE ROOM.

_____ I want to learn to sky-dive.

_____ I want to take a course in photography.

_____ I need a vacation.

_____ I need to buy new clothes.

_____ I need to learn how to relax.

_____ I need to exercise more.

_____ I need a new car.

_____ I want to get more involved in church.

_____ I want to visit my grandparents.

_____ I need to clean out my flower beds.

_____ I need to stop watching so much television.

_____ I need to call friends more often.

about the community. By jumping too quickly to
responses and judgments, you may miss important nu-
ances and needs.

• **Identifying major needs.** When the planning
task force has gone through all the questions, ask
them to identify families' top needs and concerns.
Many of these needs may be obvious because of high
percentages. Others may surface in the open-ended
questions or other responses from the respondents.
List these needs on a new sheet of newsprint. You
may need separate sheets for families in the congregation and the community. After you've compiled this
list, have the planning task force members reach a
consensus, ranking families' needs and concerns.

• **Assessing current programs.** How well do current programs in the community and congregation already meet each of these needs? Divide the group
into pairs and assign them to discuss one or more of
the needs on the list. Have each pair think about current programming in the church and community. Give
them one copy of the "Current Programs Assessment"
sheet (Diagram 12) for each problem to guide their
discussion and report back to the group.

• **Brainstorming.** When the pairs complete their
worksheets, bring the group back together and have
each pair report on its discussion. On newsprint, list
all the suggestions they have for how the church
could address these issues. After each pair reports, ask
the whole group to think of other ideas.

After people share their worksheets, tell them these
ideas will be the basis for drawing the blueprint for
the new ministry during the next planning task force
meeting. Ask them to think of other ideas before that
meeting.

• **Closing.** Remind the group that meeting people's
needs is an important part of the church's mission.
Read aloud Matthew 25:31-46. Close with this prayer:

Dear Father: All around us we see families in need. Some are hungry and thirsty, either literally or spiritually. Some feel like strangers in an impersonal world. Others feel naked to the many forces that reshape them. Some are sick with serious problems, while others are imprisoned by unhealthy habits and relationships.

Guide us as we seek to minister to these families in appropriate ways. May we learn to see your Son Jesus in their faces, and may they see you working through us. Amen.

Chapter 15

*F*rom Blueprint to Building: Designing Your Ministry

*I*magine your family has decided to build a house. You've talked with all family members, and you have a list of everything you need and want. So you're ready to build, right? Well, not quite. You first have to design a house you can afford. Chances are good that your dream house isn't within your budget. Moreover, you have to design a building that is structurally sound. It has to meet building codes, and all the pieces must fit together logically. And you want it to fit in with the other houses in the neighborhood.

Building a ministry to families with teenagers is, once again, similar. It's not enough to know what everyone wants and needs, and it's impractical to build a ministry you can't afford or manage.

This chapter helps you design a well-rounded and realistic ministry. It doesn't offer you a ready-to-build blueprint, but it does suggest a process for designing your program. It also suggests some critical elements to include so that your "customized" ministry will address families' needs in practical and faithful ways.

The process suggested in this chapter is not only

designed for beginning a new ministry, but also is effective for re-evaluating an existing ministry. Once you've established a ministry to families with teenagers, use a similar process each year to assess progress and ensure that your ministry stays on track.

We've divided the chapter into the following sections: Understanding the Blueprint; Foundations; Critical Elements; Mission Statement; Committee Structure; Objectives; Limitations; Ministry Priorities; Programs; Task Force Meeting #3: Drawing the Blueprint.

*U*nderstanding the Blueprint

To build an effective and well-rounded ministry to families with teenagers, step back briefly and try to understand how all the pieces of your ministry will fit. Diagram 14, "A Family Ministry Blueprint," illustrates the basic process and structure involved in ministering to families with teenagers. Many of the pieces will vary between congregations, and many will change within a congregation as years pass and families change.

Here, briefly, are the elements in the structure:

• **Foundations.** The foundations are your reasons for planning a ministry to families with teenagers.

• **Critical elements.** Including these elements ensures a balanced and well-rounded ministry.

• **Mission statement.** A mission statement succinctly defines the church's purpose in ministering to families with teenagers. The congregation should develop its own mission statement, which will, in turn, affect all other parts of the structure.

• **Committee structure.** Who will carry out the mission statement? By designing a committee structure based on parts of the mission statement, you build a balanced ministry.

• **Objectives.** Objectives spell out what you hope

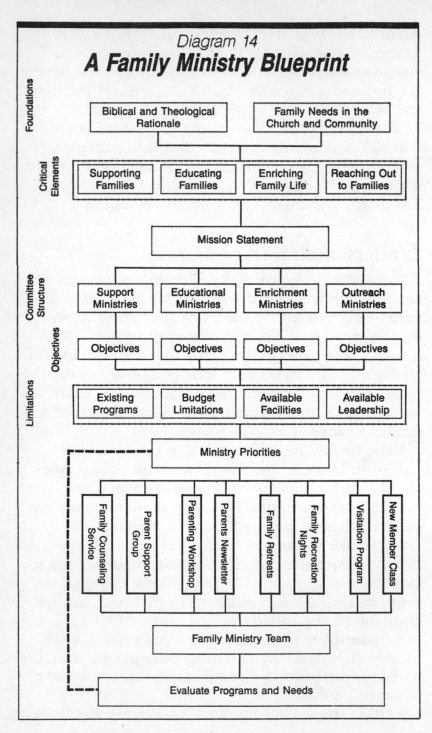

Diagram 14
A Family Ministry Blueprint

Foundations

| Biblical and Theological Rationale | Family Needs in the Church and Community |

Critical Elements

| Supporting Families | Educating Families | Enriching Family Life | Reaching Out to Families |

Mission Statement

Committee Structure

| Support Ministries | Educational Ministries | Enrichment Ministries | Outreach Ministries |

Objectives

| Objectives | Objectives | Objectives | Objectives |

Limitations

| Existing Programs | Budget Limitations | Available Facilities | Available Leadership |

Ministry Priorities

Family Counseling Service • Parent Support Group • Parenting Workshop • Parents Newsletter • Family Retreats • Family Recreation Nights • Visitation Program • New Member Class

Family Ministry Team

Evaluate Programs and Needs

to accomplish through your various programs for families. They give a bench mark against which you can evaluate specific programs.

• **Limitations.** The congregation must examine whether specific programs are feasible and appropriate within the limitations it faces due to existing programs, budget, facilities and leadership.

• **Ministry priorities.** Because there are so many needs to meet with limited resources, the congregation should decide what's most important for it right now and in the future.

• **Programs.** These are the specific avenues through which the church ministers to families in the congregation and community.

• **Family ministry team.** The family ministry team—which can be the same as or different from the planning task force—is responsible for implementing and evaluating the total ministry.

• **Evaluation.** Evaluation involves critiquing specific programs to ensure that the ministry is fulfilling its objectives effectively and faithfully. The family ministry team and evaluation are explained in greater detail in Chapter 16.

By examining each element of this basic blueprint, you'll find step-by-step plans for designing and building a ministry to families with teenagers that fits the specific concerns of your congregation and community.

As you read these steps, keep in mind the following two important points:

1. No two structures will be identical. "No two congregations are alike," Roland Martinson writes in *Ministry With Families*. "The individuals and families within congregations belong to a particular time and place. Each congregation will have its own priorities, resources, and circumstances for ministry with families. What is fitting in one congregation may not be in another."[1]

2. The process isn't necessarily linear, but circular. Each step influences the one before and after it. No step is self-sufficient. Therefore, keep other points in mind as you focus on a specific issue. For example, the diagram shows that objectives precede ministry priorities and limitations. But the three steps must be taken together in your planning, since your limitations will help define your priorities, and your objectives may be influenced by both your priorities and your limitations.

*F*oundations

Why do you want to minister to families with teenagers? That question is critical for each congregation to answer before it begins its ministry. Otherwise, misunderstanding, miscommunication and a lack of purpose will undercut the quality of your ministry.

• **Theological and biblical rationale.** What does the church have to do with families? What do your Christian beliefs say about families? How does the church help or hurt families? What can or should the church do for families?

Your family ministry task force should talk about some of these kinds of questions in light of your congregation's unique history and circumstances. (Refer to Chapters 2 and 3 for more insight into a biblical perspective on the family and its relation to the church.)

Unless you answer these theological questions, your ministry can lose its roots, leaving it to drift between whatever issues happen to "grab the headlines" at the time. But by addressing these questions, the task force can examine and respond to family needs from a solid faith perspective.

• **Family needs.** After gathering information about families in the congregation and community through various surveys, the family ministry task force should understand the importance of listening to the families' needs before trying to minister to them. See Chapter 14 for more details on gathering this information.

Critical Elements

While each congregation's ministry to families with teenagers will be unique, each ministry should include several critical elements. Because of their understanding of mission and their community, some congregations will emphasize some elements more than others. Other congregations may add additional elements as critical. Every congregation will flesh out each element with a unique mixture of programs. And some programs will simultaneously address two or more of the elements.

But in the midst of all the variations, core issues should be identified and followed. Here are critical elements we believe a ministry to families with teenagers should include:

• **Supporting families.** In addition to educating families, the church should support them, particularly in times of crisis. Support can take various forms and involve various situations. It may occur through informal contacts and networks, support groups, counseling services or emergency food relief. Chapter 6, "Supporting and Educating Parents," suggests several ways the church can support families.

• **Educating families.** Christian education is a central part of congregational life in most churches. A ministry to families with teenagers should include this same emphasis. It's not enough just to use counseling and support groups to pick up families when they fall. The church should teach families the skills and knowledge they need to enjoy a healthy family life. Many of the educational services congregations provide can also provide support, enrichment and outreach.

(Chapter 6 elaborates on ways to educate parents.)

In his book *Planning Family Ministry: A Guide for a Teaching Church*, Joe Leonard Jr. suggests six areas in which the church should educate families:

1. Growth in faith. The church is called to teach families to grow and mature as Christians. Leonard writes: "A central focus of family education needs to be helping persons grow toward the kind of moral maturity and vision we see portrayed in the living and teaching of Jesus Christ."

2. Sexuality. The family is the primary context for people learning about sexuality. In the midst of the changing sexual values in the culture, the church must help families deal with their feelings and values regarding sexuality.

3. Family relations. This area deals with how family members relate to each other, and how the family as a whole relates to the community. The goal of the ministry, Leonard writes, is to help families "choose and grow into patterns of living together that liberate, fulfill, and satisfy each member."

4. Communication skills. "Probably no aspect of family life education is so important and so practical," Leonard writes. By teaching families to communicate, the church enriches family life and helps avert crises. (See Chapter 9, "Helping Families Communicate.")

5. Planning skills. In today's busy and complicated world, families confront numerous situations that require planning—financial planning, recreation planning, planning for the future. By helping families plan, the church encourages them to make intentional choices about their time together and their resources.

6. Organizational skills. Families sometimes feel isolated and stressed because of outside forces and institutions. The church can help families work together for positive change and mutual support.[2]

• **Enriching family life.** It's not enough to support families in crisis—as important as that support can be. The church should also work to prevent crises from ever occurring by working to enrich family life. As Royce Money writes in *Ministering to Families: A Positive Plan of Action*: "The traditional response of the church to family troubles has been 'reactive'— waiting for problems to surface, then (when it's really too late) trying to do something about them. The church's family ministry needs to be more "pro-active" in its approach: recognizing the forces at work before family conflicts become serious, and working to promote healthy family relationships and patterns all the time."[3]

Family enrichment can involve many things. First, it can guide what the congregation *doesn't* do. Enriching families may mean cutting back on programs so family members have time to spend together. Second, it involves bringing families together in the church so that parents and teenagers can interact with each other. Third, it involves providing fun, recreational activities that allow families to relax and enjoy being together.

• **Reaching out to families.** As the body of Christ, the church is not called just to meet its own needs. It's called to reach out to the world in service and mission. A faithful and well-rounded ministry to families with teenagers should include this dimension of the gospel.

Different congregations interpret their call to outreach in different ways. For some, it is primarily evangelism and witnessing. Others focus more on service and advocacy in the community. Regardless of how your congregation interprets this aspect of its calling, it should be a part of this particular ministry as well.

*M*ission Statement

Once the planning task force has worked through its understanding of the foundational issues and the critical elements to a balanced ministry, write a mission statement that succinctly summarizes the purpose and focus of its ministry to families with teenagers. Every program and idea the planning task force considers should then be tested against this mission statement.

A mission statement summarizes a congregation's response to the foundational and critical issues in one or two sentences. The statement answers the questions: What is the purpose for this congregation to minister to families with teenagers? Does the program help the church accomplish its mission to families?

Keep several points in mind as you prepare your mission statement:

1. It should be well-rounded to reflect the various elements of a balanced ministry.

2. It should be short and succinct, making it easy to refer to and use as you develop specific programs.

3. It should be shared. Unless everyone is comfortable with the mission statement, it will have little value to the planning.

Since your mission statement will become the guide for all family programming, take time and care as you design it. Ask all the task force members to contribute their insights. Develop a consensus in the group on what should be said and how to say it. Examine whether each word accurately conveys your purpose. This careful examination will not only help shape your programming, but it will also ensure that all task force members share a common vision of the ministry.

For the example in Diagram 14, the mission statement might read: "First Community Church seeks to apply the gospel to the needs of families by supporting and educating families, by enriching family life, and by reaching out to families in the community through a variety of programs."

Another mission statement could be an adaptation of the suggested definition of ministry to families with teenagers in Chapter 1: "Oak Street Church seeks to support and strengthen families by bringing parents and teenagers together in the church and equipping them to live out their faith in their relationships with each other and in all areas of life."

Committee Structure

Once you've developed a mission statement, you can design a committee structure to meet those needs. Our sample mission statement, for example, naturally breaks into four areas: support, education, enrichment and outreach.

The ongoing family ministry team (that takes over after the initial plans have been set) can be made up of a coordinator for each area. You can choose to include more than one person in each position by teaming an adult with a teenager to coordinate an area. (See page 283 for more about choosing the family ministry team.) In our example, we would have coordinators for support ministries, educational ministries, family enrichment and family outreach. Each coordinator can recruit other parents and teenagers to serve in his or her interest area.

Objectives

Ministry objectives put your mission statement in concrete terms based on specific needs you discovered in the congregation and community. You may have several objectives based on each aspect of your mission statement. Each objective addresses a specific need within a specific time frame. Diagram 15, "Defining Objectives," expands the first part of our sample mission statement with several objectives designed to meet specific needs.

Use the format in Diagram 15 with the planning task force to develop your own objectives based on your mission statement. Make the objectives specific and measurable. Give each objective a timetable. By doing this, you allow for evaluation and reassessment in the future.

*L*imitations

In an ideal congregation with unlimited resources, you could take your mission statement and do everything to meet its goals and purpose. In reality, though, every congregation must minister within certain limitations. It's important to face these limitations honestly and work creatively within them and around them.

• **Leadership.** Too many times congregations start programs without leaders. Usually someone is co-opted into leading the program, but a lack of enthusiasm or motivation makes the program more of a burden than a blessing. And too often a youth worker ends up doing all the work alone.

When organizing your ministry to families with teenagers, ask whether the congregation has the leadership to run a specific ministry. If no one feels called to lead a ministry, perhaps God isn't calling the congregation into that ministry at that time. Rather than trying to organize programs without leadership, concentrate on organizing programs people feel called to.

• **Budget.** Like every other ministry in a congregation, a ministry to families with teenagers requires money. In considering specific programs, ask whether the church can financially support the program. If not, consider other alternatives for meeting the needs.

Diagram 15
Defining Objectives (Sample)

Mission Statement: First Community Church seeks to apply the gospel to the needs of families by supporting and educating families, by enriching family life, and by reaching out to families in the community through a variety of programs.

Area	Need	Objective
Enriching family life.	For families to spend time together.	1. To re-evaluate by December 1 current age-specific programming to see whether it asks families to spend more than two evenings apart each week. 2. To begin a monthly church event during which families learn together. Begin the program in September.
	To enhance family communication.	1. To hold a special one-day seminar on parent-teenager communication this fall. 2. To design "table-talk sheets" for families to use during meals to stimulate conversation. Design these sheets by January 15.

By thinking creatively, you can discover ways to meet needs within your budget limitations.

The following examples illustrate the kinds of choices you can make based on your budget limitations:

1. Hiring a full-time counselor might be an important ministry you could offer the community. But if you can't afford to pay another salary, you could organize support groups around various family problems.

2. Perhaps families in your community could benefit from a series of seminars on parenting skills. But if you don't have funds to hire a parenting expert to lead the sessions, you could schedule seminars using videos and discussion groups to share the same kinds of information an expert could provide.

• **Facilities.** Does the congregation have adequate and appropriate facilities for a particular program? If not, is it willing to invest in building, purchasing or renting the facilities? Are there creative ways to use existing facilities to meet the needs? As you consider families' needs and your facilities, start with the resources you already have. Be a good steward of your existing resources—as elaborate or simple as they may be.

For example, your planning task force may want to start a family basketball tournament, but if you don't have a court, such a program could require a major investment. However, if you have a large church lawn, you could start a volleyball tournament that would accomplish the same purposes much less expensively.

• **Existing programs.** Existing programs are not so much restrictions as releases. The question this limitation asks is: Are other programs already meeting this need effectively? If so, there's no reason to duplicate these existing programs. Your ministry will be more helpful and effective in addressing other unmet needs.

For instance, if your community has an interdenominational family counseling center, your congregation doesn't need to provide similar services. Rather, you can simply refer people who need those services to the existing center. Other examples could include support groups for various crises and emergency food pantries.

Of course, some programs may address needs that are so prevalent that the existing programs can't adequately meet the needs. And some community programs may have perspectives that are inconsistent with your congregation's biblical foundation. In these cases, you may choose to duplicate the ministry in order to address unmet needs.

*M*inistry Priorities

The entire process thus far has helped you set priorities for your ministry. No congregation can meet all the needs of families. And no congregation can launch every ministry at once. Instead, the family ministry planning task force should establish priorities based on its own limitations, knowing that some important needs may remain unmet for the present. As Money writes: "In building a family ministry, you don't have to build a whole 'house' at once. But you should plan far enough in advance so that the different parts of the house go well together."[4]

In establishing your priorities, ask yourself the following questions:

• What does my congregation sense as God's specific callings in ministering to families with teenagers?

• Where are the greatest needs for families?

• What important ministry is not being done that my congregation could do?

• What ministries would best use the resources God has given me?

• What groups of people are in most need of the church's ministry?

• What priorities will result in a balanced, well-rounded ministry to families with teenagers?

*P*rograms

Once you've taken the time to develop your mission statement, priorities and objectives, starting to develop specific programs should be straightforward. Think creatively about ways to meet each specific need and objective. Keep in mind the limitations you have in terms of leadership, personnel and facilities.

In the sample structure we've used for this chapter, you could develop a variety of different programs to meet the different objectives. You could support families with particular support groups, a counseling service or through emergency food banks for families in crisis. For education, you could organize a parent-teenager Bible study, a series of parenting workshops or a parents newsletter. Family enrichment programs could include family retreats, picnics or family fellowship meals. And you could reach out to families through a neighborhood evangelism program, a new members class and publicity in the community for church events. Various chapters in Part 4, "Elements of a Successful Ministry," elaborate on numerous program ideas for different needs and objectives.

Think of a variety of programming that fits all elements of your mission statement. Keep in mind different needs of different families. Avoid designing so many programs that none can be carried out effectively.

As you develop specific program ideas, you'll discover that some programs overlap under different areas of your mission statement. For example, a workshop on conflict resolution would deal with educational, support and enrichment issues. Take advantage of these overlaps. Remember, keep your limitations in mind and think of the most creative, effective and efficient ways to meet the needs of families with teenagers. *Fast Forms for Youth Ministry* (Group Books), includes several planning checklists and guides for various types of programs.

The task force is responsible for outlining the general ideas for your ongoing program. Task force members have developed the structure and will have lots of ideas for programs to meet the needs. However, task force members didn't make a long-term commitment to run the ministry. So after the ministry structure is in place and has been introduced through the housewarming party (see Chapter 16), turn over the responsibilities for fine-tuning and maintaining the ministry to the new family ministry team.

*T*ask Force Meeting #3: Drawing the Blueprint

In the previous meeting, the task force analyzed the data you gathered from the congregation and community. This meeting is designed to help the task force translate that data into specific goals and objectives for the church's ministry to families with teenagers. It's also designed to begin generating ideas for specific programs. Because of the importance of your goals and objectives, it may be useful to design this meeting as an afternoon or evening workshop.

• **Objectives.** This meeting is designed to:

1. Help the task force pull together foundational issues into a well-rounded ministry.

2. Develop a mission statement for the ministry to families with teenagers.

3. Establish an effective structure for fulfilling your mission.

4. Define objectives and priorities for the ministry.

5. Begin thinking about and constructing programs.

• **Preparation.** Gather blank paper and pencils for all task force members. Have newsprint and markers available. Photocopy the "Program Objectives" worksheet (Diagram 16) and the "Designing Programs" worksheet (Diagram 17). Type the list of family needs you developed at the previous meeting and photocopy it for each task force member. Design a "Family Ministry House Title" based on Diagram 18 and photocopy it for all task force members. Fill in each person's name on a title.

• **Opening.** Open the meeting with a prayer asking God to guide the task force as it develops its structure for your family ministry program. Then divide the task force into groups of three. Ask each group to sketch an ideal house floor plan. Include three bedrooms, a kitchen, a dining room, a living room, a den and two bathrooms. Have the groups work quickly, and tell them not to share their plans with other groups.

After about five minutes, ask the small groups to share their plans with the whole task force. Ask the group to discuss the different plans. Are all the plans the same? What's different about each plan? Do different plans show different priorities and emphases?

Then say to the group: "Each small group designed a similar house, yet all of the designs were quite different. Similarly, there are many different ways we can design our ministry to families with teenagers. Each plan would emphasize different needs and interests. Our task today is to develop a plan that best fits our collective sense of ministry to families."

• **Developing your mission statement.** Briefly discuss as a group the foundational issues for family ministry as well as the suggested critical elements for such a ministry. Distribute copies of the list of priorities of family needs you developed at the previous meeting. Do members agree with these foundational and critical issues? Would they add other issues?

Based on this information and their own understanding of the envisioned ministry, have task force members each write their own mission statement for the ministry. Urge members to be short and concise. You may want to read the sample statements on page 262 to get them thinking. Give them several minutes to write their statements. Then ask them to share their proposed mission statement with the group. Write all the ideas on newsprint.

When everyone has shared his or her statement, work with the group to pick the critical parts from the different visions. As members mention elements, write important phrases, concerns and issues. Gradually lead the members to a consensus on their central purposes. As the group discusses its statement, ask questions like the following:

1. Is this idea central to our understanding of our ministry to families?

2. Is this idea a concept we'll be comfortable with as a central task in 20 years?

3. Does this statement describe a balanced and well-rounded ministry?

4. Is everything in the statement a central part of our task?

5. Is everyone in the group comfortable with the statement? If not, what changes would make people more comfortable?

• **Establishing a structure.** What is the best structure for fulfilling the various elements of the mission statement? Divide the mission statement into its key phrases (for example, education, outreach, support and spiritual growth). Do these different phrases suggest an appropriate committee structure? Are there more effective and balanced ways to divide the work among various committees?

Have the group brainstorm the best structure for your ministry to families with teenagers. When several ideas have been suggested, have the group think through which one (or which combination) would work best.

• **Defining objectives.** Once the group has developed a structure, ask task force members to choose which area they'd like to work with. Assure them that they aren't making a long-term commitment to that area of the program. Rather, they are simply developing objectives for that area. Later they will have opportunities to join the family ministry team in a specific capacity. If too many people want to work in one area, ask for volunteers to work in another area.

When the group has evenly divided itself into the different ministry areas, distribute the "Program Objectives" worksheet (Diagram 16) to each group. Have each group develop specific objectives and think through the limitations it has toward meeting those objectives. Ask groups to fill out the chart for each objective.

When all the groups have brainstormed objectives, bring the whole group back together. Have each small group tell about its work. Have the whole group respond with other ideas, questions and concerns. Write the ideas on newsprint. After each objective is discussed, bring the whole group to a consensus on the objectives the family ministry program should address in each area. Urge the group to be realistic in thinking through its limitations. Keep a list of the final objectives on newsprint.

When all the groups have reported on their work and the task force has come to a consensus on the objectives, ask the task force members to look at the objectives and to prioritize them. Ask members to keep their limitations and the need for balance in mind as they plan. When they've agreed on the priorities, rank in order the different objectives on the newsprint.

Remember, the groups aren't outlining specific programs yet; they're just saying what they want to ac-

Diagram 16
Program Objectives

Area of mission statement: Enriching Family Life (Example)

Objective	Needs It Addresses	Limitations
To help families grow together spiritually.	Lack of spiritual unity in families in the family survey.	May compete with existing educational opportunities at church.

Diagram 17
Designing Programs

Use this worksheet to plan specific programs in your ministry to families with teenagers.

1. What is the title for this activity? _____

2. What are the objectives for this activity? _____
_____

3. What is the subject to be addressed? _____
_____

4. What approach, methods and resources will be used? _____
_____

5. Who do we want to attend? _____
_____

6. How will we get the word out? _____
_____

7. Where will this activity be held? _____
_____

8. When and for how long will this activity be offered? _____
_____

9. Is child care needed? If so, how will it be offered? _____
_____

10. Will participants need transportation? If so, how will it be provided?
_____

11. What funds are needed?
   a. Materials: _____
   b. Leadership: _____
   c. Advertising: _____
   d. Refreshments: _____
   e. Facilities: _____
   f. Child care: _____

12. Who will be leaders, and in what areas will they lead? _____
_____
_____

complish in each area.

• **Getting programs going.** When the task force has agreed on the objectives for each ministry area, have participants get back into their small groups. Ask the groups to brainstorm programming ideas to meet the specific objectives the task force has set. At this point the goal is just to begin thinking about specific programs. After the housewarming party, the family ministry team will develop and run the programs.

Distribute enough copies of the "Designing Programs" worksheet (Diagram 17) for each group to use for several different programs. Ask members to decide which programs they'd like to begin developing. Then have them use the worksheet to think through some of the basic elements of the program. Encourage them to be innovative and to use resources efficiently and effectively.

If they discover problems with a particular program, have them find creative ways around obstacles. Otherwise, encourage them to try other alternatives. It's better to deal with potential problems now— before you've done much work—than to discover them after the family ministry team has carefully planned and started a program.

When groups have discussed programs they think would realistically and effectively meet the objectives, have them report to the task force. Discuss the ideas, including any ways to improve them or any questions about them. Have someone keep notes on all the programs to use in your publicity about the new ministry. Pass on these initial plans to the family ministry team to flesh out and begin.

• **Closing.** Planning task force members have built a basic structure for your congregation's ministry to families with teenagers. Conclude the meeting by symbolically giving task force members ownership of the program.

Diagram 18
Family Ministry House Title

We, the undersigned, do give to   _____
                                   (task force member's name)

title to the ministry to families with teenagers at   _____
                                                      (church name)

_____

   We hereby attest that said titleholder has fulfilled all obligations necessary to hold this title through his/her hard work, creative ideas, prayer support and good sense of humor through the planning process.

   Furthermore, we covenant with said titleholder to maintain and support this ministry together from this time forth through prayer, participation and leadership.

   Signed on this _____ day of _____
                                             (month)
in the year of our Lord _____.

_____   _____

_____   _____

_____   _____

Distribute copies of the "Family Ministry House Title" (Diagram 18) to each family member. Say: "Building a house isn't easy. But you've put in the 'sweat equity' that gives you ownership of this family ministry house. We give you this title as a symbol of your hard work. It reminds you that this ministry is *your* ministry." Then ask each person to sign everyone's title. Explain that the signatures symbolize the members' promise to work together to support and maintain this ministry they've built together.

When everyone has signed the certificates, close the meeting in a prayer of thanks for the members' hard work, participation and creativity.

• **After the meeting.** Work with volunteers from the task force to write the job descriptions for each family ministry team member. Be sure each job description includes expectations, areas of responsibilities and time commitment. [For a variety of sample job descriptions, see *Fast Forms for Youth Ministry* (Group Books).] Also have someone type the complete list of suggested programs. Use the job descriptions and programs in your next planning meeting.

Chapter 16

The Housewarming Party: Beginning Your Ministry

What if you built a house to sell but didn't advertise it, list it with a real estate company, hold an open house or tell anyone about it? Chances are good that no one would buy it. Similarly, you won't get much interest or enthusiasm for the ministry you've built unless you tell people it's "on the market."

This chapter outlines how to introduce your ministry with a "housewarming party," how to get a family ministry team going, and how to evaluate ongoing programs. It's divided into the following sections: Going Public; What to Include; Choosing the Party Theme; Publicity; After the Party; Family Ministry Team; Evaluation; Making It Work; Task Force Meeting #4: Presenting the Ministry.

Going Public

Throughout your planning process, people probably have been aware that you're forming the ministry. Parents and teenagers completed surveys. You had announcements about it, and you detailed progress in the church newsletter. However, the low profile is no longer adequate once you're ready to begin your ministry. As Royce Money writes in *Ministering to Families: A Positive Plan of Action*: "When the committee is ready to implement its programs, it is time to go public. Widespread congregational support for and understanding of the family ministry is necessary for its long-term success."[1]

First impressions are lasting impressions. The messages you send families through your initial publicity and your first program will greatly affect acceptance and support for your ministry. It's important, therefore, to put extra energy and planning into your housewarming party or kickoff event.

A housewarming party has several important purposes. They include:

• Giving families an opportunity to begin getting acquainted.

• Drawing attention to the new program.

• Building enthusiasm for the program and drawing continued attendance.

• Attracting unchurched families through an appealing, non-threatening program.

• Sharing the ministry vision with parents and teenagers.

• Giving families a feel for the program and how it will operate.

• Offering people opportunities to express interest in specific programs.

• Allowing people to volunteer for programs.

What to Include

You can design many different kinds of housewarming parties, depending on your own interests, ideas and needs. However, there are several important elements to include in any structure. Here are some of them:

• **Attractiveness.** In order to draw people, your housewarming party should be fun and unusual. Plan activities that grab people's attention and get them interested in the program.

• **Getting acquainted.** Give parents and teenagers opportunities to get acquainted during the party. These can be in the form of informal mingling or through structured community-building activities. Some parents may never have met other parents, and many won't know all the teenagers. You're more likely to see them come to future meetings if they're acquainted with other people in the group.

• **Preview.** Your housewarming party should give participants a taste of the new program. Share information about the overall ministry as well as specific programs. Use the same kinds of activities, formats and leadership you'll use throughout the ministry. When you tell families about the new program, simplify and condense the information. Don't give them all the details, but tell them how the program will help families.

• **Promotion.** Distribute fliers and calendars that promote specific programs and upcoming events. Make the publicity attractive so families will read it and remember it.

• **Spiritual.** Since the emphasis of your ministry is spiritual, don't plan an opening event devoid of a spiritual base. Include a brief, creative worship or devotional time.

• **Gather information.** Be sure you get the name, address and phone number of everyone who comes to your housewarming party. Have a guest book near the entrance, and have a parent and teenager invite people to sign the book as they arrive.

• **Introductions.** Introduce people who have already agreed to serve on the family ministry team. In this way you show participants that the ministry is indeed run by their peers.

• **Sign-ups.** Participants who are enthusiastic about the program may want to serve on the family ministry team or help with a specific program. Give them these opportunities through a "Family Ministry Involvement Card" (Diagram 19) or sign-up sheets.

Choosing the Party Theme

Selecting the theme and activities to include in a family ministry housewarming party is a critical decision. Spend lots of time considering and evaluating different options. As the task force decides what to plan, have members ask these kinds of questions:

1. Does the event sound fun and exciting for families?

2. Would the event appeal to a broad spectrum of people? Avoid choosing events that would alienate some people or that appeal only to a certain segment of parents and teenagers.

3. Can the event take place at church? It's important to launch the ministry at the church to help people identify the ministry with the church.

4. Does the event include plenty of time and opportunities for people to get acquainted? An event such as a movie night or concert wouldn't be appropriate since they involve little interaction among participants.

5. Is the timing right? Pick a time that the survey indicated would be best for most families. Carefully check calendars to ensure there are no major conflicts with the time you've chosen.

There are dozens of creative activities you could use for your housewarming party. Use your imagination and be creative. Some ideas to build your party around might include:

• **Family fair.** Hold an outdoor fair at the church for families. Create a festive carnival atmosphere with balloons, clowns and light music. Have a colorful booth for each new program where volunteers tell interested people about the opportunity. Enlist "street performers" to juggle, sing and entertain people. Serve hot dogs, cotton candy and other carnival-type foods.

• **Family feud.** Have friendly games in which families compete against each other. Some could be physical activities such as crazy relays or team sports. Others could be mind games designed after TV game shows.

• **Family vacation.** Invite all families to take a mini-vacation at church. Set up different rooms like different kinds of vacations. One could be a beach setting with beach chairs, umbrellas, sun-tan lotion and a background tape of waves. Another could be a trip to an amusement park. Have families wear their "vacation clothes" and visit each room where they'd learn about the different programs.

*P*ublicity

Publicity is always important for family events. But since the housewarming party is critical to the early success of your ministry, publicity for this event should be exceptionally creative and thorough. Start several weeks in advance, and use many different strategies.

Try some different publicity methods for your housewarming event. Because you're beginning a major new ministry, contact local media (newspapers, radio or television) to see whether they're interested in doing a story about your plans. Contact community organizations that help families, and ask them to spread the word. Use skits, posters, announcements and letters to tell people in the congregation about the plans. Make buttons about the event for parents and teenagers to wear. A button that says something like "I'll be there" invites questions from people who don't know about the new program. (Refer to Chapter 5 for more information on how to publicize family programs.)

After the Party

Soon after the inaugural event, send letters to participants thanking them for participating. Invite them to upcoming meetings and remind them of the time and place for each activity. Send them copies of the calendars and brochures that were distributed during the event. Send similar information to families you know about who didn't attend the event. Tell them they were missed, and encourage them to participate in upcoming events.

Compile information from the interest surveys. Make lists of people who volunteered for different tasks, and keep a file of people with specific needs. These names will be valuable for future programming and planning.

Finally, if you haven't already lined up the coordinators for the family ministry team, work with the church's committee structure to find and enlist the appropriate people. If new people are interested in serving on the family ministry team, contact them to find out what roles they can fill, and fit them into the structure appropriately. When the team is complete announce the members to the congregation.

Family Ministry Team

After the family ministry program has been introduced at the housewarming party, the family ministry team fulfills long-term leadership needs. Planning task force members may not want to work with the day-today leadership of the ongoing program after the housewarming party. Furthermore, other people who didn't commit to the task force may be ideal for leading specific programs once they're in place.

• **Choosing team members.** Recruit individuals from the task force and congregation to join the permanent family ministry team. Use the same types of criteria for choosing the team members you used in choosing task force members. These criteria include the following:

1. Include people from different kinds of families (single-parent families, two-career families, blended families, traditional families).

2. Include both parents and teenagers.

3. Include family experts in the congregation, if possible.

4. Limit the team's size to eight people.

5. Limit the length of members' commitments.

• **Dividing responsibilities.** Each family ministry team member will have specific responsibilities. Carefully cover all the responsibilities in written job descriptions so that you as youth worker don't get stuck with constantly picking up responsibilities that fall between the different job descriptions.

There are numerous ways to organize your family ministry team. A simple structure is to include team coordinators, area coordinators and any consultants who agree to participate. Here are the responsibilities for each of these positions:

1. Team coordinators. Youth workers shouldn't be responsible for running the family ministry. Find a capable person (or couple) and a youth group member to coordinate the ministry.

Including a young person as a team coordinator helps ensure a partnership between parents and teenagers in the ministry. This person should be mature and relate well to adults. The young person can be a representative from the youth council, or he or she can be a person chosen by the youth group. Be sure that the adult coordinators don't dominate planning. Help them learn to work as a team.

2. Area coordinators. Area coordinators head up specific areas of your ministry. You could assign an area coordinator to each program (support groups, family potlucks, workshops). Or you could assign an area coordinator to each ministry objective (support, education, enrichment, outreach). The area coordinators can work with a crew of volunteers who actually plan and implement specific programs such as retreats, workshops and family nights. You may also have area coordinators who are responsible for publicity or for coordinating volunteers.

3. Youth worker. As youth worker, you should serve as consultant to the family ministry team, leaving the planning and implementation to the team. By stepping back and letting other people run the program, you not only give parents and teenagers ownership of the program, but you also free yourself for other responsibilities. You may choose to arrange weekly or biweekly meetings with the team coordinators to share ideas and give feedback.

4. Consultants. If you have family specialists in the congregation (such as social workers or psychologists) who would be willing to contribute their insights but who can't commit to coordinating a particular part of the ministry, ask them to serve as informal consultants to the family ministry team. They can attend meetings and be available for telephone consultations when needed. Their participation can be an important check to ensure that your programming is appropriate and on target.

5. Other church staff. Other members of your church staff such as a pastor or education director may want to participate on the family ministry team.

If so, ask them to be consultants and to share their insights.

6. Other volunteers. The small family ministry team will not be able to do all the details involved in planning and implementing the ministry. Recruit other volunteers to work with each area coordinator to plan and implement specific programs. You'll need people to help with publicity, setup, refreshments and other elements involved in each program. Ask parents and teenagers at your housewarming party to fill out a "Family Ministry Involvement Card" (Diagram 19) so you can discover people who would be interested in helping with the program.

*E*valuation

How do you know if your programming is on target? What programs work? What programs do families enjoy? What ministries are helpful to families? These are important questions to answer as you develop your ministry. It's critical, therefore, to evaluate each program periodically to make sure you're meeting families' needs. Here are some possible ways to gather this information:

• **Written evaluations.** Ask program participants to fill out a brief survey after a special workshop or series of meetings. Ask what was useful and what wasn't useful about the program. Ask for their suggestions for improving future programs.

You can also use written forms to evaluate ongoing ministries such as counseling services. Have evaluation forms available in the church office or counseling center for people to fill out throughout the year. Or include an evaluation form in a parents newsletter once a year and ask families who used the service to evaluate it.

• **Interviews.** Another way to get feedback about

Diagram 19
Family Ministry Involvement Card

Name _____

Address_____

City, State, ZIP _____

Work phone _____ Home phone _____

Parents only
Your teenager(s)' name(s): _____

Your teenager(s)' grade(s): _____

Teenagers only
Your parent(s)' name(s): _____

_____

Check (✓) any of the following areas in which you'd be willing to help with the church's ministry to families.

☐ Leading discussions
☐ Helping with setup for events
☐ Coordinating events
☐ Telephoning families
☐ Teaching classes
☐ Editing/writing a newsletter
☐ Preparing refreshments for meetings
☐ Providing child care during events
☐ Facilitating a parents support group

☐ Hosting meetings
☐ Driving a bus or van for events
☐ Visiting families in the community
☐ Keeping records
☐ Designing publicity
☐ Leading sports
☐ Preparing snack dinners for families
☐ Helping plan retreats
☐ Other: _____

Please list any special skills you have such as cooking, teaching crafts, working with computers or camping expertise.

1. _____   3. _____

2. _____   4. _____

your ministry is through informal interviews. Have team members ask various parents and teenagers about their impressions and feelings about the programs you offer. These interviews could take place over the phone or after events.

• **Small group discussions.** At the end of a special series or a workshop, divide the participants into small groups. Ask them to discuss their reactions to the program and to give you their overall impressions.

Making It Work

Occasionally someone from a small church will hear about developing a family ministry team and say: "The program may be fine for a large church. But I don't think our little congregation could pull off that kind of a program." In a sense, these people are correct. Small churches can't develop several different programs for families with teenagers. But any church that has parents and teenagers can minister to its families. Just keep the following five points in mind:

• **Share leadership.** We've already mentioned this several times, but it bears repeating. Without sharing the responsibilities of your ministry, your efforts to "do it yourself" will "do yourself in." Even churches with a small leadership core of six or eight people can conduct an effective ministry.

• **Go for high returns for your efforts.** You could probably think of dozens of things—many of them useful—that families could do. But your time and families' time are valuable. So be selective in choosing activities that will offer high returns for the time and energy you invest. Whether you're planning educational, inspirational or recreational events, plan activities that you think will have the greatest impact on families with teenagers.

• **Limit your options.** Don't try to do everything.

When you try to provide too many options and programs, the family ministry team won't know where to start planning. By choosing activities carefully, you can concentrate your energies on worthwhile programs.

• **Follow up.** Work with the family ministry coordinators to ensure that various team members are following through with their responsibilities. Offer them support, suggestions and encouragement long before their task is due. This extra effort will ensure well-planned programs.

• **Express affirmation and appreciation often.** Don't let family ministry team members feel unnoticed or unappreciated. Recognize their contributions to the ministry through announcements during worship and meetings and through newsletters. Drop them notes expressing your appreciation. Let them know that their contribution is a valuable part of the church's ministry to families.

*T*ask Force Meeting #4: Presenting the Ministry

After weeks of behind-the-scenes planning, the family ministry task force must prepare to step on stage to present its new program. Much of the work involved in getting programs ready doesn't need to involve only the task force. Instead, individuals and subcommittees can take responsibility for various tasks and report to the task force. This meeting sets the detailed planning in motion.

• **Objectives.** This meeting is designed to:

1. Finalize job descriptions for the family ministry team and to invite task force members to fill some of those roles.

2. Decide a theme for the housewarming party.

3. Assign responsibilities for planning the housewarming party.

• **Preparation.** Cut out of magazines a variety of pictures to use in the opening exercise. Paste them on separate sheets of construction paper. Make one for each task force member.

Have someone type and photocopy the list of suggested programs from the previous meeting. Make enough copies of the proposed family ministry team job descriptions for each task force member. (See Diagram 20 for a sample job description.)

Bring the "Designing Programs" worksheets (Diagram 17) the task force completed at its previous meeting for the programs you're developing. Have newsprint and markers available. Bring several blank copies of the "Designing Programs" worksheet to use to plan the housewarming party.

Cut a house out of construction paper for each task force member for the closing exercise.

• **Opening.** Begin the meeting with a prayer. Ask God to guide you as you finalize plans for your ministry and your housewarming party.

This opening exercise is designed to help people loosen up before the final planning push. Gather everyone into a circle. Distribute a picture, face down, to each person. Tell people not to look at the picture or show it to others. Then tell participants they're going to "spin a yarn" about an ideal family ministry. One at a time, they turn up their picture. Based on their picture, they tell what makes an ideal family ministry.

For example, a person could show a picture of a building and start the story by saying: "Once upon a time in a faraway state was a quaint, old church. The people in this church wanted to start a family ministry . . ." The person must keep talking until the leader says, "Change!" Then the next person must turn up his or her picture and—inspired by the picture—continue the story. Let each person add to the story before stopping.

Diagram 20

Job Description for
Family Ministry Team Coordinators

By volunteering to coordinate the ministry to families with teenagers in our congregation, you've stated your belief that families are important to the life of the church and community. As a team coordinator, you'll give a significant amount of your time and talents. Our family ministry team recognizes your commitment and pledges to support your efforts. Following are our expectations of you and your expectations of us.

As a family ministry team coordinator, you will:
• Work with a team of adults and young people to plan and implement the congregation's ministry to families with teenagers.
• Maintain regular contact with area coordinators on the family ministry team.
• Work with coordinators in all assigned responsibilities.
• Inform the youth minister of all family ministry plans.
• Coordinate family ministry plans to be consistent with the goals of the youth program and congregation.
• Coordinate family ministry activities to avoid conflict with other church activities.
• Help lead family ministry team meetings.
• Be prepared for all assigned tasks to which you agree.
• Call young people and parents or visit them as time permits.
• Inform team members when you can't attend a family ministry meeting or event.
• Serve for one year.
• Give at least one month's notice of resignation, except in an emergency.
• Be a Christian example in conduct and speech for families.
• Pray for team members and for families in the church and community.

The congregation, family ministry team and youth minister agree to:
• Keep you well-informed of all family ministry plans and programs.
• Provide you with training to be a family ministry leader.
• Provide resources such as books, materials and films, and share their ministry experience to help you do your job.
• Provide babysitting for your preschool and elementary children during family meetings and other events, either at church or in your home.
• Pay your expenses on family ministry events and trips.
• Listen to your needs and concerns.
• Pray for you.

continued

Other agreements or expectations:

_____

_____

_____

_____

_____

_____

_____

_____

_____

Signature of youth minister:_____

Signature of family ministry team coordinator: _____

_____

Date: _____

• **Job descriptions.** Pass out copies of the family ministry team job descriptions. Ask task force members to comment and make suggestions and changes.

When everyone is satisfied with the job descriptions, ask if any team members want to fill any of the positions. Remind volunteers that team members will be chosen formally through the church's committee structure. Don't pressure people to fill spots they aren't comfortable with. If people don't want to continue on the task force, ask if they'll help with planning until after the housewarming party when other people volunteer.

• **Choosing a party theme.** Explain the purpose and importance of the housewarming party. Ask task force members to brainstorm theme ideas. You can get them started by mentioning some of the ideas listed in this chapter. Then let the team's imagination go. What would be fun, inviting and appropriate? How could you attract busy people? What are some good, creative ways to introduce families to the program?

After several minutes of brainstorming, have the task force members evaluate different options based on the checklist on page 281. Keep notes on their ideas. Since you haven't developed the specific elements for the program, think of creative ways to make various programs work.

Based on the answers to the checklist and your discussion, have members decide on a specific theme for the event. Make sure everyone understands and accepts the theme.

• **Planning the party.** Distribute blank copies of the "Designing Programs" worksheets (Diagram 17). Have the whole group work together to answer the first five questions on the worksheet as they pertain to the housewarming party.

Then divide the task force into teams of two or three people. Have each team work through the different questions that remain on the worksheet. For instance, one group could deal with publicity while another deals with budget or leadership. If groups encounter major obstacles, have them discuss the problems with the others to discover creative solutions.

When the groups have finished their questions, bring the task force back together to discuss the details. Make sure everything is covered and answer any other concerns on the task force.

• **Assigning responsibilities.** With so many jobs to accomplish to put on the housewarming party, ask task force members to volunteer to cover all the specific responsibilities. Write each responsibility on newsprint, then fill in the name of a person who will take charge. Encourage each person to enlist help from other parents and teenagers as needed. Responsibilities could be publicity, materials, leadership, refreshments, facilities, child care, activities and presenting the program ideas.

• **Closing.** Since this is the final meeting of the planning task force, allow each member to affirm each other's work and creativity.

Give each person a house-shape piece of construction paper. Have each participant write his or her name at the top of the house. Say all members get to write one thing they've appreciated about each person during these past few weeks. Everyone passes his or her house to the person on the right. Allow a moment for each person to write an affirmation on his or her neighbor's house. Then pass the house to the next person to write an affirmation. Continue until the house returns to its original owner. Encourage task force members to keep their houses as reminders of their individual contribution to the formation of your ministry to families with teenagers.

Close the meeting with a prayer of thanksgiving and hope for the future of the ministry.

Part 4
Programming Ideas

Chapter 17

*P*rograms for Parents and Teenagers Together

*I*n Chapter 5 we discussed the elements of effective family programs. This chapter consists of four models of successful programs for parents and teenagers together. As you use these meetings and retreats keep in mind the following guidelines, which we introduced in Chapter 5:

• Don't assume that all teenagers will have two parents—or that their parent or parents will participate.

• Keep programs balanced so that both parents and teenagers participate equally.

• Plan in advance so families can set aside time on their schedules.

• Be creative. Make the programs fit your own situation.

Bible Study: **Getting Along With Parents**

It's natural for parents and kids to experience some difficulty in getting along. Expect it. Getting along with each other can be better accomplished, however, when parents and kids understand each other's needs and responsibilities and have the tools necessary for effective communication.

Use this Bible study with your teenagers and their parents to help them better understand each other and learn how to communicate their feelings.

In this Bible study parents and teenagers will:

• view family situations from a parent's and kid's perspective.

• discover God's expectations for parents and kids.

• practice communication skills.

• evaluate their progress in areas of responsibility and communication.

*P*reparation

Gather pencils, paper, scissors, jars, newsprint, markers, Bibles, plain paper cups and refreshments. Copy all handouts. Cut apart the "Playing the Role" situations (Diagram 21). You'll need one set and a jar for each group of six to eight people. Fold each situation and place one set in a jar for the "Playing the Role" activity.

If some parents can't attend the meeting, ask them to complete the "Great Expectations" handout (Diagram 22). List their responses on newsprint and have it ready for the "Great Expectations" activity.

*B*ible Study

Building community—Welcome people as they come in, and form groups of six or eight. Make sure each group has both adults and kids, but try to mix up families. Display the following questions on newsprint:

• When was a time you felt particularly close to your parents?

• Think about a favorite family Christmas, vacation

Diagram 21
Playing the Role

Situation 1—You want to go on a weekend ski or camping trip with friends. Your parents insist that you stay home and babysit your younger brother. What do you say to them? How do they respond?

Situation 2—Your mom remembers your birthday with a special surprise party and includes some of your friends. You're thankful. What do you say to your mom? How does she respond?

Situation 3—You skip a day of school to go skiing or to the beach. The school office calls your dad to report your absence, and your dad confronts you with what he knows. What does he say to you? How do you respond?

Situation 4—Your parents are out of town for the weekend, and you invite some friends over for a party. Someone brings alcohol, and your parents find out about it. What do you say to them? How do they respond?

Situation 5—You tell your mom that you're going to attend a youth activity at church. Instead, you go out with a friend. The next day you feel guilty and decide to tell her. What do you say? How does she respond?

Situation 6—You bring home your report card with a failing grade. Your dad is upset. What does he say to you? How do you respond?

Situation 7—Prayer is important to your family. You know your parents pray for you daily. You want to tell your parents how that makes you feel. What do you tell them? How do they respond?

Situation 8—You have an accident with your mom's car. Although she's upset, she doesn't get angry. What does she say to you? How do you respond?

Situation 9—There's something you want—a role in a play, a spot on the team, a position in the band, but you don't get it. You tell your mom or dad about your disappointment. What do you say? How does she or he respond?

Situation 10—You come home from school and no one else is home. You decide to clean the breakfast dishes. What does your parent say to you when he or she comes home? How do you respond?

or birthday celebration. Why was it special?

Have everyone pick a partner and share the answers. After a few minutes, have partners tell their small group something they learned about each other.

Playing the Role—Give each group a jar filled with the "Playing the Role" situations, a sheet of paper and a pencil. Have everyone select a partner within his or her group. Have each kid pick an adult partner if possible. Ask each pair to draw a piece of paper from the jar, read the instructions and do a one-minute role play on the chosen situation. After each role play, have group members discuss the key issues represented from a parent's perspective and a kid's perspective. Issues to discuss include trust, independence, understanding, selfishness, responsibility and cooperation. Have each group list key issues on paper.

When small groups are finished, list all responses on newsprint in two columns: "Parent's Perspective" and "Kid's Perspective." Ask the kids: "What are some frustrations in your relationships with your parents? What are some joys?" Ask the parents: "What are some frustrations or fears in your relationships with your kids? What are some joys?" Ask the total group: "What are some positive attributes you bring to your family relationships? How do these attributes work within your family?"

Great Expectations—Give each person a pencil and a copy of the "Great Expectations" handout (Diagram 22). Assign each small group four or five verses from the handout, and have groups each complete their assignment. If some parents aren't present, display their answers from the previously completed handouts.

Give each small group two sheets of newsprint and a marker. Have each group create two 20- to 30-word classified ads with an appropriate heading. Ask groups to use the key issues they found in their scripture pas-

Diagram 22
Great Expectations

Instructions: Look up your assigned passages. For each, write the key issue from a parent's perspective and the key issue from a kid's perspective.

Passage	Parent's Key Issue	Kid's Key Issue
1. Exodus 20:12		
2. Deuteronomy 4:9		
3. Deuteronomy 32:46		
4. Proverbs 19:18		
5. Proverbs 22:6		
6. Proverbs 23:13-14		
7. Proverbs 27:11		
8. Proverbs 29:17		
9. Proverbs 31:28		
10. Luke 2:48-52		
11. Ephesians 6:1-3		
12. Ephesians 6:4		
13. Philippians 2:3-4		
14. Colossians 3:20		
15. Colossians 3:21		
16. 1 Thessalonians 2:11-12		
17. 1 Timothy 3:4		
18. 1 Timothy 4:12		
19. 1 Timothy 5:8		
20. 1 Peter 3:8-12		

sages. One ad should be for parents, the other for kids. For example, part of one ad might say, "Diligent Father Wanted: must be able to give instruction and discipline children without making them mad" (Ephesians 6:4).

When they're finished, have groups each read aloud their ad to the whole group. Display the ads.

Do you see what I'm saying?—Encourage participants to consider an area of their relationship with their kids or parents where they need help. Say: "None of us is perfect. We all have areas in our lives in which we need wisdom and encouragement. God wants to help us live Christlike lives, to love and support each other. Because of that, we're challenged to improve our relationships with our parents or children. One way to do that is to improve our communication and listening skills."

Have groups stand in small circles. Display a list of "feeling" words on newsprint. The list should include words such as peaceful, frustrated, overwhelmed, excited, afraid, brave, reliable, unhappy, depressed, enthusiastic, proud and thankful. Ask everyone to pick a word but not reveal the choice to anyone. Then have group members each take turns pantomiming a feeling while others try to guess what it is.

It's in the "I"s—Give each person a copy of the "I's and Ears" handout (Diagram 23). Read the following explanation of "I" messages: "Psychologists say that parent-child relationships can be helped best through improved communication. While body language and facial expression enhance communication of your feelings, one helpful skill is learning to express yourself through 'I' messages. 'I' messages communicate a position or feeling in a non-judgmental manner. A statement that begins with 'you' is usually a blaming statement. Beginning a statement with 'I' is non-judgmental and usually leads to better under-

Diagram 23
I's and Ears

Instructions: Read the information about "I" messages. Write one of your own in the space provided. Ask a partner to check if all steps are included.

I's

"I" messages are helpful to communicate a position or feeling in a non-judgmental manner. "I" messages can be a good beginning toward understanding a situation or resolving a problem. "I" messages include the following steps.

1. *Clarity*—Clearly state the issue.
2. *Feelings*—State how you feel about the issue.
3. *Reasons*—State why you feel it's an issue.
4. *Action*—State what you want done about the issue.

The following format is helpful in developing the "I" message.

"When you _____, I feel _____ because _____
_____. I would like _____
_____
_____."

Instructions: Read the information about "Ears." Share your "I" messages with another partner, using the reflective listening techniques suggested. Be prepared to discuss your experience with the total group.

Ears

Reflective listening is a skill to use if the other person is stating an issue. It lets the person know you understand and care. Reflective listening includes the following steps.

1. *Attention*—Focus on what the person is saying; give undivided attention to that person and the message being communicated.
2. *Acknowledgement*—Gesture and say "yes" and "uh-huh" to indicate you understand.
3. *Empathy*—Use facial expressions and an attitude of "I know how it feels" to indicate that you're experiencing the impact of what's being said.
4. *Feedback*—Communicate understanding of the message by putting it into different words and feeding it back to the sender.

standing between two people."

On the "I's and Ears" handout, have everyone create an "I" statement that refers to one of the role plays from the "Playing the Role" activity. Be sure to have the jar of situations available to refer to. Have everyone say his or her "I" statement to a partner. The partner can use the worksheet to assess whether all of the elements of the "I" statement are there.

That's using your ears—Refer to the "I's and Ears" handout and say: "Reflective listening is a skill that lets the other person know you understand. Read the four elements of reflective listening. When you're finished, pick a partner and share your 'I' messages again. This time, however, ask your partner to use the reflective listening skills and give you feedback on what he or she understood." When everyone is finished ask:

• What was different between your communication during the original role play and this time when you used the "I" messages and reflective listening?

• What new understanding did you gain by using these two skills?

• How can you use these new skills at home?

Self Checkup—Give each person a copy of the "Self Checkup" handout to complete (Diagram 24). When everyone's finished, have parents and kids stand in a circle, hold hands and pray silently for one area in which they would like God to help them improve and become more Christlike. Then invite participants to share what they prayed for.

Refreshments—Serve punch and cookies. Have parents and kids each draw a symbol or picture on their cup that represents the area of life they'd like to improve. Discuss the symbols.

Diagram 24
Self Checkup

Instructions: How closely are you living up to biblical standards in your relationship with your parent or teenager? Rate yourself from "0" to "10" with "0" meaning "I've never even thought about it" and "10" meaning "I've got my act together on this one."

1. Trust	0	1	2	3	4	5	6	7	8	9	10
2. Love	0	1	2	3	4	5	6	7	8	9	10
3. Respect	0	1	2	3	4	5	6	7	8	9	10
4. Good listening	0	1	2	3	4	5	6	7	8	9	10
5. Responsibility	0	1	2	3	4	5	6	7	8	9	10
6. Open communication	0	1	2	3	4	5	6	7	8	9	10
7. Cooperation	0	1	2	3	4	5	6	7	8	9	10
8. Honesty	0	1	2	3	4	5	6	7	8	9	10
9. Unselfishness	0	1	2	3	4	5	6	7	8	9	10
10. Understanding attitude	0	1	2	3	4	5	6	7	8	9	10

Meeting: Parent Appreciation Night

Many high school young people find themselves deeply enmeshed in a struggle for autonomy and independence from the parents they love. It's often difficult for them to express the love and appreciation they secretly feel. This activity provides an opportunity for kids to say thanks in a tangible and enjoyable manner. For those young people who have difficulty relating to their parents, this activity provides an opportunity for them to reflect on their parents' love, recognize the valuable role their parents play and reach out to them in a special and moving way.

During the meeting teenagers will:

• Serve their parents (and siblings) dinner and be the waiter or waitress at the family table.

• Present parents with certificates of appreciation for parenting well-done.

• Present recorded speeches of appreciation.

*P*reparation

Besides the kitchen equipment necessary to cook a meal and the chairs, tables and table settings necessary to serve it, gather a tape recorder, a short cassette for each teenager, a camera, and enough film to take several pictures or slides of each person's family. You'll also need a slide projector and screen or a spotlight to highlight photographs taped to a wall. Borrow or purchase tapes of soft music to play during the meal. Purchase certificates of appreciation, name tags and place cards from your local office supply store, or design your own.

Ask someone to prepare a talk about Malachi 4:5-6, substituting "parents" for "fathers." Talk about the importance of this promise to God's people both in Malachi's day and in our own. Challenge parents to make every attempt to keep in touch with their kids, especially through the teenage years. Challenge kids to remember this attempt to let their parents know how much they appreciate them and to make an effort to stay in touch with the parents they love.

Divide preparation into three parts. Enlist the services of an older group such as college students or young adults to help with planning as well as preparations.

1. Food committee. Ask two or three group members to meet with your food committee to plan, prepare and serve the meal. Suggest easy-to-prepare meals such as a spaghetti dinner with tossed green salad, garlic bread, and carrot cake for dessert; barbecued burgers and hot dogs, baked beans, macaroni or potato salad, and ice cream for dessert; or oven-fried chicken, baked potatoes, green salad, and ice cream for dessert. Include drinks as part of your planning.

Have the committee make a list of all food and quantities needed. Check the list before any purchases are made.

2. Setup committee. This crew will make arrangements for and set up tables, chairs, tablecloths, name tags, place cards, table settings and all serving pieces. They'll work with the food committee to schedule when help is needed both before and after the dinner.

3. Presentation committee. Work with each teenager to write a two-minute speech of appreciation for his or her parent or parents. You may need to offer ideas, but leave the speech in the kid's own words. The more the speeches sound like their own teenagers, the more parents will be moved. Once speeches are written and practiced, record them on individual cassettes and label them. Use the tapes in the program and present them to parents at the end of the evening. Make sure each teenager has also prepared his or her certificate of appreciation prior to the dinner.

Create a slide show or a picture wall of youth group members with their families. Ask several young people to be photographers and take pictures of each group member's family. Instruct photographers to provide a flavor of life at home. Ask them to snap pictures of families assembled at dinner, the parents themselves, just Mom, just Dad, brothers and sisters, pets or the kid's room. (If this isn't possible, simply ask families to supply the slides and photographs.) Show each person's slides or spotlight pictures as you play that person's tape at the dinner.

Encourage young people to dress up for this occasion. Offer tips on how to serve and remove dishes from the table.

*A*ppreciation Night

Welcome—Greet families as they arrive. Ask them to find their name tags. Serve punch and play a get-to-know-you game such as "Find the Facts." Allow 10 minutes for participants to talk to as many people as they can and discover one fact about each person (favorite hobby or where he or she lives or works).

Dinner—When everyone is present, invite kids to escort their families to preassigned seats. Open the evening with prayer. Then say: "This dinner is your young people's attempt to let you know how much their families mean to them. Your own young person will be your waiter or waitress. The meal will be served family style so you'll have a chance to talk with each other. Enjoy this time together."

As people finish the meal, have your young people remove plates and serving dishes and serve dessert. Make final preparations for the program to begin.

After a few introductory remarks about the importance of families, invite your first presenter to come forward. The teenager will ask his or her parent(s) to come to the front of the room and read to them his or her certificate of appreciation. Dim the lights and play that young person's tape while you spotlight photographs or show slides of that family. When the tape is finished, raise the lights and invite the next young person to repeat the same process. Continue until each family has had a turn.

Be prepared for various reactions. Hugs, tears or laughter may be typical expressions of the deeper feelings inside.

Conclude the program with the talk about Malachi 4:5-6. Emphasize a challenge to kids and parents to "stay in touch" with one another.

Closing—Ask the group to sing together "Blest Be the Tie That Binds" as you pass out tapes to parents.

Variation—Get with the parents and brainstorm for ideas for a "Youth Appreciation Night." This is an easy-to-do, fun-to-present program for parents to show they care about their teenagers.

Retreat: *The Family: Past, Present and Future*

A family changes constantly. As young people grow up and parents experience more of life, the family can't remain the same. Instead of looking at these changes as something negative, a family can examine its changes as opportunities for growth. As family members interact with one another, they'll have opportunities to look at the past, the present and their future together.

In this retreat family members will:
• spend quality time talking and interacting with one another.
• share memories.
• discuss current thoughts and feelings.
• plan for the future.

*P*reparation

Gather the following supplies: Bibles, two colors of construction paper, paper, envelopes, staplers, markers, pencils, posterboard, tape, scissors and newsprint. Individual family groups will also need three shoe boxes. Provide crayons, watercolors, tempera, brushes or art supplies you select for the final activity.

Read the retreat thoroughly. At least one month before the retreat notify each family to bring memorabilia related to the family's past. Suggest they include special pictures, clothes a family member used to wear, souvenirs from a trip, gifts they've received from each other—anything that represents some special memory for family members.

Prepare journals (Diagrams 28 and 29). Copy questions and staple them inside a construction paper cover. Use different-color covers to distinguish between parents' and young people's journals.

Prepare time capsules. Wrap shoe boxes and lids with newsprint. Label lids Past, Present and Future. Each family will need a Past, Present and Future capsule. Copy instructions for each capsule. Prepare capsules according to the following list:

Past
- Instructions—one per capsule (Diagram 25)
- Journals—one for each parent (Diagram 28)
            one for each student (Diagram 29)
- Family memorabilia—Once you obtain memorabilia, label this capsule with the correct family name and seal it so items won't be lost

Present
- Instructions—one per capsule (Diagram 26)
- Paper—one sheet for each family member

Future
- Instructions—one per capsule (Diagram 27)
- Paper—one sheet for each family member per person
- Envelopes—one for each family member

Make posterboard signs to designate each family's space. Arrange family spaces far enough apart to be somewhat private.

Make sure each family space has pencils, markers, scissors, tape, one sheet of posterboard, one sheet of newsprint and the art supplies you decide to use.

Mark your calendar and mail "love notes" to family members to arrive one month after the retreat. These notes will be welcome affirmations and polite reminders of commitments made during the retreat.

Retreat Schedule

Friday		Saturday	
6:00 p.m.	Leave for retreat	7:00 a.m.	Get up and get ready
7:00 p.m.	Arrive and get settled	8:00 a.m.	Breakfast
		8:30 a.m.	Morning activity
7:30 p.m.	Welcome and instructions	9:00 a.m.	Time Capsule 2—Present
		10:30 a.m.	Snack
8:00 p.m.	Time Capsule 1—Past	10:45 a.m.	Sharing session (family)
		11:30 a.m.	Prepare for lunch
9:30 p.m.	Sharing session	Noon	Lunch
10:00 p.m.	Snacks	1:00 p.m.	Family activity
10:30 p.m.	Games	2:30 p.m.	Snack
11:30 p.m.	Lights out	2:45 p.m.	Time Capsule 3—Future
		4:05 p.m.	Sharing session
		4:30 p.m.	Pack up and return

*R*etreat
Friday

Welcome—Welcome families to the retreat. Ask family members to join hands. Each person will be responsible for introducing the family member on his or her right. Individuals should be introduced by name and one other positive thing about them. For example, "This is my dad, Mark Murphy, and he loves to play golf." Say: "One of the main objectives for this retreat is to spend quality time together. You'll have opportunities to grow in understanding and accepting one another."

Begin the meeting with prayer. Ask for openness and a willingness to listen to other family members as they share their thoughts and feelings. Say: "One of the best ways to examine your thoughts and feelings is to write them on paper. In your first time capsule each of you will receive a journal. Respond to each question or open-ended statement in writing. No one will read your journal, so be honest with yourself.

"You'll be asked to write in your journal as you begin each of the three sessions. This is a time for you to think before you begin talking. Get in touch with your own thoughts and feelings, then share what you feel comfortable with."

Diagram 25
Past

Instructions

1. Begin this family time by writing in your personal journal. Record some of your memories as you respond to the questions and open-ended statements in your journal. After 10 minutes, share your responses with other family members.

2. Take time to reminisce. Use the objects in your time capsule as catalysts to spark stories of the past. As each person finishes a story, ask other family members to share what they recall about that same experience. You may be surprised at the different ways your family members experienced some of the same events with different feelings and associations.

3. Use markers, scissors and the posterboard in your family space to create a family coat of arms. This symbol should communicate to others who you are as a family. Design your coat of arms to include a space for each family member. Each person should draw a picture to represent what's most meaningful to him or her about the family. Be prepared to explain your coat of arms to the rest of the group. After the sharing session, tape your coat of arms to the wall in your family space.

---

*T*ime Capsule 1—Past

Read Leviticus 25:10. Say: "God asked the Israelites to celebrate where and what they had been in the past. They were instructed to return to their families as part of a jubilee—a celebration of God's involvement in their lives.

"God is with our families at all times. Open your first time capsule and remind yourselves of how God has been with you in the past."

Have families locate their family space for the retreat. Then instruct them to open their time capsule labeled Past and follow the instructions inside.

Sharing session—Ask a person from each family group to talk about the family shield and what it means. Assure families if some things are private, it's not necessary to share those with the total group.

After all families have shared, close the meeting with a circle prayer. Ask the total group circle to say, "Thank you, God, for giving us such special families."

Saturday

Morning activity—Before families begin their family time for the Present, demonstrate the following exercise. This activity presents a powerful image for identifying things that "pull at" individuals, causing tension and pressure in their lives.

Ask for a parent volunteer. Have that person sit in a chair facing the group. Say: "Teenagers may be unaware of what's going on in a parent's life. Let's brainstorm about all the things that demand a parent's attention and 'tug on' him or her until the matter is taken care of. When you think of something, call it out. Then come up to the parent volunteer, hold on to part of his or her shirt or pants and pull on it. For example, I might say, 'Work pressures' and then take hold of the volunteer's sleeve and pull lightly. Think of other things that pull at a parent." When several people have surrounded your volunteer and are pulling in all directions, ask the volunteer, "How do you feel?"

After his or her response, say: "It's easy to forget how many things tug at and demand parents' attention these days. Perhaps this experience can remind us to be more sensitive." Thank the volunteer and ask people to return to their seats.

Next ask a teenage volunteer to sit in the chair. Follow the same procedure. Have participants name the pressure and come up to pull at the teenager's clothing. Ask the teenager how he or she feels. Conclude with a similar remark about a need for sensitivity for the many things that cause tension in a teenager's life.

*T*ime Capsule 2—Present

Dismiss families to go to their family space. Tell them to open the time capsule marked Present and follow the instructions inside.

Diagram 26
Present

Instructions
1. Begin this family time by writing in your journal. As you write your responses to the Present, think about the activity you just experienced.

2. Write your name on a sheet of paper. Draw a stick figure of yourself. Write some things that pull at you on the figure.
Pass your drawing around the family. Ask each person to list one specific way he or she can lessen the pull of your stresses.

3. After your drawing is returned, look over the family members' ideas. Talk honestly to each other about how these ideas for help will or won't work for you. Listen carefully to what each person is saying. For each family member, establish one way each person can help.

4. Tape your drawings to the wall in your family space.

Sharing session—Read Joshua 4:4-6a and Exodus

20:24. Say: "Take your journal on a walk with your
family. Build a family altar to God with real stones. As
each of you places a stone on the altar, read your
response to number 5 in your journal. Let your family
know what you like about your family life right now.
Talk about what others have shared. Close by holding
hands or putting your arms around each other and
saying, 'Thank you, God, for giving me such a special
family. Amen.' Return your journals to your family
space at the end of your walk."

Family activity—Plan games or activities in which
a family can compete or interact as a team. A family
olympics or a game show in which family members
must help and support each other is an excellent way
to utilize the team concept and build a sense of unity.

*T*ime Capsule 3—Future

Before you ask families to begin their final session,
say: "After looking at where you've been and where
you are as a family, it's time to think about where you
want to be in the future. Use this session to give your
family direction and to develop specific ideas on what
each of you can do or say to make your family life
more effective." Dismiss families to go to their family
space. Tell them to open the time capsule marked Future and follow the instructions inside.

Sharing session—Collect envelopes. Read Eccle-
siastes 3:1-11a. Say: "Everything is beautiful in its time.
The concept of family is a beautiful concept, and we
can celebrate our family life in numerous ways." Ask
family groups to share their creations and what they
mean to them for the future.

When families have finished sharing, say: "During
this retreat, you've learned to celebrate all of life as an
opportunity for growth. In recognition of this unique
approach to family life, talk with family members

Diagram 27
Future

Instructions

1. In your journal complete the open-ended statements in the Future section. Share your responses with the rest of your family after everyone has finished writing.

2. Using the art supplies provided, work together as a family to create a picture that represents the hopes you have for your family as you move into the future. Use whatever style (realistic, impressionistic, dramatic) and subject (a nature scene, a family portrait, a colorful design) you decide. Paint a picture that reminds your family of a hope-filled future.

3. Write your name on one of the envelopes in your capsule. Then write love notes (notes of appreciation and affirmation) to each family member at the retreat. Place each note in the correct envelope. After all love notes are complete and in the envelopes, seal and address the envelopes. Turn them in during the final sharing session. You'll receive the notes one month from today.

4. Close by holding hands or putting your arms around each other and saying: "Thank you, God, for giving me such a special family. Amen."

Diagram 28
Parent's Journal

Instructions: Respond in writing to the questions and open-ended statements for each part of your journal. Be honest with yourself. Share as much as you feel comfortable sharing with your family.

Past

1. Recall a special occasion when your son or daughter was a small child. What made that time special?

2. What do you remember doing as a family that you found meaningful? What made it meaningful?

3. Recall one of your child's birthday celebrations that was especially fun. What made it so fun?

4. Recall a time you were particularly proud of your son or daughter. What was it that made you so proud?

5. What have you enjoyed doing with your family that you would want to do again?

continued

Present

1. List the stresses that "pull at" you every day.

2. How can your teenager lessen the "pull" of your everyday stresses? Be specific. For example, get a schedule of your teenager's activities for the week so you can make meal plans when everyone can be home.

3. List the stresses that pull at your teenager.

4. How can you help lessen the pull of your teenager's everyday stresses? Be specific. For example, take care of the dishes during your teenager's finals week.

5. What do you like about your family right now? Why?

continued

Future

1. As a result of the things I've learned on this retreat, I'm willing to change

2. I'm willing to do more

3. I wish the following for other family members:

Name	**What I Wish**
_____	_____
_____	_____
_____	_____
_____	_____
_____	_____
_____	_____
_____	_____

4. I hope I'll be able to give my family

Diagram 29
Young People's Journal

Instructions: Respond in writing to the questions and open-ended statements for each part of your journal. Be honest with yourself. Share as much as you feel comfortable sharing with your family.

Past

1. What is your favorite family memory when you were in elementary school?

2. What special birthday do you recall? What made that birthday so special?

3. Recall a time you were particularly proud of your mother or father. What did he or she do, or what made you so proud?

4. What have you enjoyed doing with your family that you would want to do again? Why?

continued

Present

1. List the stresses that "pull at" you every day.

2. How can your parent help lessen the "pull" of your everyday stresses? Be specific. For example, your mom or dad could do the dishes for you during finals week.

3. List the stresses that "pull at" your parent.

4. How can you help lessen the pull of your parent's everyday stresses? Be specific. For example, help with plans for meals by giving your mom a schedule of your after-school activities each week.

5. What do you like about your family right now? Why?

continued

Future

1. As a result of the things I've learned on this retreat, I'm willing to change

2. I'm willing to do more

3. I wish the following for other family members:

Name   **What I Wish**

_____   _____

_____   _____

_____   _____

_____   _____

4. **I hope I'll be able to give my family**

about how the prayer 'Thank you, God, for giving me such a special family' has changed for you during the retreat." Once families have finished, make a large circle and repeat the same prayer, "Thank you, God, for giving me such a special family."

Retreat: *Let's Make a Deal*

Many conflicts between parents and teenagers happen because one doesn't know what the other expects. Parents fail to communicate rules clearly. Teenagers don't tell their parents how they want to be treated.

This lack of communication inevitably spells conflict.

Use this parent-teenager mini-retreat to help kids and parents learn to communicate clearly and agree on specific disagreements. In this retreat, parents and teenagers will:

- increase communication skills.
- help each family member see the other's viewpoint.
- give a pattern for negotiation.
- help families set specific rules.

*P*reparation

Proper preparation of kids, parents, facilities, small group leaders and yourself is essential for the retreat's success.

Gather construction paper, scissors, markers, straight pins, newsprint, a camera and enough film to take a picture of each family group. For every six people, make a copy of the "Offering Criticism" and "Accepting Criticism" handouts (Diagrams 32 and 33). For each person, gather a pencil, piece of paper, 3×5 card and a copy of the "What Is Communication?" handout (Diagram 31).

Ask participants to each bring a Bible, a notebook and any sports equipment or table games they'd like to use during recreation and free time.

Arrange for two meals and one snack time.

Inform parents and kids there'll be fun times, but also lots of study and interaction time.

Prior to the event, survey kids and parents to determine what conflicts they have. Adapt the "Sample Survey" (Diagram 30) for your needs. Use these conflicts to develop role plays for Sessions 1 and 3.

Find a facility with a meeting room large enough to divide the group into smaller groups in the same room.

Secure enough small tables (one for each family) and chairs (one for each person) for the "Parent-Kid

Diagram 30
Sample Survey

Instructions: Answer the following questions. Your responses may be used as part of the retreat.

1. What do you and your parents (or you and your teenagers) have the most conflict over? (For example, school, grades, chores, money, curfew.)

2. Describe your latest conflict. Did anything precede or follow this experience that would be important to understand what happened?

3. Can this conflict be used as a sample role play if names and places are changed?   Yes ☐   No ☐

Negotiations."

Assign leaders for the Bible studies and monitors for the "Parent-Kid Negotiations." Give Bible study leaders a copy of the two handouts ahead of time so they can prepare.

Find songs kids and parents can sing together.

Retreat Schedule

10:00 a.m. Beginnings
10:30 a.m. Session 1: Communication
   Noon Lunch
 1:00 p.m. Session 2: Criticism
 2:30 p.m. Snack time
 2:45 p.m. Session 3: Contracts
 4:00 p.m. Recreation and free time
 5:30 p.m. Dinner
 6:30 p.m. Session 4: Celebration
 8:00 p.m. Adjourn

*R*etreat Beginnings

Name tags—Provide construction paper, scissors, markers and straight pins. Have each person make a name tag that includes his or her name and a symbol describing his or her family. One person might use a fan blade to describe how his family members reach in all directions but are linked together by their love for one another. Have participants use straight pins to pin on the name tags.

Singing—Begin with a prayer for God's guidance. Gather the group in a circle and sing favorite songs both teenagers and parents know.

Getting acquainted—Form a circle of chairs facing outward; ask parents to sit in them. Form another circle of chairs with each chair facing a parent's chair; ask teenagers to sit in the outer circle. If there's an imbalance in numbers of parents and teenagers, intersperse the extra people so everyone shares with a partner at least every other time.

Diagram 31
What Is Communication?

Instructions: Read the following information about communication and follow your leader's instructions.

People communicate at one of five levels.

1. Cliché—"How's your new car?" "Okay."

2. Selected facts—"There's a dent in the right front fender of my new Mustang."

3. Idea or judgment—"I think I'd like to pay for having the fender fixed."

4. Feelings and emotions plus pertinent facts—"Since I'm the one who hit the fire hydrant, I feel I'm the one who should pay for the repair."

5. Intimate words—"I love you, Dad. Thanks for listening to my story and helping me work through this accident without judging me. I feel bad enough."

Communication is accomplished in a variety of ways.

1. Verbally—with words, voice inflection, tone, volume.

2. Bodily—with gestures, posture, expression.

3. Silently—as in "the old silent treatment."

Begin by having parent-teenager pairs tell each other about their name tags. After about one minute, have teenagers each move one chair to the right and repeat the process with their new partner until they arrive back at their original chair.

Session 1: Communication

Role plays—Ask kids and parents to role play several conflict situations you've developed from the pre-retreat survey. Reverse roles so kids act like parents and parents act like kids.

Communication methods—Give everyone a "What Is Communication?" handout (Diagram 31) and review the methods of communication. Ask group members to give additional examples of each item.

What are you doing?—Divide into smaller groups of no more than eight people. Have an equal number of parents and teenagers, all from different families, in each group. Hand out pencils.

On the back of the handout, have group members list ways of asking, "What are you doing?" Have them use the different levels and ways to communicate on the "What Is Communication?" handout.

Conversation levels—Have each small group choose two group members to carry on a conversation about an everyday topic such as the weather. After a couple of minutes, have other group members analyze the level of their statements by using the "What Is Communication?" handout.

Don't condemn—Tell participants that an "I" message expresses personal emotions and facts, but doesn't condemn the listeners. Ask participants to think of two things they'd like to say to their parents or teenagers. Ask them to turn over their "What Is Communication?" handouts and write two "I" messages. For example, "I feel angry when you won't let me use your car because my friends will think I'm a nobody without wheels." Have them each write what they'd say to their parent or teenager. Then have them write what they think their parent or teenager would say to them. (These messages may become the subject of "Parent-Kid Negotiations" later.)

Have the small groups discuss what they've learned from these communication methods. Ask volunteers from different groups to tell the total group what they learned.

Session 2: Criticism

Bible study—Divide into groups of six with only parents or only kids in each group. Hand pre-assigned leaders the "Offering Criticism" and "Accepting Criticism" handouts (Diagrams 32 and 33) and have them lead the small group Bible studies. Groups will study James 3:1-18 to learn how to *give* criticism and 1 Kings 16—18 to learn how to *accept* criticism. Make sure everyone has paper and a pencil.

After the Bible study, have someone from each small group report to the total group two things group members learned.

Session 3: Contracts

Parent-Kid negotiations—Contracting between parents and teenagers helps participants practice what they've learned. Explain these steps of the contract exercise:

• Each family group sits together around a table. (Provide newsprint and markers.)

• Each family group chooses two family conflict situations or the "I" messages in Session 1 to discuss. For example: use of the family car, leaving dirty dishes in the sink, curfew, music and choice of clothes.

• For each situation, either a parent or teenager gives his or her expectations. The other person(s) then gives his or her expectations.

• Discussion continues, using the methods in the "What Is Communication?" handout (Diagram 31). Have trained adult leaders monitor the negotiations

Diagram 32
Offering Criticism
James 3:1-18

This Bible study will help participants:
- learn how criticism affects relationships.
- learn how to be more constructive and less destructive in their criticism.

1. Tell others' criticisms. Have parents groups talk about what their kids criticize them for. Have teenagers groups talk about what their parents criticize them for. Ask: "Which criticism bothers you most? Why?"

2. Be careful how you talk. Have a volunteer read aloud James 3:1-12. Ask: "What images does James use to illustrate control of the tongue? What does each illustration tell about the power of criticism?"

- Horse and bit—verse 3
- Ship, wind and helm—verse 4
- Fire—verses 5-6
- Animals—verse 7
- Poison—verse 8
- Fountain—verse 11
- Fruit trees—verse 12

Ask: "Which image best describes your best and worst criticisms of your teenager (or parent)? How does criticism affect your relationship with your teenager (or parent)?"

3. Break a cycle. Read aloud James 3:6, 16. Ask: "What cycle does James outline? Where can you most easily break the cycle?"

4. Tell and show. Read James 3:13. In the parents groups say: "It's not enough to *tell* our children what they need to do. We must *show* them."

Then have parents talk about areas in which they're critical of their teenagers. Write these areas of criticism on newsprint. Opposite them, write parents' actions that may be hypocritical. Examples:

Areas of Criticism	Parents' Hypocritical Actions
Listening to rock music	Listening to country-western music
Abusing drugs	Drinking 15 cups of coffee a day
Drinking	Drinking a cocktail at a party
Being lazy	Failing to attend church
Being dishonest	Cheating on income taxes

In the teenagers groups say: "It's not enough to tell our parents what we need from them. We need to explain in specific terms what bothers us and why we're bothered by their actions or words."

continued

Then have teenagers talk about areas in which they're critical of their parents. Write these areas of criticism on newsprint. Opposite them, write teenagers' actions that may be hypocritical. Examples:

Areas of Criticism	Teenagers' Hypocritical Actions
Limiting time on phone calls	Urging a parent to get off the phone when you're expecting a call
Talking about your friends when they don't know them	Talking about adults and friends' parents when you don't know them

5. Remove covetous attitudes. Ask a volunteer to read aloud James 3:14-16.

In parents groups, say: "What do you envy about your teenagers? Do you wish you had their free time? their energy? their romance? their age? their opportunities? Explain. How can these attitudes affect your relationship with your teenagers?"

In the teenagers groups, say: "What do you envy about your parents? Do you wish you had their free time? their money? their authority? their age? their experience? their opportunities? Explain. How can these attitudes affect your relationship with your parents?"

6. Live wisely. Have a volunteer read aloud James 3:17-18. Then have participants define these words: pure, peace-loving, considerate, submissive, full of mercy, good fruit, impartial and sincere. Ask: "How can each of these characteristics help you give criticism?"

7. Develop guidelines for criticizing. Have participants list guidelines they think are important for criticizing other family members. Then ask each person to choose one guideline to follow next week.

Close with prayer.

Diagram 33
Accepting Criticism
1 Kings 16—18

This Bible study will help participants:
- see that all criticism isn't harmful; in fact, some is helpful.
- determine what criticisms they should accept or reject
- react properly to criticism.

1. Legitimate criticism. Ask each person to make a list of things he or she has been criticized for. Ask: "Which of these criticisms are legitimate? Which aren't? Who gives you the most legitimate criticism? the most unjust?" Have participants each talk about their list with a partner.

Say: "Elijah was God's man during the rule of Ahab. But that didn't exempt him from criticism. Everyone is criticized at one time or another. Your job is to discern what criticisms you should listen to and what you should ignore."

2. The criticism of Elijah. 1 Kings 16—18. Tell participants when they're criticized, they need to:
- *Consider the criticism's source.* Ask a volunteer to read aloud 1 Kings 18:16-17. Say: "The king of Israel accused Elijah of causing trouble for the nation. But Elijah didn't let that bother him because he knew the source of the criticism."

Ask someone else to read aloud 1 Kings 16:30-33. Ask: "What problems had King Ahab created?"
- *Consider the criticism's nature.* Have a participant read aloud 1 Kings 18:7-15. Say: "The prophet Obadiah had a valid concern. Elijah accepted his criticism and assured the prophet that he'd keep his word. Elijah wasn't offended at Obadiah's criticism but accepted it, because it was valid."
- *Consider the critic's situation.* Have someone read aloud 1 Kings 17:17-18. Say: "Elijah saved this widow from starvation. But the woman turned on him with vengeful criticism. The source was valid; she was a friend. But the criticism wasn't. Elijah hadn't killed the boy as the widow complained."

Ask: "Why did she say something like that? Why did she have such bitter criticism?" (Note the circumstances: This woman, a widow, just lost her son. She probably didn't mean what she said.)

3. How to judge criticism for yourself. Assign one of the following scriptures to each pair in your group: Matthew 16:21-23 (Peter disputes Jesus); John 18:28-40 (Jesus before Pilate); and 1 Corinthians 5:1-5 (church discipline). Have the pairs talk about the source and nature of the criticism and the critic's situation in each scripture. Have each pair report its findings to the other pairs in

continued

the small group.

4. Unjust criticism. Say: "Unjust criticism is part of life. Remember you're not responsible for the criticism, but you are responsible for how you react to it. Jesus was more unjustly criticized than anyone."

Ask one person to read aloud 1 Peter 2:22-25. Ask: "How did Jesus react to unjust criticism? How should you react?"

5. Reaction to criticism. Have participants choose one just criticism and one unjust criticism from the list they wrote earlier. Ask several people to tell how they reacted to each criticism. Ask: "What reaction could have been better? Explain."

Have volunteers share what they've learned.

Close with prayer.

and help family groups think of new ways to look at the conflict situations. The family's goal is to reach an agreement on how to resolve each conflict situation.

• When a family group reaches an agreement for each situation, a family member should write the agreement on newsprint and have all family members sign it. This is the contract. Celebrate!

• Continue discussing other conflict situations. Have someone take pictures of each family group.

Role plays—Bring family groups together. Role play the same situations role played in Session 1. This time, have parents and kids role play themselves. Ask: "How was communication different from the first role plays?"

*S*ession 4: Celebration

Singing—Sing group members' favorite songs.

Learning—Have participants tell what they learned about themselves, others and the different kinds of communication.

Committing—Give each person a 3×5 card and a pencil. Have participants write what they'll do to improve communication in their home. For example, one young person might say, "Because I don't like it when my parents get angry about my staying out later than expected, I'll call within 30 minutes of my curfew to talk with them about changes or unexpected occurrences." Encourage volunteers to share what they wrote and why.

Encouraging—Remind parents and teenagers that they haven't solved all their problems in one day. They'll still have disagreements. They may even break their contracts. But now they have a foundation to build on. They can renew their contracts from the "Parent-Kid Negotiations" or even make new ones.

Praying—Have family groups join hands in small family circles. Ask individuals to pray for each family member.

Chapter 18
Programs for Parents

If you've never sponsored programs for parents, you may be a little nervous and uncertain. The ready-made meetings and the retreat in this chapter give you everything you need to conduct successful programs for parents. Keep the following points in mind as you prepare your programs:

• Remember that parents are adults. Their learning skills, needs and inhibitions are different from teenagers' skills, needs and inhibitions.

• Involve parents in discussions and activities.

• Plan well. Parents can tell the difference between well-organized and thrown-together programs. Their time is valuable to them, so make your programs worth their time and effort to participate.

• Some parents don't have a spouse or their spouse isn't an active Christian. Be sensitive to their unique concerns and needs as you lead programs for them.

• See Chapter 5 for more information about programming for parents.

Meeting: Rx for a Healthy Family

Parents are always searching for ways to make family relationships healthy. In her book *Traits of a Healthy Family*, Dolores Curran describes 15 traits that contribute to a healthy family. One trait she suggests is teaching morals. She elaborates on this trait with five directives on how parents can teach morals to their children. This meeting is based on an adaptation of those five directives.

In this meeting parents will:

• talk about what it means to be a healthy family.

• recall the healthy relationships in their own family life when they were teenagers.

• discuss how to teach moral values.

• examine their current family life to see if moral values are being taught.

• write prescriptions for what they need to do to make their family relationships healthy.

*P*reparation

Gather 25 sheets of newsprint, markers, masking tape and for each person, a 3×5 card, pencil, handout, Bible and chair.

Ask three or four parents to help by greeting other parents and making them feel comfortable.

Set up stations with chairs and a place to write. Label the stations one through five clockwise around the room. Photocopy one "Station Instructions" handout (Diagram 34) and cut it apart. Distribute the descriptions to the appropriate stations. Place five sheets of newsprint, tape and a marker at each station.

*M*eeting

Opening—After parents arrive and are introduced to one another, give each person a pencil and a 3×5 card. Ask individuals to list traits they admire in their own parents.

After a few minutes, have each individual read his or her list to the group. After all lists are read, have individuals each circle the parental trait they see in

Diagram 34
Station Instructions
Station 1

Instructions: Read the directive and discuss the questions that follow. Have one person record different answers on the newsprint provided.

To teach moral values, parents need to agree on which values are most important.

1. What values did you learn from your parents? Which values seemed to be most important to them?

2. What values do you want to pass on to your own kids? Why?

3. How can you teach these values to your teenagers? In what specific ways are you teaching these values now?

4. What do you do when you and your spouse disagree on moral values to be taught?

Station 2

Instructions: Read the directive and discuss the questions that follow. Have one person record different answers on the newsprint provided.

To teach moral values, a parent needs to offer clear and specific guidelines about right and wrong.

1. What guidelines did your parents provide when you were a teenager? Were they clear and specific? Explain.

2. What clear and specific guidelines do you offer your kids in areas such as safety, health, education, relationships, responsibility and faith?

3. How can you offer these guidelines in a way your teenager will accept them? How can you communicate these guidelines as goals rather than demands?

4. What do you do when your teenager ignores, rejects or forgets your guidelines?

continued

Station 3

Instructions: Read the directive and discuss the questions that follow. Have one person record different answers on the newsprint provided.

To teach moral values, a parent needs to hold the teenager accountable for his or her moral decisions and behavior.

1. As a teenager, what did you learn from experiences in which you "got away with something"? What did you learn from experiences in which you "got caught"? Explain.

2. *Natural* consequences occur as a result of a particular behavior. For example, a young person who drives too fast can lose control and have an accident. *Logical* consequences are imposed by some authority figure. For example, a young person who drives too fast may get a traffic ticket.
   What would be a natural and a logical consequence for each of the following typical teenage behaviors?
   • Coming in after curfew
   • Getting a bad report card
   • Being dishonest with a parent
   • Having a "fender bender" car accident
   • Being too busy to follow through on commitments
   • Having a messy room
   • Hanging around with friends who abuse drugs

3. Which type of consequence do you use most often with your teenager? Why? Give an example.

Station 4

Instructions: Read the directive and discuss the questions that follow. Have one person record different answers on the newsprint provided.

To teach moral values, family members need to realize that motive plays an important part in judging a parent's or teenager's behavior.

1. Did your parents ever punish you for something you did and then discover that your intention was good? For example, perhaps you messed up the kitchen while trying to bake a birthday cake for your dad. Share your story with the group.

2. Has your teenager ever become angry with you when you were trying to help? For example, perhaps you cleaned up his or her room but threw away some important papers. Talk about this experience. *continued*

3. How can family members effectively determine the motivation behind one another's actions?

4. What kinds of motives are appropriate or inappropriate for disciplining a teenager?

Examples:

Appropriate	**Inappropriate**
For safety.	For hurting the "family name."
To offer an opportunity to think about the behavior's effect on others.	When self-anger is projected toward the teenager.
To make restitution.	When punishment is more convenient than conversation.

5. What do you do when you're unsure about your teenager's motive for his or her behavior?

Station 5

Instructions: Read the directive and discuss the questions that follow. Have one person record different answers on the newsprint provided.

To teach moral values, a parent must help his or her teenager live a moral life.

1. How did your parents help you live a moral life when you were a teenager? Did they lecture, offer rules, talk with you, allow you to struggle, respond to your needs, respect your independence?

2. How do you help your teenager live a moral life? Give specific examples.

3. What specific concerns do you have about helping your young person live a moral life?

4. After listening to others' concerns, do you have any suggestions or ideas that have worked for you? Share these with your group.

themselves and write a personal example of this trait on the back of their 3×5 card. Ask them to share the example with the rest of the group.

Stations—After everyone has been affirmed, say: "This meeting will revolve around five stations based on how to teach those values you admire. In each station you'll look at your past family experiences and then examine the present."

Divide into five groups and assign each group to a station. Instruct groups to follow the instructions at their stations. When you give a signal, have them roll up the newsprint, leave it there and move clockwise to the next station.

Review—When all groups complete the five stations, ask individuals to tape onto the wall all five sheets of newsprint at their last station. Ask groups to look for similarities and differences in responses. After 10 minutes have volunteers from each group read the directives and give a one-minute report on what they found.

Responses—Give each parent a photocopy of the "Rx for My Healthy Family" handout (Diagram 35). Say: "After listening to and discussing all these ideas on how to teach moral values, write a prescription for your family describing what it needs to be healthy. Answer the questions for each part. After writing your prescription, read the suggested scripture passages to see if your prescription agrees with God's guidance."

Closing—After parents complete their prescriptions and check them against God's guidelines, ask parents to form one large circle of chairs and say: "To close this meeting, we need to acknowledge the fact that we can't make our family relationships healthy on our own. Let's pray silently for God's guidance."

Guide this silent prayer with the following statements:

"God, help us teach those moral values we see as most important. (Pause) Help us offer clear and specif-

---

Diagram 35
Rx for My Healthy Family

Instructions: On this form, write a prescription for your family by answering the questions for each part. Be specific on what you'll do and how you'll do it. Complete the activity by comparing your prescription to what God expects.

Rx

The_____family   Date_____

Diagnosis: (What needs do my family members have?)

Rx: (What kinds of actions, behaviors or teachings can I offer to make the relationships between my family members healthy?)

Application: (In what ways can I offer these actions, behaviors or teachings to my family members?)

Refill: (How often should I offer these actions, behaviors or teachings to family members?)

Physician: (By whose authority can I use this prescription with my family? Read Ephesians 5:1-2, 15; 6:4. Does your prescription agree with what God would have you do? If not, amend it to agree. Pray for his guidance.)

---

ic guidelines about right and wrong. (Pause) Help us hold our teenagers accountable for their moral behaviors. (Pause) Help us be open to understanding our teenagers' motives before judging their behavior. (Pause) Help us support our teenagers' attempts to live moral lives. (Pause) God, with your guidance and support, we can teach our teenagers moral values. Our kids can experience growth and our families can celebrate the joy of spiritual health. Thanks for your presence and concern in all we do. In your Son's name we pray. Amen."

Meeting: *The Thrill of Parenting*

Recent studies indicate that parents receive the most joy and satisfaction out of parenting when their children are between ages six and nine. These studies also indicate that parents find the most difficult parenting years are when their children are between ages 10 and 18. Many parents see the adolescent years as being full of turmoil. They need reassurance that their family isn't the only one experiencing change or difficulty. This meeting can help parents understand today's young people, accept the struggles common to the adolescent years and celebrate the opportunities the teenage years offer for growth and insight.

During this meeting parents will:

• meet with other parents and begin to build relationships with them.

• learn that it's normal to see the adolescent years as changing and difficult.

• learn about teenagers' heroes and develop an awareness of what's happening in contemporary youth culture.

• talk about the ideal teenager and the myths that foster a lack of understanding.

• discover what "real" teenagers are like and what

to expect from them.

● recognize their young people as gifts from God.

● develop an action plan for nurturing and understanding their teenagers.

*P*reparation

Gather cassette tapes, music videos, a tape player, a VCR and color television, adhesive name tags, markers, a basket, chairs, newsprint, paper, pencils, tape, white construction paper, glue, scissors and Bibles. Purchase eight different magazines your teenagers read (such as Seventeen, Sports Illustrated or Teen).

Prepare eight puzzles by gluing the covers of the magazines you purchased to white construction paper. To make each cover a puzzle, wait until all parents have arrived at the meeting. Then cut enough pieces so each parent will get one piece.

For each parent, prepare one "Name Guess" name tag on an adhesive name tag by writing the name of a rock star, cult hero or movie idol on it. Use the magazines you purchased to get ideas. Be prepared to identify each famous person and to give parents information about why that person is popular with their teenagers. Be prepared to tell about the movies, videos, song lyrics, TV shows, sports or whatever these people are involved in that kids admire.

Make one copy of "Myths About Teenagers" (Diagram 36) and cut them apart. The myths are adapted from *Thank God I Have a Teenager* by Charles S. Mueller. Make a copy of the "Reward Poster" (Diagram 37) for each participant.

Borrow favorite cassette tapes and music videos from teenagers for the evening. Play them as parents arrive. Give parents a chance to hear the music their kids listen to.

Meeting

Welcome—Welcome parents as they arrive. Play the cassette tapes or music videos you borrowed from their teenagers. Ask each parent to make a name tag to wear. Stick a "Name Guess" name tag on each parent's back without letting the person see who he or she is supposed to be. When all "Name Guess" name tags are in place, say: "Each of you has a name tag on your back that identifies you as someone who's currently popular with teenagers. Mingle throughout the room, asking others one question at a time. Try to find out who you are by asking questions that can be answered yes or no."

After 10 minutes, stop the game and the music and ask everyone to sit down. Ask those who think they've guessed who they are to identify themselves and tell the others what they know about that individual. Ask the rest to look at the name on their back and share any information they might know about the person. Use this opportunity to educate parents about the musicians, TV stars or other famous people who are popular with their kids.

Sum up this section of the meeting by challenging parents to stay aware of what's happening in the youth culture. Offer suggestions to make that happen such as reading kids' magazines, listening to their music, watching videos, TV shows and movies and asking questions when they don't know or understand.

The ideal teenager—Pass a basket containing the puzzle pieces you made ahead of time. Ask each parent to take one piece. Say, "When the music starts, find the other parents who have the pieces necessary to complete your puzzle."

When parents have located the others in their group, have each group complete the puzzle on the floor and arrange chairs in a small circle around the puzzle. Play the music while parents complete this task.

When all groups have finished their puzzles, stop the music and say: "The teenage years are often puzzling to parents. Let's take time to talk about what we understand and don't understand about our teenagers. Let's discuss what the teenage years are all about."

Have members in each small group respond to the following questions one at a time. (Allow two minutes' discussion time for each question.)

• What is your name and what are the names and ages of your teenagers?

• What has been your greatest joy as a parent of a teenager?

• What has been your greatest frustration as the parent of a teenager?

• What puzzles you most about the teenage years?

Give each group a sheet of newsprint and markers. Ask group members to work together to draw a picture of the ideal teenager. Have them draw and label all necessary ingredients, including personality traits and personal habits. Give groups 10 minutes to complete this task. When all groups finish their pictures, have each group select a spokesperson to explain the picture to the total group.

After all groups share and tape their pictures onto the wall, ask the following discussion questions:

• Is it right to have an established ideal for who and what your teenager should be? Why or why not?

• What are the dangers of setting up an ideal?

• What are the advantages?

• Have you ever met the ideal teenager?

The real teenager—After a brief discussion of the ideal teenager, say: "All of us have hopes and dreams for our teenagers. Many of us have created an ideal picture in our minds of what our teenager should be. We have a problem when the ideal picture we create is different from the real picture that exists. This difference can cause many of us to be frustrated with our teenager. Tension builds. The parent-teenager relationship is strained. By taking time to understand what "real teenagers" are like, we can eliminate much of the strain and build stronger relationships with our kids. We can also assure ourselves that our kids are similar to other teenagers."

Give each small group one of the eight "Myths About Teenagers." Have a group member read the myth aloud. Have group members create a one- or two-minute skit that communicates both the myth and the truth. Tell parents to act out an actual incident (illustrating their myth and truth) that occurred in a group member's family. Offer the following rules:

1. Groups will have 10 minutes to prepare their skit.
2. Everyone in the group must have a part.
3. The skit must be one to two minutes long.

Have groups present their skits. After each skit, have parents restate the myth and make summary statements regarding the reality of the teenage years.

Give parents each a sheet of paper and a pencil. Have them fold the paper in half. Ask them to label the left side "Ideal" and the right side "Real." Then say: "Think about your dreams or plans for your teenager. Write these in the 'Ideal' column. Look at each plan or ideal and think realistically about your teenager. Is this his or her plan? Is this his or her dream? Or does it belong to only you?

"In the 'Real' column, write your teenager's dream or plan for the same issue. For example, you may feel that your son should become a doctor because he not only has the ability but would be an excellent addition 'to this fine profession.' Your teenager, however, may feel uneasy about committing himself to all that schooling and therefore may choose a career in nursing or physical therapy.

Diagram 36
Myths About Teenagers

Myth 1: The teenage years are a period of severe personality maladjustment.

Truth 1: Most young people pass through their teenage years unscathed and unscarred, excited about the possibilities of their tomorrows. Studies show that a majority of all teenagers adjust to their daily new experiences with ease and suffer minimal tension through it all. While some have difficulty, only a small fraction represent the extreme most generally featured in dramas, remembered best from books and portrayed clearly on television.

There are many adjustments in the teenage years and a lot of changes. Some of them take place at dizzying speeds. But most young people move from challenge to challenge, from change to change, from choice to choice, with little difficulty. Severe personality maladjustments aren't normal for teenagers; change is. Don't confuse the two.

Myth 2: It's best to grow up as speedily as possible.

Truth 2: Compared with the overall maturation rate of animals, people mature at a leisurely pace. It should seem obvious that the Lord didn't intend the growing process to be hurried, hustled or hastened. No one thinks that a cake can be baked in half the time if the oven is set at twice the recommended temperature. Some tasks (to be done right) take time. Developing a teenager and helping him or her through the early phases of young adulthood is one such task.

Myth 3: Constant conflict between parents and teenagers is normal.

Truth 3: There's nothing normal about constant conflict, no matter who it's between. Constant conflict indicates a problem. Get help. The overwhelming majority of kids don't constantly squabble with their parents. There isn't perpetual tension and deep-seated animosity in the relationship either. Most teenagers love and respect their moms and dads, hold them in high esteem and seek to serve them.

Strange to say, when conflict is present, the parent can actually

continued

initiate it for reasons that have nothing to do with the son or daughter and that are in no way related to the son or daughter. Sometimes parents stir up the pot because they're getting older and think they need some reaffirmation. When that reaffirmation is sought through dominance, there will be conflict.

However, not all conflict is malicious, intentional or negative. Everybody in the house experiences growing pains. Peace and tranquility ultimately come, but they come through a process of inner searching, experimenting with communication between each other and joyfully discovering that the best relationship between parents and teenagers carries the common name "friendship."

Myth 4: It's impossible for teenagers and parents to communicate.

Truth 4: Some teenagers and parents have worked hard at developing necessary communication skills and practice those skills with intensity. Others of us need lessons.

The lesson most of us need is in listening. It shouldn't surprise us that listening is the key to communication. If you can clearly hear what the other person says, the possibility of making a useful response improves dramatically.

If I'm careful about how I speak, I can help teenagers as they travel from where they are to where I am (or where we both ought to be) in the least complicated and most helpful fashion possible. Because I want to do that, I recognize that communication skills are critical. The better the communication, the less the conflict.

Myth 5: Young people today aren't as moral as they used to be.

Truth 5: Do you believe that? Most people seem to. Some adults forget that there were homes for unwed mothers when they were young.

Alcohol is now a severe problem. Yesterday too! What do you think Prohibition was all about? Murder. Rape. Red-light districts. Crime. Delinquency. There was plenty of all that in the past. Read any old newspaper. Search through historical documents. The facts are clear. The texture of life today is no worse than it was yesterday.

But there's something radically different about today's moral dilemmas compared with yesterday's. I was shielded. Weren't you? The average teenager today is confronted with more specific

continued

temptation before noon than I faced through all my high school years. If that's an exaggerated statement, then it's only mildly so.

In our yearning to maintain constitutional safeguards, we permit an inexcusable pressuring of young people that boggles the mind. Teenagers are surrounded by filth, immorality and decadence. Most handle it just fine. Many teenagers chart a course of decency their parents should emulate—in the midst of all that immorality. It's sad that our young people are forced to grow up in a society where what their parents know is wrong surrounds them every moment—an adult-operated society that they didn't make, but must deal with.

Myth 6: The teenage years aren't a period of turmoil.

Truth 6: There's a lot of turmoil going on during the teenage years. That turmoil can't and shouldn't be glossed over. But much of that turmoil has at least one other dimension: It's normal to life. Job described it: "Yet man is born to trouble as surely as sparks fly upward" (Job 5:7).

Acne is turmoil. Menstruation is turmoil. Self-consciousness and awkwardness are turmoil. Physical plainness is turmoil. Ignorance of social skills is turmoil. But all that turmoil is easily controllable. It can be turned around—advantageously.

Acne keeps a lot of kids unattractive at a time in their lives they aren't ready to handle what it means to be attractive. Right? Isn't menstruation a monthly reminder of femininity and sexuality, and doesn't it offer a forced moment for reflecting upon those things and what they could mean? Plainness, self-consciousness and minimal social skills are the stuff out of which growth takes place, *if we exert effort.*

Each of the cited turmoils (and so many others) can turn into a positive moment in the hands of a caring person. They are superb subjects for discussion and sharing. They are the specifics integral to the teenage experience. Out of each exciting perception a new understanding can develop.

Myth 7: Teenagers like to spend a lot of time alone.

Truth 7: Not unless they're forced to. Not unless no one will talk with them. There are times they'll want to be away from parents and family. There are times they'll want to go to their room, listen to their radio or records, and times they'll want to think privately. Private moments are important to life, but so is community time,

continued

especially when that community is the family.

Talk with your teenagers in the subject areas they're most comfortable. Make sure you're in a conversation, not delivering a lecture. Make sure you listen at least as much as you talk. Try to learn.

Myth 8: The teenage years are idyllic, filled with free time.

Truth 8: Many young people have complex schedules and must satisfy intense time demands. Many teenagers have more daily obligations and responsibilities than some adults.

Test it out. Write out your teenager's daily schedule. Don't evaluate it, write it. List the time-consuming obligations he or she has. Total the hours for school, meetings, travel, work, study, satisfying social necessities, church, family and the like.

Teenagers are busy. They have many commitments. Recognize that and help teenagers meet them.

"List your dreams and plans for your teenager in areas such as career choice, life partner, expression of talent and grades. Then take a realistic look at your teenager's view. Ask yourself:
- Am I listening to what my teenager wants?
- Am I forcing my own ideals or dreams on my teenager?
- Am I realistic about what I expect from my teenager?
- Am I open-minded enough to accept my young person's decision?
- Will I affirm my young person no matter what decision he or she makes?"

Response—Ask a volunteer to read aloud Psalm 127 to the entire group. Have parents discuss the following questions:
- What does it mean to understand children as a heritage and reward from the Lord?
- What are some creative ways to cope with and respond to these gifts and rewards from God while they're teenagers? (Encourage parents to talk about creative ideas that have worked for them.)

Closing—Distribute copies of the "Reward Poster" (Diagram 37). Ask parents each to create a "Reward Poster" for their teenager. After five minutes ask parents to share part of their teenager's "Reward Poster" with the rest of the group.

Have parents talk about what they're most thankful for about their young people. Listening to what others are thankful for may trigger new appreciation for others. Conclude this meeting with prayer, asking God for wisdom, courage and strength for these parents as they return home to understand and raise their teenagers.

Diagram 37
Reward Poster

_____
(Your teenager's name)

_____
(State your teenager's value to you in monetary or personal worth such as billions of dollars, a lifetime of joy or an opportunity for celebration.)

(Draw a picture of your teenager emphasizing personal attributes such as a smile if a happy person or a big heart if a caring person.)

Wanted for: (Include things he or she has *done* such as winning first place in the debate tournament, coaching the Special Olympics or serving communion to shut-ins.)

Personal characteristics: (Include descriptions such as being sympathetic with a friend's problems, enthusiastic about family activities or supportive of family members' struggles.)

Personal note: (Write one specific way you want to celebrate with this person who's your reward from God. Think about what would make your son or daughter know he or she is valuable in your eyes.)

Retreat: **Getting Them Through It**

When children reach adolescence, the task of parents and other adults is to "get them through it." This three-session retreat involves parents of teenagers in a unique opportunity to explore the needs and concerns they share. The retreat setting provides a caring experience in which parents can talk with one another and receive support.

In addition to exploring the significant role parents play with their teenagers, participants also will examine personal issues they face when they're called on to parent their teenagers.

After this retreat, you may want to schedule a follow-up session with teenagers and their parents or establish a regular gathering of parents for support and sharing of resources.

In this retreat parents will:

• share stories and concerns about being the parents of teenagers.

• listen to the stories and concerns of other parents of teenagers.

• explore their place in life's journey.

• examine how their personal struggles and concerns affect their feelings and reactions.

• understand the significance of the role they play as adults in the lives of other teenagers.

• understand the need for other significant adults in the lives of their teenagers.

• realize they're not alone in their needs and concerns.

• create a caring support group.

*P*reparation

Gather name tags, newsprint, markers, masking tape, paper, pencils, Bibles, food, snacks and copies of the handouts.

Recruiting parents is the key to this event. A group of 10 to 12 parents works well, and single parents should be encouraged to attend. This retreat has three sessions. An overnight retreat is suggested for a Friday evening and all day Saturday. A night away at a retreat center can help parents experience informal times—at meals, before and after sessions, and during free time—when they can talk about the sharing that has taken place.

Distance to the retreat center will determine when beginning and ending sessions should be held. If the group wants to stay a second night, conclude the event with a worship service Sunday morning after breakfast. If time and travel are an issue, the retreat can be condensed to one intensive day.

Write the retreat schedule and objectives on newsprint. Tape it to the wall at your retreat site.

Write Merton P. Strommen's five cries of youth across the top of a page of newsprint: Loneliness, Family trouble, Outrage, Closed minds and Joy. Leave room under each cry to make a list. Use in Session 3.

Resources that may help you prepare for this retreat include Merton P. Strommen's *Five Cries of Youth* and Henri Nouwen's *Reaching Out: The Three Movements of the Spiritual Life*.

Retreat Schedule
Friday
      6:00 p.m. Dinner
      7:00 p.m. Session 1
      8:30 p.m. Snacks
      Midnight Lights out

Saturday
      8:00 a.m. Breakfast
      9:00 a.m. Session 2

10:30 a.m. Snacks
10:45 a.m. Session 2 continued
    Noon Lunch
 1:00 p.m. Recreation
 2:45 p.m. Snacks
 3:00 p.m. Session 3
 5:30 p.m. Dinner

*R*etreat
Session 1

Welcome—Welcome parents and have them fill out name tags. Invite them to enjoy the fellowship and sharing of other parents plus this time away from their teenagers. Discuss the retreat schedule and objectives.

Encourage an atmosphere of trust. Ask that information shared in the retreat not be discussed with others outside the retreat. Give parents permission not to share if they feel too uncomfortable. But help them understand that the more they trust and become involved, the more they'll gain from the retreat.

Open the session with prayer. Ask God to bless this time together and make it an opportunity for support and fellowship.

Family sketches—Distribute newsprint and markers. Ask parents to sketch their family. (Assure them that stick figures are fine; artistic skills aren't required!) Ask them to identify each family member by first name and age. Under each person's name, have them list three words that describe the person. (Give single parents the choice to omit or list their spouse's name and note if he or she is deceased, divorced, separated or absent from home.)

Discuss the information on the sketches with the total group. Post sketches around the room where they'll be visible throughout the retreat.

Exploring the past—Divide the group of parents

into smaller groups of four. (Spouses should be in the same group.) Pass out paper and pencils and invite individuals to reflect on their experiences as teenagers. Ask each person to make notes and be prepared to talk about how family decisions were made on each of the following topics: money, dating, sex, substance abuse and church life. Read each topic and wait for participants to write their responses. Then ask:

- How were family decisions usually made?
- Was there a standard response handed down as the only possible answer? Explain.
- Was your input requested and listened to before a response was offered? Explain.
- Did anyone care about what you thought? Explain.
- Did anyone know what you thought? Explain.

After a brief discussion, ask for any general observations that surfaced when the small groups shared. Then have group members discuss the following questions:

- How have your past family experiences affected the way things are done now in your family?
- How have different past experiences complicated how you do things and how your family makes decisions?

After 10 minutes, ask small groups to come together and offer a brief report of their discussions. Write discoveries on newsprint, noting similarities.

Break

Roots and wings—When parents return from their break, read the following minilecture.

Minilecture

In an article titled "Roots and Wings," Karen Tye, a seminary student in religious education, responded to the title of the book *Will Our Children Have Faith?* by asking another critical question: "Do *we* have faith?"

As Christian parents, we're deeply concerned about

our teenagers' faith and moral development. Tye reminds us: "The two greatest gifts parents can bequeath to their children are roots and wings . . . roots so that they know who they are and where they came from, and wings so that they can become that which they were created to be!" Though young people may or may not study their Bibles as much as we feel they should, they will examine the lives of the adults they meet—at home, in the church, at school and within the community.

A central issue in Christian parenting is to help our teenagers grow in faith. Put another way, Christian parents want to help their teenagers grow as people who value life. When individuals value life, their actions will benefit themselves and others, and their faith in God will become a guiding force in their lives.

What we do will have more influence than what we say. The interaction we have with our kids and other teenagers must contribute positively to their lives as they grow and develop as human beings and as Christians.

Faith family tree—Give parents each a sheet of paper. Ask them to draw a line from one edge to the other about one-third from the bottom of the paper. This line represents soil. Next ask them to draw a tree trunk from the soil up. Have them put several branches on the tree. Then ask them to draw some roots under the tree in the soil.

Ask parents each to write their name on the tree trunk. Have them write on the roots the names of individuals who've encouraged them in their faith journey—church school teachers, pastors, neighbors, family, friends—any people who've positively influenced them. After the names are added, invite parents to choose a partner other than their spouse and tell about at least two of the people who've encouraged their faith. Allow 10 minutes for sharing.

Closing—Ask participants to tape their trees to the wall and then form a circle with their chairs. Read Galatians 3:1-5, 10-14. Say: "Christ is the example of how individuals who are our roots can give us wings and free us to become the best we can be. Think about the people you listed as your roots, and silently complete the following prayer: 'Thank you, God, for the roots provided by (insert the names you listed earlier).' "

After a few moments invite parents to complete the following phrase: "Thank you, God, for wings that have helped me become . . ." Tell participants to insert words or phrases such as sensitive, caring, a risk taker or a questioner. After several individuals have shared aloud, close with prayer. Ask God to help the parents each recognize their roots and celebrate their wings by being the best that they were created to be.

Snacks—A "make-your-own-sundae" or "make-your-own-pizza" party will offer an informal time for participants to talk together and share personal stories. Be aware of the general feeling level of the parents. Help clarify anything that may have confused them in the opening session.

Session 2

Affirmation and clarification—Review the first session and clarify any schedule or content questions before Session 2 begins. Sing a hymn and open the session with prayer. Encourage participants to maintain their openness and trust in God and in one another.

Issue identification—Say: "During the past week each of your families faced a variety of issues, problems and concerns. List three such issues that confronted your family. Recall how each was resolved." Ask:

- Who made the decision?
- How was the decision received?
- What feelings were present before, during and after the decision? Identify the source of the feelings.

Ask parents to reflect alone for three minutes. Have them make notes on the following questions:

- What values were used to resolve the situation?
- Were religious principles involved? Explain.
- Was personal safety an issue? Why or why not?
- Was peer pressure a factor? Why or why not?

Have participants meet with a partner to discuss their reflections. (Married participants should meet with their spouse.) Then ask each family unit to meet in small groups of four people to talk about one of the situations on its list. Encourage participants to give a brief description of the situation and a more specific explanation of how it was resolved.

After 15 minutes, say: "If teenagers are to grow into responsible adults, they must experience freedom and the responsibility that's part of that freedom. As parents, it's often difficult to see our teenagers experiment with freedom. We don't want them to be hurt, so we become protective, sometimes overly so.

"When we have faith in God, we trust that he'll guide us and give us the strength we need to make good choices with the freedom we have. If we follow God's role model, we must support our teenagers and expect them to make good choices with the freedom they have.

"A major struggle for parents of teenagers is finding the right balance between freedom and control." Give parents each a copy of "The Parenting Conflict" (Diagram 38). Ask them to read it and respond to each statement according to the instructions.

After most people have finished their responses and read the material at the bottom of the handout, say: "This handout illustrates a complex set of tensions. As

Diagram 38
The Parenting Conflict
Freedom and Love Versus Authority and Law

Instructions: Read each statement and respond in one of the following ways:
- Write "X" by the statements you agree with.
- Write "O" by the statements you disagree with.
- Write "?" by the statements you're unsure about.

_____ 1. I want my teenager to experience life.

_____ 2. I want my teenager to have the freedom to develop his or her life in an atmosphere of love.

_____ 3. I don't want my teenager to experience any pain when he or she makes mistakes.

_____ 4. I want lots of rules and regulations so my teenager will know his or her limits.

_____ 5. I expect my teenager to react against me during these years.

_____ 6. I won't allow my teenager to rebel.

_____ 7. I want my teenager to know and live by the rules in our house.

_____ 8. I want to work with my teenager to set limits and make decisions in our family.

_____ 9. I want to retain all authority in our home.

_____ 10. I want my teenager to find out through experience what's good or bad.

Freedom and love—If you agree mostly with statements 1, 2, 5, 8 or 10, you support a freedom approach to parenting. This parenting style offers a creative approach for parents and teenagers to discuss appropriate issues such as curfews, bedroom condition and length of phone calls.

Authority and law—If you agree mostly with statements 3, 4, 6, 7 or 9, you support an authority approach to parenting. This parenting style is appropriate when discussing dangerous situations, illegal actions or potentially self-destructive experiences.

Both parenting styles are appropriate in different situations. Creative learning takes place when parents and teenagers realize that different situations call for different types of parenting.

parents, our task is to know at what point on the
spectrum between freedom and law we can appropriately respond to each child in each situation we face.
There's no easy answer. As the last sentence on the
handout says, 'Creative learning takes place when parents and teenagers realize that different situations call
for different types of parenting.' "

Family situations—Ask parents to choose one of
the three issues they listed at the beginning of Session
2. Have them talk with a partner (spouses, if married)
and determine which style of parenting (freedom and
love or law and authority) affected the situation and
its outcome. Ask family units to share their discussions in groups of three or four.

After a few minutes, say: "No matter what parenting
style you use most often, remember both styles are
appropriate, depending upon the circumstance. The
key is to know which choice you've made and why
so you can talk about it with your teenager."

Snacks—Serve something nutritious such as fruit or
juice.

Midlife parenting—Ask parents to listen to the following statements and think about what they mean:

• Various authorities agree that adults spend the
first half of their lives trying to find out who they are
and the last half living out that identity to the fullest.

• Just when adults begin to change their roles and
expectations for themselves, their children grow older,
become less dependent and begin to make choices of
their own.

• Jesus' description of spiritual rebirth explains
what happens in the midlife transition, that continu-
ous process of changing into a new and different
being.

After a few minutes, ask people to share their
thoughts. After several individuals have shared, say:
"Just when we're called on to parent our teenagers,

most of us reach midlife. This is a period of change and growth, many times described by studies as a crisis.

"In midlife the inner self seeks consciousness, and we begin a personal journey. During this time we realize that all of life isn't related to our social usefulness. We begin to experience moments of reflection and spiritual growth as reality."

Ask parents to share other things that are part of their midlife experience. List these observations on newsprint. After several minutes, summarize the group's expectations of midlife.

Then say: "Just when we're called on to parent our teenagers, we're in the process of personal rebirth. Just when our kids choose to test their freedom and the limits of parental authority, we're struggling with our own transition. At this point in our lives we're vulnerable, even without the challenges of our teenagers!"

Have participants form small groups of three or four people. Ask, "How does our midlife crisis affect our parenting?" Allow 15 minutes for discussion. As each group reports its conclusions to the total group, write the conclusions on newsprint. When all groups have reported, note the similarities.

Then say: "Remember the observations about parenting we made earlier. We talked about how important the actions of parents and other adults are to children and teenagers. We're in a midlife transition precisely the same time our teenagers learn from our actions. They'll naturally challenge any rules and limitations we set. And their challenge will come just when we've determined these are the rules and limitations we choose to live with. It's not easy to be a teenager!"

The influence of other adults—Ask individuals to retrieve their faith family tree from Session 1 from

the walls. Have them look at the adults other than
their parents who were important in their faith journey. Ask them to circle the adults who were important
during their teenage years such as relatives, teachers,
ministers, youth leaders, church school teachers,
coaches, employers or neighbors.

Have parents list five adults who are important to
their teenagers. Then say: "These are the adults your
teenager learns from by example. You may want to
visit with these individuals to share the concerns and
needs you perceive your teenager has. You may want
to talk with them about the needs and concerns you
have as a parent. These individuals may be able to
help both you and your teenager when they gain your
insights."

You as a significant adult—Say: "You're an important adult to your teenager's friends. You're also an
important adult to your friends' teenagers. Therefore
be diligent and strong in expressing your faith.

"Think about the teenagers who might list you as a
root on their faith family tree. Write their names in
the branches of your tree." Tell parents to circle three
names then answer the following questions:

• How and where do you witness to these young
people?

• What are three specific ways in which you can
and do influence their lives?

• Are there things they learn from you that you
wouldn't want your teenager to learn from other
adults?

Allow five minutes for reflection. Ask if anyone
would like to talk about observations he or she has
made during this time.

Closing—Pass out Bibles to each group of three.
Invite participants to read 1 Corinthians 13, the love
chapter. Have parents rewrite this chapter as goals for
parents of teenagers. For example, they might rewrite

the first verse as "I'll make sure that what I say to my teenager is backed by positive action."

Allow 10 minutes for this activity.

Then form a large circle and have the groups share their rewrites of each verse. Close with a prayer.

Session 3

Take a look—This final session offers parents a chance to use the insights they've gained about themselves and their teenagers.

Give each parent the handout "A Look at My Teenager" (Diagram 39). Say: "Our teenagers aren't always the same with us as they are with others. It's important for us to look at our kids carefully—through our eyes, through others' eyes and through God's eyes.

"When you look at the handout, you'll notice three pairs of glasses that represent the different views of our teenagers. Take a few minutes to think about your teenager's positive qualities and those he or she needs to improve. Look at the qualities from all three viewpoints. At the bottom of the page, list specific ways you can affirm your teenager and ways you can help him or her improve."

After five minutes, ask parents to meet in small groups of four to talk about what they wrote. After 10 minutes, bring all groups together and ask:

● Which viewpoint was most critical? Why?

● Which viewpoint was most accepting? Why?

● Which form of affirmation would be most appropriate for your teenager? Why?

● Which form of help would be most acceptable to your teenager? Why?

● What did you learn about yourself through this experience?

Listen to the cries—After looking at their teenagers, it's important for parents to evaluate what they see.

Diagram 39
A Look at My Teenager

Instructions: In the left lens of each pair of glasses, list your teenager's good qualities that you, others and God would see. In the right lens of each pair of glasses, list your teenager's qualities that need improvement. At the bottom of the page, list specific ways you can affirm your teenager and help improve his or her other qualities.

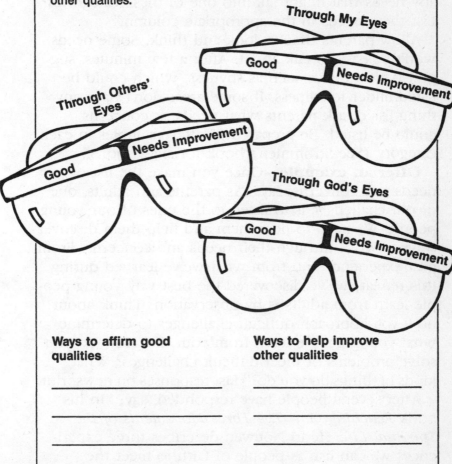

Ways to affirm good qualities

_____

_____

_____

_____

Ways to help improve other qualities

_____

_____

_____

_____

Turn to the newsprint on which you listed the five cries of youth. Say: "In the book *Five Cries of Youth*, Merton P. Strommen identifies the five deepest concerns and needs of young people as loneliness, family trouble, outrage, closed minds and joy.

"Look again at the lists you made of areas in which your teenager needs to improve. Can you determine any needs that might fall into one of these categories? List these needs in the appropriate column."

Allow parents time to look and think. Some needs won't be easy to talk about. After a few minutes, suggest typical needs such as shyness, which could be listed under loneliness. If some areas don't have anything listed, ask parents what needs or concerns could be listed. Be prepared to offer examples in each category. (See Strommen's book for suggestions.)

Offer an example—Once you make the list of needs and concerns, say: "As parents and adults, one of our challenges is to listen to the cries of our young people. We need to hear them and help them discover ways to work through their needs and concerns. From past experience and from what we've learned during this retreat, we've discovered the best way young people learn from adults is by observation. Think about how you approach difficult challenges to determine what young people learn from your life. How do you solve problems or meet difficult challenges? What kinds of things do you do?" List responses on newsprint.

After several people have responded, say: "In his book *Reaching Out: The Three Movements of the Spiritual Life*, Henri Nouwen describes three experiences we can use as people of faith to meet the challenges in our lives: solitude, hospitality and prayer. Give each person a Bible and an "Our Example" handout (Diagram 40). Have parents form three groups, and give each group one of the assignments on the handout. Ask participants to read their assign-

Diagram 40
Our Example

Instructions: Read your assignment and list the scripture passages you find. Be prepared to share your findings with the other groups.

Assignment 1:
Solitude is the experience we have when we get away from the everyday rush of our busy lives. To grow in our faith we need to spend time alone with ourselves and God. We need time to think, to reflect and to dream. We also need time to open ourselves and listen.

Look through the Gospels. See when, why and how Jesus spent time in solitude. He's our example.

Assignment 2:
Hospitality is the experience of reaching out to a growing circle of people to discover more of God's magnificent differences. The more people we meet and relate to, the richer our lives will be.

Look through the Gospels. See how many kinds of people Jesus associated with. Discover how wide Jesus' circle of relationships was. He's our example.

Assignment 3:
Prayer is part of the experience of our relationship with God—of realizing our Creator is in control and ultimately sustains life. We live a life of prayer when we recognize our human limitations and ask for God's presence and guidance in every aspect of life.

Look through the Gospels. Find evidence that Jesus was aware of God's presence and availability as guardian and guide. He's our example.

ment and follow the instructions on the handout.

After all three groups have completed their assignments, regroup and ask volunteers to report each group's findings. Then ask participants to turn their handouts over and individually respond to the following:

• List ways you currently use solitude, hospitality and prayer in your life.

• In what ways do these experiences influence the time you spend with your family or other young people?

• List three things you've learned from this retreat. Did it cause you to rethink something? Was there a new thought? Was one point especially helpful for your family situation?

Allow 10 minutes for this time of reflection. Then ask participants to join with someone (other than their spouse, if married) to talk about what they've learned. After five minutes of talking in pairs, invite volunteers to share what they've learned with the rest of the group.

Closing—Ask participants to form a circle with their chairs. Make sure everyone has paper and a pencil. Say: "We've looked at our teenagers, along with their needs and concerns. We've examined ourselves, including our own needs and concerns. We also looked at Jesus and how he handled his needs and concerns.

"We've acknowledged and celebrated our roots— those individuals who've lifted us up and given us support in our faith journey. Now it's time for us to use our wings—to 'fly' with purpose and direction toward those young people who need our support and affirmation.

"Just to 'get them through it' isn't enough. We must make a conscious effort to work with our teenagers. We must answer their questions, clarify their confusion, and encourage them to initiate action that will help them grow and develop in their own faith journey.

"Think of one specific way you can love, nurture and support your teenager. Write it on your paper. Once you've written your response, make an airplane out of your paper and give your idea wings. Fly your airplane around the circle. To show your support for other parents, pick up their planes and fly them around the circle. When I say stop, pick up the plane nearest you. I'll ask individuals to volunteer to read these ideas to the group." After everyone has shared, read Isaiah 40:28-31. Close with prayer and a group hug.

Chapter 19
*P*rograms for Teenagers

*T*eenagers want to understand their families and build family relationships. This chapter consists of two meetings and a lock-in to help teenagers understand family issues. Keep the following guidelines in mind as you lead these programs:

• Kids come from different types of homes. Avoid making generalizations about their parents.

• Some family issues may be difficult for teenagers— particularly those from dysfunctional families. Be sensitive to these unique problems as you lead activities and discussions.

• Make meetings constructive. Kids may need to air their frustrations, but challenge them to move beyond their complaints to build better relationships.

• Encourage teenagers to share with their parents what they learned.

Meeting: **Hearing Assistance Lab**

When Jesus says, "He who has ears, let him hear" (Matthew 11:15), he refers to more than our physical ears. He's speaking to human beings and their need to listen to one another. The Bible offers numerous "hearing aids" that can help individuals learn how to listen and respond to what they hear. The ability to listen is especially valuable within the family.

During this meeting teenagers will:

• listen to the parable of the sower and discuss different ways of hearing.

• talk about who they should and shouldn't listen to.

• develop a list of hearing aids that help in receiving messages.

• practice the art of listening.

• make a commitment to use their ears as God intended, both within and outside the family.

*P*reparation

Gather songbooks, copies of the handouts, newsprint, construction paper, scissors, glue, staplers, markers, paper, pencils, tape and, for each person, a Bible and 10 small gummed labels.

Make construction paper ears or hearing devices such as headphones for participants to copy. Place the construction paper, scissors, markers, glue, staplers, tape and string on a table near the entrance.

Write the following situations each on a separate slip of paper—or create your own. These will be used in the "Response" section.

• Sally's mother just heard disturbing news about her daughter, but it's only partially true. Sally tries to decide how to talk with her mother about the situation when her mother confronts her with what she's heard.

• In spite of his father's warnings to be careful with the car, Dave had an accident that seemed to be his fault. While his dad expresses his disappointment, Dave tries to explain what happened.

• Brenda received a letter from her boyfriend and left it on the table. Brenda's mother returned home from work and cleared the table. She stuffed the letter in the envelope and placed it on Brenda's bed. Brenda is concerned that her mother has read the letter.

• Margaret finds it difficult to listen to her mother's disparaging remarks about her father. Since her parents' divorce, Margaret feels many of their misunderstandings would be resolved if they'd listen to what each other was saying. She wants to get her parents together to talk.

Ask four young people to act out the "Bible Study Skit" (Diagram 41). Give them copies of the skit and schedule a practice when you can be there to help.

Make two lists on newsprint:

Who Should I Listen To?	**Who Shouldn't I Listen To?**
Proverbs 4:1	Ecclesiastes 7:5
Ecclesiastes 7:5	Ephesians 4:27
Ezekiel 3:10	2 Peter 2:7-8
Romans 10:17	

*M*eeting

As everyone arrives—Have individuals each design a pair of ears or a listening device like the samples. Ask them each to write their name on the back and take it to the meeting area.

Opening—Begin the meeting by asking a small group to start singing "Listen to My Heart Song" from *Songs* (Songs and Creations). As others move into the meeting area, include them in the singing. Open with the following prayer: "God, thank you for listening to us. Sometimes we don't listen to you or to one another. Show us how to be better listeners. Help us put what we learn into practice. Amen."

Ask a volunteer to read Matthew 11:15. Say: "Although we all have ears, we often fail to use them properly. To help us become more aware of our ears, look at the

Diagram 41
Bible Study Skit

Narrator: Mom watches through the window as Cindy and Jane climb out of Dave Turner's car. The girls come into the house laughing and talking, obviously having a good time.

Mom: Cindy, Jane, why were you out with Dave Turner? You know I don't approve of you being with him.

Cindy: We didn't really go out with him, Mom. He just gave us a ride home.

Mom: Well, don't let it happen again. He isn't the kind of boy I want you to associate with.

Cindy: All right, Mom.

Jane: Oh, Mom, what's wrong with him? You wouldn't approve no matter who we came home with. You never approve of anything we do.

Mom: That's not true, Jane, and you know it. Dave Turner doesn't have a good reputation, and I don't want you involved with him in any way. Is that clear?

Cindy: Yes, Mom.

(Jane casts her mother a belligerent glance.)

Mom: Jane, did you understand me?

Jane: Yes, "Tyrant."

(Jane stalks away from her mother, followed by Cindy.)

Mom: (Sighing and shaking her head): Why can't Jane be like Cindy?

(When the girls are some distance from their mother, they stop to talk.)

Jane: Cindy, how can you stand to listen to Mom? I think she's really being unfair.

Cindy: Don't let what she says get to you, Jane! Just do what I do—let it go in one ear and out the other. [Exit]

(Across the room Mom looks shocked, frowns and shakes her head. [Exit].)

paper ears or listening devices you created. What are
some blessings you've received from your ability to
hear? What opportunities are provided by our ears?"
If people need help to get started, suggest opportunities such as hearing news to pray about, responding to
someone's need or responding to a sermon.

Bible study—Read Luke 8:4-15. Ask participants to
watch the skit and look for examples of what Jesus
was talking about.

Discuss the skit by asking the following questions:

• How does the skit relate to the parable of the
sower?

• Which character most resembles the seed that fell
by the wayside or among thorns? Why?

• Which character most resembles the seed that fell
on the rock? Why?

• Was the mother a good listener? Why or why not?

• Should we always listen to our parents? Why or
why not?

After a brief discussion of the last question, say:
"How do we know who we should and shouldn't listen to? The Bible gives guidelines to help us with this
decision." Call participants' attention to the two newsprint lists: "Who Should I Listen To?" and "Who
Shouldn't I Listen To?" Form up to seven groups. Give
each group a scripture passage to read and report on
to the others. After the groups have reported their
findings, ask:

• Who else should we listen to? Why?

• Who else shouldn't we listen to? Why?

After a brief discussion, say: "You've talked about
who you should and shouldn't listen to. It's also important to think about what kind of listener you are.
Think about the parable of the sower and the seed
that fell on good soil. How can you become the 'good
soil' in your family, the kind of listener that responds
and produces an abundant crop?"

Give each participant 10 gummed labels. Say: "Think about the hearing aids you use to help you receive messages in the proper manner such as not talking when someone is speaking or watching body language as someone speaks. List on your gummed labels the hearing aids you use, and attach them to the ears or listening device you created earlier. Hearing aids could include keeping an open mind, meditating or thinking about a problem, trying to understand and love others, and praying in all situations.

Response—Ask participants to pair up. Give each pair a slip of paper that describes a situation in which one individual conveys a message to the other. Ask each pair to prepare a dialogue, implementing as many hearing aids as possible. Hearing aids could include an open mind, mutual respect, compassion and a willingness to listen. Give pairs about 10 minutes to prepare their dialogues.

Encourage several pairs to share. Highlight the hearing aids they used. If the group is small, listen to every pair.

Closing—Ask participants each to choose one hearing aid they intend to use during the week. Ask them to take the ears or devices home to remind them to listen to others.

Pass out copies of the "Responsive Reading" (Diagram 42) and form two groups. Ask one group to read "Side 1" and the other group to read "Side 2." Have everyone read "All." Lead the reading.

Ask the group to sing "Open My Eyes That I May See" from *Songs* (Songs and Creations).

After the song, ask a volunteer to give the following prayer of dedication: "God, we offer our ears to you. Help us use them to promote understanding with one another and within our families. Amen."

Diagram 42
Responsive Reading

All: In all my relationships, especially in my family, I promise to "be quick to listen, slow to speak and slow to become angry" (James 1:19b).

Side 1: I pledge to listen to what others say. I'll refrain from passing judgment until I hear the whole story.

Side 2: I pledge to hear my parents' and other adults' instructions and try to understand the reasons behind the decisions they make.

All: I pledge to place my ears—my ability to listen—in God's hands and ask for his guidance to listen as he intended.

Meeting: **Excuses, Excuses**

The adolescent years provide teenagers and their parents with numerous opportunities for misunderstandings and attempts to clarify what was said or what really happened. Parents think they've heard every excuse possible, but teenagers create more. Parents suddenly find themselves explaining their own decisions or actions to young people who no longer accept the response, "Because that's the way it is."

Although this stressful time produces tension, it also gives family members a chance to recognize one another as human beings. Parents no longer sit on a pedestal, and teenagers have the skill to make many decisions on their own. Their relationship has changed and grown. Parents and teenagers can not only look at and talk about their misunderstandings, but they can also laugh at them.

In this meeting teenagers will:
- enjoy a non-threatening game show format.
- listen to excuses teenagers use.
- listen to excuses parents use.
- evaluate excuses in different ways such as humorous, believable or emotional.
- talk about why and when excuses are needed.
- discuss the value of forgiveness.
- initiate the opportunity for forgiveness to occur within their families.

*P*reparation

Gather a tape recorder, cassette tapes, two long tables, four chairs, four pads of paper, pencils, newsprint, posterboard, markers, tape, scissors and paper (five sheets for each participant). A video camera, videotape and VCR are optional. Make copies of the "Certificates of Forgiveness."

Make a large sign on newsprint that says "Excuses, Excuses." Then prepare four smaller signs with the numbers 1, 2, 3 and 4 on separate sheets of newsprint. Make a sign that says "Applause."

Tape the "Excuses, Excuses" sign on the front wall. Under the sign, set up one long table with four chairs facing the audience. On the table in front of each chair, tape a number. Place a pad of paper and a pencil at each place. Set the other long table near the entrance. Place paper and several markers on it.

Read the meeting thoroughly. Choose four teenagers to be game show panelists. Prepare your welcome and your introductions of the panelists ahead of time.

Ask a young person to serve as announcer and scorekeeper for your program. Give him or her instructions ahead of time. Have this person interrupt the game to announce the "Double-Point Round" in which the winner receives twice as many points as usual.

Tape game show music ahead of time to be played as you walk onto the stage.

Ask a parent or volunteer to videotape the program for later viewing. The tape provides an optional but fun activity to show at the end of this meeting or to show at a parents meeting.

On newsprint, prepare one large certificate for the winner. Design your own or adapt the idea shown in Diagram 43.

Meeting

As teenagers arrive—Have kids go to the table by the door. Ask them to get four sheets of paper and use the markers to write the numbers 1, 2, 3 and 4 on individual sheets. Ask the first two people who arrive to help you by explaining these same instructions to others.

When most have arrived, ask the audience to be seated. Instruct one person in the front row to raise and lower the "Applause" sign when you give the cues.

The game—To begin the game, ask your announcer to introduce you by saying: "It's time for the #1 game show in America—'Excuses, Excuses.' And now, here's America's #1 game show host— ____(your name)____!" Have the announcer play the music as you walk on stage. Cue your sign holder to raise the "Applause" sign so everyone will cheer. After a few seconds cue your sign holder to lower the sign. Then explain the game.

Welcome your viewing audience with the typical grandiose statements most game show hosts make about being the best, the most interesting, the most realistic program on the air. Introduce your four panelists with a crazy story about each one. Then say: "All of you know how to play 'Excuses, Excuses,' but I'll explain it to our audience. I'll read some hypothet-

Diagram 43
Excuses, Excuses

This certificate frees

_____

from having to have an excuse.

Valid for one year from this date.

_____

(Date)

ical situations involving parents and their teenagers. Then I'll give our panelists one minute to write the best excuse they can. Sometimes I may ask for the most believable excuse. Other times I may ask for the funniest excuse. The panelists must listen carefully to the type of excuse I ask for.

"After one minute, panelists will each read their excuse. Then the audience will vote on which excuse is best.

"Remember, panelists, your goal is to win the vote of the audience. The panelist with the most votes for each situation will win 100 points. If that panelist wins with over half the votes from the audience, he or she will double the winnings and earn 200 points. And don't forget that 'Double-Point Round' that can happen at any time!

"And now, if there are no questions, let's play 'Excuses, Excuses'!"

Alternate between parent and teenager excuses. Take a vote after each set of excuses is read. Have the scorekeeper tally the vote so the audience (and video camera) can see who's ahead.

Ask for different kinds of excuses after each of the following situations. Rather than ask for the best excuse, you might ask for the worst excuse, the most believable, the least believable or the most apologetic. Use your imagination.

Situations

You're a teenager and . . .

1. You've been out late with several of your friends. You ended up going to a movie that your mom told you not to see. Unfortunately, it ran later than you thought, and you're coming in one hour after your curfew. Your mom is still up, waiting in her robe. She doesn't look happy!

2. You're in love. Because of your romance, you've neglected your studies. You've dropped two grades in math, which is typically your best class. This report card eliminates your graduating with honors and forfeits a large scholarship to the university. Your financially struggling parents were counting on this scholarship to get you through college. When you walk in, your dad smiles and asks to see your report card.

3. You finally got your drivers license! You made the highest grade in your drivers education class. Each time you drove with your dad he was impressed with your attentive, defensive style of driving.

On the first weekend after getting your license, your dad gave you the keys because he knows you drive better than any of your friends. Unfortunately, when challenged at a stoplight by a popular high school athlete, your ego got the best of you and you accepted the challenge. You're not sure exactly what happened, but you temporarily lost control, went over the curb, knocked over a trash can and customized the right front fender of your dad's pride and joy. When you walk in he asks, "Well, how did it go, #1 safe driver?"

4. Your parents have planned an evening out. Although they've always told you not to have anyone else in the house when they're gone, you figure your own home is the safest place for you and your sweetheart to have some fun. You set the alarm clock so your sweetheart can get out of the house before your parents get home. Then the kissing begins! With the dim lights in the living room and soft music on the stereo, the situation feels like it's getting a little out of control. Just when the two of you decide you'd better cool it before you're both sorry, you hear the back door open. Your parents have come home early, and they're coming through the kitchen. They'll be in the living room any second now. What do you tell them

when they see you there with your sweetheart?

You're a parent and . . .

1. You're so proud of your daughter who's gone to her first school dance. No one asked her to go, but a lot of her friends were going together, so you took her to the gymnasium. When you let her out, she reminded you to pick her up at 9 p.m. when the dance was scheduled to end.

You went home and relaxed on the couch to watch television. That's the last thing you remember until you heard the phone ring. You looked at the clock and realized it was 10:15 p.m. Rushing to the school, you find your daughter, sitting outside alone. Her outfit is a mess, and her mascara is smeared down her face. She tells you she called and called, and you never answered. What excuse do you give for being late?

2. You've invested hundreds of dollars in your son's piano lessons. He practices religiously for two hours a day, sometimes longer on weekends. He's even said he wants to become a concert pianist.

Tonight his new band is going to play at a club. You're so proud of him that you invite the minister to share in a surprise celebration you've planned to wish your son luck before he leaves the house. When the minister arrives, you call your son into the den to see this secret admirer who wants to wish him well. As you're complimenting the minister on last Sunday's sermon, your son walks into the room. His hair is pink and standing straight up. He's wearing heavy makeup, dressed in an all-black leather outfit and wrapped in several pounds of chains. He smiles, obviously pleased to see one of his favorite people, then extends his hand with brightly painted fingernails and numerous rings. After the handshake, your son hears a horn outside and rushes out the door. The minister turns and looks at you. What do you say?

3. You're excited. It's the first time the high school

administration has asked you to chaperon a party. You remember how much fun the dances were when you were in school. The night of the dance, you're getting ready to go. Your daughter is also getting ready. She notices you're getting dressed up and asks, "Hey, where are you going tonight?"

You tell her the principal asked you to be a chaperon at the school dance tonight. When she hears this, your daughter starts screaming and runs into her room. "I can't believe it!" she yells. "Why didn't you tell me? Why didn't you ask me first?" Apparently she's unhappy about your being at the dance. What excuse do you give her for not checking with her?

4. You think it's the best-looking jacket in the world! You wore it to your high school graduation, and now your son gets to wear it to his. He'll be so proud! He's been asking for a new jacket because everyone else is getting one and he wants to be in style. You've told him you want to surprise him on graduation day with the most stylish jacket there.

It's time to leave for the graduation exercises, and you hand him a box with the jacket inside. He opens the box enthusiastically, anticipating a fashionable article of clothing. When he sees the checkerboard pattern and the wide lapels and then smells the mothballs, his mouth opens wide. He looks at you and says, "This is a joke, right?" What do you say?

At the end of the game, tally the score and announce the winner. Give that person the certificate you prepared ahead of time. Say: "Because you've proved you can devise any kind of excuse in any kind of situation, this certificate frees you from having to have an excuse for one year. Of course, you'll have to explain to others how and why this certificate is good for an excuse, but that should be no problem for you."

Stop videotaping here.

Response—Ask group members to choose a partner. Give each person a pencil and paper and ask, "Why do we need excuses?" When people say that it's usually for forgiveness for something we've done or haven't done, say: "Think about the last time you needed an excuse for what you did or didn't do. Perhaps you watched television instead of cleaning the kitchen as you promised.

"Think about the last time your parent needed an excuse for something he or she did or didn't do. Perhaps your father used your car keys and dropped them in his coat pocket instead of putting them back in your purse.

"Use the next five minutes to write about your experience. Share your story with your partner. Have partners respond with the best excuse they can think of. If the excuse is acceptable to you, draw a happy face on your partner's paper. If the excuse is unacceptable, draw a sad face and explain why that excuse is unacceptable."

Ask two volunteers to read aloud Matthew 18:21-22 and Mark 3:24-25. Ask partners to discuss how these scripture passages apply to forgiveness in families. After a few minutes ask pairs to briefly share their discussions with the total group.

Closing—Give each person a copy of the "Certificates of Forgiveness" handout (Diagram 44).

Say: "Within our families there are times to forgive and times we need to ask for forgiveness. Complete both certificates of forgiveness. Decide on a time to meet with that family member to talk about the situation and how it can be resolved. Plan a way the two of you can celebrate the forgiveness.

"Discuss your certificates with one other person in the group. Pray for each other and plan to check with each other later in the week to see how plans went." After a few minutes, close the session with prayer.

Diagram 44
Certificates of Forgiveness

Certificate of Forgiveness
To

_____

**Because I want our home to remain
undivided, *I'm* willing to forgive *you* for**

_____
_____
_____

To celebrate this forgiveness, let's

_____
_____

_____   _____
(Name)   (Name)

_____   _____
(Date)   (Date)

Certificate of Forgiveness
To

_____

**Because I want our home to remain
undivided, I hope *you* will forgive *me* for**

_____
_____

To celebrate this forgiveness, let's

_____
_____

_____   _____
(Name)   (Name)

_____   _____
(Date)   (Date)

Snack on refreshments while you watch the video-tape of the game show.

Lock-In: The Burning-Coals Approach to Confrontation

Even the best parents sometimes deal with their teenagers unfairly. When teenagers react angrily or defiantly, the situation usually escalates, damaging family relationships further. When teenagers respond with the burning-coals approach—offering a positive, patient response to a frustrating, negative confrontation—parents can feel free to examine their own words or actions. This approach encourages family relationships to grow beyond the pain of injustice.

During this lock-in teenagers will:
- learn how to react to unfair treatment.
- discover Bible verses to use as guidelines.
- explore examples of interaction in difficult situations.
- accept the challenge to build better relationships with family and friends.

*P*reparation

Gather copies of handouts, pencils, paper, Bibles, construction paper, scissors, glue, sacks, markers, a trash can, an offering plate and for each person, 12 gummed labels.

Prepare enough sugar cookie dough for each person to make six or more cookies. Keep dough and rolling pin chilled until ready to use. Use a collection of cookie cutters or let participants create their own out of construction paper. Make several colors of "paint" when you're ready for refreshments. Use 1 egg yolk, ¼ teaspoon of water and enough food coloring to make desired colors. Supply small paintbrushes for each color.

Make arrangements for all snacks and a pancake breakfast.

Ask two teenagers ahead of time to present the skit at the beginning of the lock-in (Diagram 45).

Cut orange construction paper into the shape of flames of fire. Tape a long sheet of newsprint horizontally across one wall.

Optional: Order the film *When Heroes Fall* from Audience Planners, Inc., 5107 Douglas Fir Rd., Calabasas, CA 91302 (1-800-624-8613). Arrange for a film projector and screen. Preview the film. Check material that accompanies it and revise discussion questions to fit your group.

Lock-In Schedule

8:00 p.m.	Welcome
8:30 p.m.	Introduce the theme
8:45 p.m.	Puppet plays
9:45 p.m.	Break
10:00 p.m.	Bible study
11:00 p.m.	Refreshments
Midnight	Exercise break
12:15 a.m.	"How Would You React?"
1:00 a.m.	Movie (optional)
1:30 a.m.	Discussion (optional)
2:00 a.m.	Relaxation and sleep
6:30 a.m.	Morning exercise
7:30 a.m.	Breakfast
8:30 a.m.	Closing worship

Adapt the schedule to suit your group. If an activity is going well, extend the time. In small groups, sharing times may be shorter.

Lock-In

Welcome—As teenagers arrive, point out the long sheet of newsprint taped to the wall. Ask individuals to write descriptions of unfair treatment that bothers them. For example, parents not listening to their side of the story when they have a problem with a teacher at school.

When everyone has arrived, welcome the group and explain the schedule for the lock-in. Discuss the descriptions on newsprint.

Introduce the theme—Have the teenagers you asked ahead of time present the skit "Playing With Fire" (Diagram 45).

After the skit, say: "In the Bible, fire is often referred to as a cleansing agent. Many times throughout the Old Testament, the Israelites were instructed to offer a burnt offering to the Lord. In the New Testament, the cleansing power of the Holy Spirit is often associated with fire.

Puppet plays—Divide students into four small groups. Assign each group one of the following scripture passages. Ask members to make puppets and dramatize the story. (Supply sacks, construction paper, markers, scissors and glue.)

Moses and the burning bush—Exodus 3:1-6

Elijah and the fire from heaven—1 Kings 18:30-38

Isaiah's vision—Isaiah 6:1-8

Three Hebrews in the fiery furnace—Daniel 3:19-27

Allow at least 30 minutes for the small groups to prepare their puppets and presentations. As each group presents its puppet play, have members of the audience hold up their hands as soon as they know which story is being portrayed. Freeze the action and see how many details of the story the audience can recall. Then let the puppet play continue.

Bible study—Reread Proverbs 25:21-22. Say: "We're going to read several real-life situations and talk about responses we might have. We'll listen to several scripture passages. Then we'll see how a warm response melts antagonism and difficulty in a relationship and how a cold, harsh response only intensifies the struggle between people."

Distribute copies of "Burning-Coal Situations" (Diagram 46). As you introduce each situation, ask for vol-

Diagram 45
Playing With Fire

Brenda: Debbie, weren't you on the planning committee for this lock-in?

Debbie: Yes, I was. Why?

Brenda: I've been trying all week to figure out what this title means, but I couldn't imagine what it was. I thought we were supposed to talk about how to handle unfair treatment. What does the burning-coals approach mean?

Debbie: We're supposed to heap burning coals on the heads of our parents, siblings, friends, whoever . . .

Brenda: (Jumps in immediately.) You're kidding!

Debbie: No, the formula comes right out of the Bible. (Hands a Bible to Brenda.) Here, read Proverbs 25:22 for yourself.

Brenda: "In doing this, you will heap burning coals on his head, and the Lord will reward you" (Proverbs 25:22). This doesn't sound like anything else I've read in the Bible. I can't imagine ever getting angry enough to put a burning coal on anyone's head.

Debbie: Read the 21st verse. Maybe that will help clear up the mystery.

Brenda: "If your enemy is hungry, give him food to eat; if he is thirsty, give him water to drink" (Proverbs 25:21). Oh, I get it. If someone is out to get us and we react with kindness, then that person will think twice about how he or she acted. That may bring about a change as great as if we'd used burning coals in the confrontation.

Debbie: Now you've got it. I just hope it works when I try it on my parents.

Diagram 46
Burning-Coal Situations

Situation 1: Mom enters your room, which isn't as neat as it should be. Snatching up one of your magazines that you left open on the floor, she rips it in two. Then she says: "Look at this room! Why do you insist on living in a pigpen? Get busy and straighten it up before you do anything else. I don't want to come home tomorrow to find this room looking like it does now!"

Scripture passages: Matthew 5:41, Proverbs 15:1

Lump of coal 1: "How dare you come in here and destroy my property! You can talk about my mess, but what about your laundry room? If you don't want to come home until I've straightened up my room, then don't come home for a long time."

Burning coal 1: "Okay, Mom, I'll take care of it. I'm sorry I upset you." After Mom leaves, you clean not only your room, but the laundry room as well. About the time you expect your parents to come home, you have a batch of chocolate chip cookies baking in the oven.

Discussion questions:
- What did you think about the lump-of-coal approach?
- What did you think about the burning-coals approach?
- What other scripture passages support the burning-coals approach?
- If you were the mom, how would you have responded to the two approaches? Why?

Situation 2: You've just picked up your check from the warehouse where you work part-time. For the third time, the paymaster has made a mistake on your check. Instead of paying you for the 14 hours you've actually worked, he's paid you for 12. You believe he's doing this deliberately because he doesn't like you.

Scripture passages: Proverbs 25:15; James 1:4

Lump of coal 2: "Look, I'm getting tired of being cheated on every paycheck. This is the third time it's happened and I think you're doing it on purpose. I want another check right now. And if this happens again, I'm going straight to the boss."

Burning coal 2: "I'm sorry I have to bother you again, but I was supposed to be paid for 14 hours. Could you please check the records and give me a new or an additional check since I'm short of cash this week?"

Discussion questions:
- What did you think about the lump-of-coal approach?
- What did you think about the burning-coals approach?
- What other scripture passages support the burning-coals approach?
- If you were the paymaster, how would you have responded to the two approaches? Why? *continued*

Situation 3: Mom has given you her charge card to pick up an item she wants at the department store. While there, you find a record album that you buy with money you earned from your part-time job. When you get home, Mom assumes you used her charge card to buy the album and loses her temper. "Young man, you're grounded for a week. I trusted you with my charge card, and what do you do? It'll be a long time before I trust you again."

Scripture passage: Colossians 3:12-13

Lump of coal 3: "How dare you talk to me like that when I'm not guilty? Here, take your old charge card! For your information, I didn't use it to buy this album. I bought it with my own money that I worked for and saved. Next time run your own errands."

Burning coal 3: "Mom, I didn't use your charge card. I bought the album with the money I've saved from my job. I hope you'll trust me to help you out again."

Discussion questions:
• What did you think about the lump-of-coal approach?
• What did you think about the burning-coals approach?
• What other scripture passages support the burning-coals approach?
• If you were the mom, how would you have responded to the two approaches? Why?

Situation 4: You've gone to the office to help your dad pack tools because he's behind in shipping. You pick the wrong tool from the shelf, and your dad catches the mistake just as you put it in the shipment. "Hey," he says, "I brought you down here to help me get ahead, not behind. If you ship the wrong item, it'll cost me all kinds of time and money to get it straightened out. I wonder how many other orders you've messed up." Angrily, he checks the entire shipment but finds no other errors.

Scripture passages: Titus 2:9-10; 1 Peter 5:5

Lump of coal 4: "All that fuss for one little mistake? Didn't you ever do anything wrong? If you're so perfect, why did you have to redo that last tool you made for Chrysler? Since there's obviously no way I can please you, I'll leave you to your packing. I'm going to round up my buddies and be with people who won't ridicule me."

Burning coal 4: "I'm sorry, Dad. I guess I hurried because I know you need to get lots of work done. But I'll slow down enough to double-check my work so I don't make any more mistakes."

Discussion questions:
• What did you think about the lump-of-coal approach?
• What did you think about the burning-coals approach?
• What other scripture passages support the burning-coals approach?
• If you were the father how would you have responded to the two approaches? Why? *continued*

Situation 5: With only a safe distance between you and the car in front of you, another driver cuts in. Some time later, changes in the traffic pattern put you ahead again. The same discourteous driver cuts into your lane with even less clearance than before.

Scripture passages: Matthew 5:44; Romans 12:14

Lump of coal 5: "You're not going to get away with that kind of driving. I'll make sure you know I don't like this!" A highway battle of control begins that could result in an accident and injury to innocent people.

Burning coal 5: "Dear Lord, be with this person. If he has a crisis, protect him on the highway. If he's just being discourteous, show him where he's wrong."

Discussion questions:
• What did you think about the lump-of-coal approach?
• What did you think about the burning-coals approach?
• What other scripture passages support the burning-coals approach?
• If you were the discourteous driver, what might have been your reasons for the erratic driving behavior?

Situation 6: Your older brother has had the family car three nights in a row. You feel tonight it's your turn, but your brother insists this is an important night for him. You object, saying it's also important for you.

Just then, your father interrupts on behalf of his older son. "Look, you can't have anything that important at your age. Let your brother have the car. I don't want to hear another word about it."

Scripture passages: Matthew 5:9; Romans 12:18

Lump of coal 6: "A lot you'd care about what's important to me. I could have an appointment with the president, and your favorite son could want to go to a movie. You'd still let him have the car."

Burning coal 6: "Okay, Dad. Maybe you and I can do something together at home. I'd be glad to help with any project you need to do."

Discussion questions:
• What did you think about the lump-of-coal approach?
• What did you think about the burning-coals approach?
• What other scripture passages support the burning-coals approach?
• If you were the dad, how would you have responded to the two approaches? Why?

unteers to read the scripture passages. Ask other volunteers to read the different reactions (lump of coal is a cold response, burning coal is a warm response). Encourage kids to talk about their reactions. Some discussions will be longer than others.

During the discussions, remind participants there may be a reason why parents sometimes jump to conclusions. The teenager may be innocent, but past behavior often programs parents with certain expectations.

Recognize the fact that resistance to the burning-coals approach is normal. Human nature calls for justice, so it's difficult to be loving when someone acts awful. Using the burning-coals approach helps build future relationships based on fair play. A good parent-teenager relationship requires give-and-take from both sides, but either side can take the first step through giving.

Remind participants that using the burning-coals approach isn't easy. Emphasize the need for prayer, especially when personal feelings call for the lump-of-coal reaction. Close this Bible study with the following prayer. "God, help us know how to react when it seems we're being treated unfairly. Help us control our emotions, and give us the ability to act on our convictions. Amen."

Refreshments—Have participants roll out the dough for sugar cookies. Suggest they each create about five different cookies that offer a message of love or affirmation to a parent or some other person who's disciplined them unfairly. Allow them to create different shapes and paint messages on the unbaked dough. They may want to shape one cookie as a heart and paint "I love you" on it. Encourage them to bake the cookies, eat some and take some home.

Exercise break—Have one individual from each of the puppet plays lead the entire group in an exercise based on an action used to dramatize the story. For

example, a person could lead jumping jacks to symbolize Moses' surprise at the burning bush. This activity will revitalize the group and remind participants
of what they've been doing.

Practical application—Give each person 12
gummed labels and the handout "How Would You
React?" (Diagram 47). Say: "For each situation on the
handout, write a lump-of-coal reaction on a gummed
label and a burning-coals reaction on another label.
Stick the labels to the handout. Be prepared to share
these reactions with the entire group."

Ask different volunteers to share a lump-of-coal reaction and a burning-coals reaction to each situation.
Discuss the different reactions. Ask for scripture passages that might clarify what to do. Talk about how
each approach would affect the other individual.

Movie (optional)—Show the film *When Heroes
Fall* and discuss it.

Relaxation and sleep

Morning exercise—Ask participants to repeat the
exercises that grew out of the puppet plays.

Breakfast

Closing worship—Gather everyone in a circle
around a trash can and an offering plate. Give each
person two sheets of paper and a pencil. Say: "You've
talked about how others can and should handle unfair
discipline. It's also important to think about how you
can handle unfair discipline when it happens to you.

"On one sheet of paper, write about a problem
you've been having with a parent, your brothers and
sisters, your friends or some other individual. Write a
way you've reacted inappropriately to that problem.
Crumple this paper and toss it into the trash can in
the center of the circle.

"On the other sheet of paper, write about how you
can cure this problem with a burning-coals response.
Remember the object of this kind of response is to in-

Diagram 47
How Would You React?

Instructions: For each situation on this sheet, write a lump-of-coal reaction on a gummed label and a burning-coals reaction on another label. Attach them to the handout.

Situation 1: Your mom promised that you could go to the youth convention. When the time comes, however, she breaks her promise. Her social club is having a meeting that same day and she needs you to stay home with your 5-year-old brother.

Situation 2: For several days you've helped with a cleanup project at church. The names of those who helped are listed in Sunday's bulletin, but your name is missing. You feel the youth group's president omitted your name because she's jealous that you worked longer than anyone else.

Situation 3: Your 14-year-old sister has been wearing your shirts again even though you've asked her not to. This time she got ink all over the one you wanted to wear on a date.

Situation 4: Your dad asked you to bring him a package that he needs to take to a customer. After waiting 15 minutes at the place you thought he specified, you leave to call the office to see if you've mixed up the instructions. While you're gone, your dad arrives, then jumps all over you for not being reliable.

Situation 5: Several reference books were listed for your sociology course. It's your understanding that you have a choice of making a report on any one of them. When you hand in the report, the teacher tells you that you reported on the wrong book and you'll not receive credit for what you did.

Situation 6: You're helping your dad hang pictures. While you're both holding a picture, it falls to the floor and the glass breaks. It's as much your dad's fault as it is yours, but he places all the blame on you.

crease understanding, not make the offender feel guilty. After you've finished writing, fold your paper and place it in the offering plate in the center of the circle."

When everyone is finished, drop into the trash can the flames of fire you made from the orange construction paper. Say: "We've talked about our human reactions, the ones that get us into deep trouble. Think of these flames as fire from heaven, purifying our hearts so we can react with a humble spirit to our experiences of injustice. We're reminded of that sacred moment when the angel of the Lord appeared to Moses in the burning bush and said, 'Take off your sandals, for the place where you are standing is holy ground' (Exodus 3:5).

"This can be a sacred moment for us as we symbolically burn our past failures and offer new beginnings in our relationships with our family and friends. We walk on holy ground when we incorporate God's power into our lives to help us keep the commitment we've made."

Close with the following prayer. "God, thank you for showing us how to deal with injustice. Help us use the tool of kindness for your glory and our own good. Amen."

Resources for Family Ministry

Organizing Family Ministry

Building Stronger Families. Royce Money. Scripture Press, Wheaton, IL 60187. Combines a discussion of what makes families strong with an outline for forming a family ministry in congregations.

A Church Guide for Strengthening Families: Strategies, Models, Programs and Resources. Jim Larson. Augsburg, 426 S. Fifth St., Box 1209, Minneapolis, MN 55440. Suggests a strategy for family ministry based on a family wellness model. Includes numerous workshop and meeting ideas.

Faith and Families. Lindell Sawyers (editor). Westminster, 925 Chestnut St., Philadelphia, PA 19107. A collection of essays about families and family ministry. Focuses on biblical, theological and sociological dimensions of the family.

Family Ministry. Gloria Durka and Joanmarie Smith (editors). Harper & Row, 10 E. 53rd St., New York, NY 10022. A collection of essays on family ministry that combine solid theory and practical suggestions. Contributors include Dolores Curran, Maria Harris and Gabriel Moran.

Family Ministry: Family Life Through the Church. Charles M. Sell. Zondervan, 1415 Lake Dr., S.E., Grand Rapids, MI 49506. Blends social, biblical and educational dimensions of the family. Emphasizes Christian education in the home supported by Christian education through the church. Challenges the church to become like a family.

Family Survival: Coping With Stress. Parker Rossman. Pilgrim, 132 W. 31st St., New York, NY 10001. Focuses on the need for family networking and support groups. Provides models for support groups in congregations as well as other settings.

Five Cries of Parents. Merton P. Strommen and A. Irene Strommen. Harper & Row, 10 E. 53rd St., New York, NY 10022. Based on Search Institute's extensive Young Adolescents and Their Parents Project Report. Examines parents' need to understand themselves and their teenager, to know what fosters close family life, to understand and model moral behavior, to make faith central to family life and to know where to find help in times of crisis. Critical reading for ministering to families with teenagers.

Ministering to Families: A Positive Plan of Action. Royce Money. Abilene Christian University, ACU Station Box 7619, Abilene, TX 79699. Provides a rationale, structure and planning process for family ministry. Includes meeting plans for a family life committee as well as sample surveys and questionnaires.

The Ministry of Listening: Ministering With a Family Perspective. J. Daryl Furlong. Buckley, 4848 N. Clark St., Chicago, IL 60640. A complete program for developing a family ministry in a congregation. Includes a 200-page manual with background on family ministry and instructions for recruiting and training leaders. Also includes a family inventory survey with 160 questions. A computer analysis and printout are available for the survey.

Ministry With Families. Roland Martinson. Augsburg, 426 S. Fifth St., Box 1209, Minneapolis, MN 55440. A booklet offering a theological rationale and several planning tools for family ministry.

A New Design for Family Ministry. Dennis B. Guernsey. David C. Cook, 850 N. Grove Ave., Elgin, IL 60120. Shows how the family is the natural and effective place for the church to fulfill its mission. The approach is based on a life cycle model.

Parents as Partners in Youth Ministry. Darrell Pearson. Scripture Press, Wheaton, IL 60187. A practical manual for supporting parents of teenagers and getting them involved in youth ministry.

Planning Family Ministry: A Guide for a Teaching Church. Joe Leonard Jr. Judson, Valley Forge, PA 19482. Provides a systematic framework for family ministry in congregations. Suggests steps for planning and implementing a family ministry. A slim but useful volume.

About Families and Parenting

All Grown Up & No Place to Go: Teenagers in Crisis. David Elkind. Addison-Wesley, 1 Jacob Way, Reading, MA 01867. Destined to become a classic on contemporary family life. Looks at stresses in culture on teenagers and their families. "Family Permutations" is a particularly insightful chapter about the struggles of teenagers in different family situations.

The American Family: It's Not Dying, It's Changing. With Dolores Curran, Argus, 1 DLM Park, P.O. Box 7000, Allen, TX 75002. A video series that presents a positive view of marriage and suggests practical ways to strengthen family relationships. The three segments are "The Myth of the Dying Family," "Changing Functions of the Family" and "Changing Value Systems in the Family." Includes a study guide.

Bringing Up Children in the Christian Faith. John H. Westerhoff III. Harper & Row, 10 E. 53rd St., New York, NY 10022. Examines the challenges of raising children as Christians. Gives biblical references about praying, celebrating, listening and talking. Stresses the importance of parental acceptance as teenagers seek a personal faith.

Facing Life's Struggles. Mike Gillespie. GROUP, Box 481, Loveland, CO 80539. A 13-week curriculum for parents and their junior high kids to study together. Deals with issues such as loneliness, faith, anger, temptation and family communication. Leaders guide and participants books available.

Family: A Changing Place. Augsburg, 426 S. Fifth St., Box 1209, Minneapolis, MN 55440. A four-part video series hosted by Bonnie Jensen and Richard Jensen. Each session focuses on a different part of family life. Session titles are "A Personal Place," "A Process Place," "A Promise Place" and "A Possibility Place."

Family Forum. Jay Kesler. Scripture Press, Wheaton, IL 60187. Based on Kesler's radio program with the same name. Seeks to answer contemporary questions about the family from a biblical perspective.

For Parents Only. Evangelical Films, 1750 N.W. Highway, Suite 250, Garland, TX 75041. Featuring John Baucom and John White, this 12-session video series equips parents to help their teenagers deal with problems such as self-image, depression, anger, sex, and drugs and alcohol.

Getting Along With Your Parents. Word, 4800 West Waco Dr., Waco, TX 76796. Dawson McAllister presents solutions to parent-teenager miscommunication and exhorts teenagers to promote family harmony. The four 30-minute sessions are "Seeing God Through Your Parents' Eyes," "Being a Peacemaker in Your Home," "Learning to Obey Your Parents" and "Seeing Life From Your Parents' Point of View."

Growing a Healthy Family. Jim Larson. Augsburg, 426 S. Fifth St., Box 1209, Minneapolis, MN 55440. Gives parents six central ingredients in a recipe for a healthy family: commitment, time, appreciation, communication, conflict resolution and faith.

Growing as Faithful Parents. Augsburg, 426 S. Fifth St., Box 1209, Minneapolis, MN 55440. In this video, host Roland Martinson explores and explains four parenting skills: bonding, listening, confronting and affirming. Shows four families interacting to live these skills in everyday life.

Growing Up Whole in a Breaking Down World. Gospel Films, P.O. Box 455, Muskegon, MI 49443. A series of four films with Kevin Leman designed to improve parent-teenager relationships. Sessions deal with parental authority, self-esteem, mutual understanding, and sexuality and marriage.

How to Live (Almost) Happily With a Teenager. Lois Davitz and Joel Davitz. Harper & Row, 10 E. 53rd St., New York, NY 10022. Despite the seemingly negative title, this book is enjoyable and insightful for parents of teenagers.

Includes information about relating to teenagers as young adults instead of as children.

How to Live With Your Teenager: A Survivor's Handbook for Parents. Peter H. Buntman and E.M. Saris. Ballantine, 400 Hahn Rd., Westminster, MD 21157. A how-to book to help parents relate to their children as young adults. Includes important information and practical suggestions.

How to Raise Parents. Mass Media Ministries, 2116 N. Charles St., Baltimore, MD 21218. A two-part video presentation to a live audience by Clayton Barbeau. Part one deals with research and insights on adolescence, communication, values and sex. Part two answers questions on topics such as parental authority and the right to privacy.

How to Really Love Your Teenager. Ross Campbell. Scripture Press, Wheaton, IL 60187. Encourages parents to look beyond material provision as a way of expressing care for their teenager.

How to Talk so Kids Will Listen and Listen so Kids Will Talk. Adele Faber and Elaine Mazlish. Avon, Box 767, Dresden, TN 38225. Though written primarily for parents of younger children, this book includes many principles and recommendations basic to healthy parent-teenager communication.

The Hurried Child: Growing Up Too Fast Too Soon. David Elkind. Addison-Wesley, 1 Jacob Way, Reading, MA 01867. A landmark book on the effects of stress on children and adolescents. Discusses the influences of parents, schools and the media, and suggests ways to help children grow up slowly.

Moms, Dads and Other Endangered Species. Concordia/Family Films, 3558 S. Jefferson Ave., St. Louis, MO 63118. Through humor, vignettes, scripture, and questions and answers, Pat Hurley encourages understanding between teenagers and their parents. He urges teenagers to appreciate their parents and approach them with respect, honesty, gratitude and love.

Parenting Teenagers. GROUP, Box 481, Loveland, CO 80539. A four-part video program to help parents of teenagers improve their parenting skills. The program covers the psychological development of adolescents, parenting styles, parent-teenager communication, and friends and peer pressure. Includes a 144-page leaders guide.

Parents and Teenagers. Jay Kesler (editor), Scripture Press, Wheaton, IL 60187. A compilation of short articles by various authors on hundreds of topics such as communication, divorce, values, spiritual development, discipline and family fights.

Preparing for Adolescence. James Dobson. Gospel Light, Box 6309, Oxnard, CA 93031. Discusses issues that adolescents face. A good book for parents and teenagers to read and discuss together.

Stress and the Healthy Family. Dolores Curran. Harper & Row, 10 E. 53rd St., New York, NY 10022. The author examines the 10 most common stresses on families and analyzes how healthy families deal with these stresses. Also available as a 50-minute video.

Traits of a Healthy Family. Dolores Curran. Harper & Row, 10 E. 53rd St., New York, NY 10022. A seminal book in which Curran identifies 15 core issues that make families healthy. The core issues include communication, trust, respect, morality, tradition and religion. She challenges parents to recognize and build on their strengths. Also available as a 50-minute video.

Try Being a Teenager: A Challenge to Parents to Stay in Touch. Earl Wilson. Multnomah, 10209 S.E. Division St., Portland, OR 97266. An easy-to-read and easy-to-understand guide to help parents lead their children through the final passage to adulthood. A useful resource for a parents Sunday school class.

*P*eriodicals

Focus on the Family. Pomona, CA 91799. A monthly periodical with parenting advice and family resources from a Christian perspective. Published by James Dobson's organization with the same name.

GROUP Magazine. Box 202, Mt. Morris, IL 61054. Published eight times a year, this interdenominational magazine for youth workers focuses on all aspects of youth work, including working with parents and dealing with family concerns.

Group's JR. HIGH MINISTRY Magazine. Box 407, Mt. Morris, IL 61054. Published five times a year, this publication includes articles and programs for junior high ministry. Also includes Parent's Page, which offers good information and tips for parents. The publisher gives congregations permission to copy the page for their own newsletters.

Living With Teenagers. Materials Services Department, 127 Ninth Ave., N., Nashville, TN 37234. A quarterly magazine for parents of teenagers with information and advice. Written primarily for Southern Baptists.

PARENTS & TEENAGERS. GROUP, Box 482, Mt. Morris, IL 61054. A bimonthly, interdenominational newsletter for Christian parents of teenagers. Designed to help parents understand their teenagers. Includes parenting tips, research about teenagers, parenting resources, and information on teenage music and movies. Available in bulk subscriptions to churches.

*B*ulletin Inserts

Dr. James Dobson's Focus on the Family Bulletin. Tyndale House, Box 220, Wheaton, IL 60189. A monthly church bulletin insert that addresses contemporary family issues from an evangelical perspective. Includes short news stories and a question-and-answer column.

Dolores Curran Talks With Parents. Alt, Box 400, Green Bay, WI 54305. Written by Dolores Curran, these provocative weekly bulletin inserts focus on family issues, church issues, social issues and humor in dealing with the family. Some columns reflect a Roman Catholic perspective.

Thinking Young. Christianity Today, 465 Gundersen Dr., Carol Stream, IL 60188. Compiled by the editors of Campus Life, this monthly bulletin insert offers suggestions and research to promote understanding between adults and young people.

Why Marriages Work. Christianity Today, 465 Gundersen Dr., Carol Stream, IL 60188. A monthly bulletin insert that provides glimpses into marriages of well-known couples, excerpts from recent books, tips on strengthening marriages, reports on trends and other resources.

Other Useful Resources

Counseling Teenagers. G. Keith Olson. GROUP, Box 481, Loveland, CO 80539. A comprehensive and practical guide to counseling young people. Includes a great deal of information about dealing with specific family problems.

Determining Needs in Your Youth Ministry. Peter L. Benson and Dorothy L. Williams. GROUP, Box 481, Loveland, CO 80539. A comprehensive survey kit for youth groups to administer and analyze. Has numerous questions about teenagers' families. Includes surveys, answer sheets, tabulation and summary sheets, and programs based on the survey. Also includes a detailed model for how to take a survey in your congregation.

Fast Forms for Youth Ministry. Lee Sparks. GROUP, Box 481, Loveland, CO 80539. Includes dozens of reproducible forms for youth ministry, including parents letters, surveys, information sheets and job descriptions.

Why Teenagers Act the Way They Do. G. Keith Olson. GROUP, Box 481, Loveland, CO 80539. Examines eight personality types among adolescents. Helps youth workers and parents understand and deal with kids with different personalities.

The Youth Group Meeting Guide. Richard W. Bimler and other contributors. GROUP, Box 481, Loveland, CO 80539. Has a detailed, step-by-step plan for designing and conducting youth group meetings. Many principles also apply to parent and family meetings.

The Youth Ministry Resource Book. Eugene C. Roehlkepartain (editor). GROUP, Box 481, Loveland, CO 80539. Summarizes the latest survey and research information about teenagers in an easy-to-read format. Includes information about hundreds of organizations involved in youth work. Lists and describes hundreds of resources for all areas of youth ministry.

Notes

Chapter 1
[1]"World Youth Survey Results," Teenage magazine (April-May 1986) pp. 52-53.
[2]Paul Borthwick, *Organizing Your Youth Ministry* (Grand Rapids, MI: Zondervan, 1988) p. 101.
[3]Jim Burns, *The Youth Builder* (Eugene, OR: Harvest House, 1988) p. 226.
[4]Teen Sex Survey in the Evangelical Church: Executive Summary Report (n.p.: Josh McDowell Ministry, 1987) p. 7.

Chapter 2
[1]Tony Campolo, "What Is the Christian Family?" Youthworker (Winter 1987) pp. 20-25.
[2]David R. Mace, *The Christian Response to the Sexual Revolution* (Nashville, TN: Abingdon, 1970) pp. 55-56.
[3]Janet Huber Lowry, "Families in Church and Society: Sociological Perspectives" in *Faith and Families*, ed. Lindell Sawyers (Philadelphia, PA: Geneva, 1986) p. 50.
[4]U.S. Department of Commerce, Bureau of the Census, *Statistical Abstract of the United States: 1987* (Washington, D.C.: U.S. Bureau of the Census, 1986) pp. 382-383.
[5]The American Chicle Youth Poll, conducted by The Roper Organization Inc. for the American Chicle Group (Morris Plains, NJ: Warner-Lambert, March 1987) p. 48.
[6]"The Family Changes Shape," USA Today (April 13, 1987).
[7]David Elkind, *All Grown Up & No Place to Go* (Reading, MA: Addison-Wesley, 1984) p. 116.
[8]Pamela P. Wong, "No Babies!?" Eternity (June 1987) pp. 12-14; and William Dunn, "The New Face of the USA Family," USA Today (December 17, 1986).
[9]Wong, pp. 12-14.
[10]Quoted in Ronald Kotulak, "Youngsters Lose Way in Maze of Family

Instability," Chicago Tribune (December 14, 1986).

[11]U.S. Department of Commerce, Bureau of the Census, *Population Profile of the United States 1984/85* (Washington, D.C.: U.S. Bureau of the Census, 1987) p. 6.

[12]The American Chicle Youth Poll, p. 23.

[13]Quoted in Kotulak.

[14]*The Ethan Allen Report: The Status and Future of the American Family* (Danbury, CT: Ethan Allen, Inc., 1986) p. 9.

[15]Joe Leonard Jr., *Planning Family Ministry: A Guide for a Teaching Church* (Valley Forge, PA: Judson, 1982) p. 33.

[16]*Statistical Abstract of the United States*, p. 383.

[17]Anthony M. Casale, *USA Today: Tracking Tomorrow's Trends* (Kansas City, MO: Andrews, McMeel & Parker, 1986) p. 86.

[18]*Population Profile of the United States*, p. 3.

[19]Louis Harris, *Inside America* (New York, NY: Vintage Books, 1987) p. 87.

[20]Gentleman's Quarterly poll, quoted in "Men Rank Marriage Over Job," Rocky Mountain News (March 24, 1988).

[21]Kaye E. Gardner and Suzanne V. LaBrecque, "Effects of Maternal Employment on Sex Role Orientation of Adolescents," Adolescence (Winter 1986) pp. 882-883.

[22]*Statistical Abstract of the United States*, p. 48.

[23]Alan L. Otten, "If You See Families Staging a Comeback, It's Probably a Mirage," The Wall Street Journal (September 25, 1986).

[24]*Population Profile of the United States*, p. 20.

[25]Ibid., pp. 33, 36.

[26]Elkind, pp. 120-124.

[27]"The Family Changes Shape," USA Today (April 13, 1987).

[28]Dean Feldmeyer, "Kids in Stepfamilies," GROUP Magazine (September 1986) pp. 12-15.

[29]Quoted in Elkind, p. 129.

[30]Lowry, p. 60.

[31]"Census Reveals Jump in Unmarried Couples," Light (February 1987) p. 14.

[32]*Statistical Abstract of the United States*, p. 42.

[33]*Population Profile of the United States*, p. 20.

[34]Leonard, p. 35.

[35]*The Ethan Allen Report*, pp. 11, 18.

[36]Alvin Toffler, *The Third Wave* (New York, NY: Bantam, 1980) pp. 215-216.

[37]Judith Kovacs, "Faith and Family in Biblical Perspective" in *Faith and Families*, p. 27.

Chapter 3

[1]Joe Leonard Jr., *Planning Family Ministry: A Guide for a Teaching Church* (Valley Forge, PA: Judson, 1982) p. 12.

[2]Sang H. Lee, "The Importance of the Family: A Reformed Theological Perspective" in *Faith and Families*, ed. Lindell Sawyers (Philadelphia,

PA: Geneva, 1986) p. 135.

[3]Leonard, p. 30.

[4]Ibid., p. 26.

[5]Peter Uhlenberg, "Adolescents in American Society: Recent Trends and Proposed Responses" (paper presented to the Annual Resource Network Conference, Family Research Council, 1986) pp. 21-22.

[6]Lee, p. 135.

[7]Uhlenberg, p. 20.

[8]Merton P. Strommen and A. Irene Strommen, *Five Cries of Parents* (San Francisco, CA: Harper & Row, 1985) pp. 11-12, 24.

[9]"The Five Cries of Parents: A Conversation With Dr. Merton Strommen," Youthworker (Spring 1985) pp. 50-57.

[10]Uhlenberg, p. 23.

Chapter 4

[1]J.C. Wynn, "Calling a Family 'Christian,' " The Christian Ministry (May 1985) p. 30.

[2]Dolores Curran, *Stress and the Healthy Family* (Minneapolis, MN: Winston, 1985) p. 8.

[3]Ibid., pp. 10-11.

[4]Anne C. Petersen, "Those Gangly Years," Psychology Today (September 1987) p. 28.

[5]Ibid., p. 33.

[6]Reginald W. Bibby and Donald C. Posterski, *The Emerging Generation: An Inside Look at Canada's Teenagers* (Toronto, Canada: Irwin, 1985) p. 96.

[7]Eugene C. Roehlkepartain, ed., *The Youth Ministry Resource Book* (Loveland, CO: GROUP, 1988) p. 31.

[8]Kate Greer, "Today's Parents: How Well Are They Doing?" Better Homes and Gardens (October 1986) pp. 38-46.

[9]Curran, p. 62.

[10]Curran, pp. 67-68.

[11]The American Chicle Youth Poll, conducted by The Roper Organization Inc. for the American Chicle Group (Morris Plains, NJ: Warner-Lambert, March 1987) p. 27.

[12]*Americans and the Arts* (New York, NY: National Research Center for the Arts, 1988) pp. 20-21.

[13]Curran, p. 158.

[14]Bettie B. Youngs, *Helping Your Teenager Deal With Stress* (New York, NY: St. Martin's, 1986) p. 27.

[15]Richard D. Parsons, *Adolescents in Turmoil, Parents Under Stress: A Pastoral Ministry Primer* (Mahwah, NJ: Paulist, 1987) p. 8.

[16]Hans Sebald, "Adolescents' Shifting Orientation Toward Parents and Peers: A Curvilinear Trend Over Recent Decades," Journal of Marriage and the Family, vol. 48, no. 1 (February 1986) p. 5.

[17]Peter Benson, Dorothy Williams and Arthur Johnson, *The Quicksilver Years: The Hopes and Fears of Early Adolescence* (San Francisco, CA: Harper & Row, 1987) p. 200.

[18]David Elkind, *All Grown Up & No Place to Go* (Reading, MA: Addison-Wesley, 1984) pp. 10-12.

[19]Benson, Williams and Johnson, pp. 168-169.

[20]Elkind, p. 13.

[21]The American Chicle Youth Poll, pp. 8-9.

[22]Ibid., p. 29.

[23]Quoted in Karen S. Peterson, "Kids Saying to Parents: 'I Need You,' " USA Today (May 26, 1987).

[24]Arlene Eskilson, Mary Glenn Wiley, Gene Muehlbauer and Laura Dodder, "Parental Pressure, Self-Esteem and Adolescent Reported Deviance: Bending the Twig Too Far," Adolescence (Fall 1986) pp. 501-515.

[25]Roehlkepartain, p. 164.

[26]Quoted in Curran, pp. 110-111.

[27]Susan and Daniel Cohen, *Teenage Stress* (New York, NY: Evans, 1984) p. 63.

[28]Benson, Williams and Johnson, p. 38.

[29]Judy Dunn, *Sisters and Brothers* (Cambridge, MA: Harvard University Press, 1985) p. 4.

[30]The American Chicle Youth Poll, pp. 28-29.

[31]Jane Norman and Myron Harris, *The Private Life of the American Teenager* (New York, NY: Rawson, Wade, 1981) p. 212.

[32]Norman and Harris, p. 214.

[33]Norman and Harris, p. 214.

[34]Quoted in Curran, p. 136.

[35]Curran, p. 137.

[36]Elkind, *All Grown Up & No Place to Go*, p. 118.

[37]"Someone You Know Feels the Suffering Caused by Sexual or Domestic Violence," pamphlet from the Center for the Prevention of Sexual and Domestic Violence (Seattle, WA: n.d.).

[38]Bruce Roscoe and John E. Callahan, "Adolescents' Self-Report of Violence in Families and Dating Relations," Adolescence (Fall 1985) p. 550.

[39]Elkind, *All Grown Up & No Place to Go*, p. 63.

[40]Alfie Kohn, "Shattered Innocence," Psychology Today (February 1987) pp. 54-58; and Donald P. Orr and Maureen C. Downes, "Self-Concept of Adolescent Sexual Abuse Victims," Journal of Youth and Adolescence, vol. 14, no. 5 (October 1985) pp. 401-410.

[41]"Children of Alcoholics," Facts for Families, vol. II, no. 6 (Washington, D.C.: American Academy of Child Psychiatry, n.d.).

[42]Greg McKinnon, "Reaching Out to the Troubled Kid (It's a Family Affair)," Youthworker (Spring 1985) p. 76.

[43]Quoted in Jim Larson, *A Church Guide for Strengthening Families* (Minneapolis, MN: Augsburg, 1984) pp. 27-29.

[44]Condensed from Curran, pp. 144-156.

[45]Larson, p. 24.

Chapter 6

[1]Parker Rossman, *Family Survival: Coping With Stress* (New York, NY: Pilgrim, 1984) p. 32.

Chapter 7

[1]Darrell Pearson, *Parents as Partners in Youth Ministry* (Wheaton, IL: Victor, 1985) p. 16.

[2]Ibid., p. 47.

[3]Quoted in David Leigh, "Are You Too Old for Youth Ministry?" GROUP Magazine (May 1987) p. 8.

[4]David Elkind, *All Grown Up & No Place to Go* (Reading, MA: Addison-Wesley, 1984) p. 205.

[5]Pearson, p. 19.

Chapter 9

[1]"What You're Not Telling Your Parents," Young Miss (December 1987) p. 78.

[2]The American Chicle Youth Poll, conducted by The Roper Organization Inc. for the American Chicle Group (Morris Plains, NJ: Warner-Lambert, March 1987) pp. 30-31.

[3]Peter Benson, Dorothy Williams and Arthur Johnson, *The Quicksilver Years: The Hopes and Fears of Early Adolescence* (San Francisco, CA: Harper & Row, 1987) p. 220.

[4]Joe Leonard Jr., *Planning Family Ministry: A Guide for a Teaching Church* (Valley Forge, PA: Judson, 1982) p. 23.

[5]Benson, Williams and Johnson, p. 212.

[6]G. Keith Olson, *Why Teenagers Act the Way They Do* (Loveland, CO: GROUP, 1987) pp. 38-43.

[7]Cited in G. Keith Olson, *Counseling Teenagers* (Loveland, CO: GROUP, 1984) p. 93.

[8]Quoted in George A. Rekers, *Counseling Families* (Waco, TX: Word, 1988) p. 107.

Chapter 10

[1]Dolores Curran, *Stress and the Healthy Family* (Minneapolis, MN: Winston, 1985) p. 152.

[2]Cited in "What Do They Fight About?" Campus Life, Leader's Guide Edition, (November 1987) p. 10.

[3]G. Keith Olson, *Counseling Teenagers* (Loveland, CO: GROUP,1984) pp. 74-89.

[4]Ibid., p. 76.

[5]"What You're Not Telling Your Parents," Young Miss (December 1987) p. 74.

[6]Olson, pp. 77, 81.

[7]Jerald G. Bachman, Lloyd D. Johnston and Patrick M. O'Malley, *Monitoring the Future: Questionnaire Responses From the Nation's High School Seniors 1986* (Ann Arbor, MI: Institute for Social Research, University of Michigan, 1987) p. 43.

[8]Eugene C. Roehlkepartain, ed., *The Youth Ministry Resource Book* (Loveland, CO: GROUP, 1988) p. 31.

[9]Ibid., p. 164.

[10]Doug Self, "Who Are the Unchurched?" Pastoral Ministry Newsletter (November-December 1987) p. 6.

Chapter 12

[1]G. Keith Olson, *Counseling Teenagers* (Loveland, CO: GROUP, 1984) p. 235.
[2]Ibid.
[3]Ibid., pp. 235-236.

Chapter 14

[1]Royce Money, *Ministering to Families: A Positive Plan of Action*, (Abilene, TX: Abilene Christian University Press, 1987) pp. 55-57.

Chapter 15

[1]Roland Martinson, *Ministry With Families* (Minneapolis, MN: Augsburg, 1986) p. 15.
[2]Joe Leonard Jr., *Planning Family Ministry: A Guide for a Teaching Church* (Valley Forge, PA: Judson, 1982) pp. 17-24.
[3]Royce Money, *Ministering to Families: A Positive Plan of Action* (Abilene, TX: Abilene Christian University Press, 1987) pp. 29-30.
[4]Ibid., p. 161.

Chapter 16

[1]Royce Money, *Ministering to Families: A Positive Plan of Action* (Abilene, TX: Abilene Christian University Press, 1987) p. 174.